TRUMP OR BIDEN: HOW WOULD CHRIST VOTE?

TIMOTHY A. JACOBSON
B.S., M.A., J.D., LTC, U.S. ARMY (RET.)

i

Trump or Biden: How Would Christ Vote?

Second edition, September 11, 2020.

Copyright @ 2020 by Timothy A. Jacobson.

All rights reserved.

Printed in the United States of America.

DEDICATION

This book is dedicated to:

The God of Abraham, the God of our Founding Fathers.
"In Him we live, and move, and have our being"
(Acts 17:28, KJV).

My parents Rev. Gerald and Jean Jacobson,
and brothers Thomas, Michael, and Daniel.

My wife Delores
and daughters Rebecca, Kristin, and Kelsey.

Herbert W. Titus,
a man who graduated from Harvard Law School
with honors, became a Christian, and as Dean of
Regent University School of Law and Government,
touched, blessed, and forever changed
the hearts, minds, and lives of so many students.

SPECIAL HONOR

The words "For to me, to live is Christ and to die is gain" (Phil. 1:20-22) epitomized the lives of my father and mother, On the day that she suffered the final stroke that silenced her forever, my mother was doing what she enjoyed most, quoting Scripture and singing hymns. Today my father, a 92-year-old retired minister, missionary, state prison chaplain, and hospital chaplain, continues to serve the Lord.

AUTHOR

Timothy Jacobson is a Christian attorney and retired Army Officer. His academic degrees include a Bachelor of Science from the United Stated Military Academy, West Point, and a Master of Arts in Theology and Juris Doctor in Law from Regent University. His 33 years of military service included 11 years of active duty and 22 years of National Guard and Reserves.

FAVORITE QUOTES

"For me to live is Christ, and to die is gain."
The Apostle Paul.

"God made me fast, and when I run, I feel His pleasure."
Eric Liddell, Chariots of Fire,
Olympic runner and missionary to China.

"Thanks be to God for the challenge and the victory."
West Point yearbook.

"Help me to never seek a crown, for
my reward is giving glory to you."
Keith Green, songwriter.

TABLE OF CONTENTS

CHAPTER 1.0

INTRODUCTION

<u>MORAL DECLINE, DUTY TO VOTE:</u> Christians bear primary responsibility for the moral decline of our nation. **<u>Every Christian has a duty to vote as Christ would vote</u>**, and to support every vote with scripture. How would Christ vote in the 2020 election? Would He vote for Trump or Biden? Would He vote for Republicans or Democrats? This book answers these simple questions with absolute certainty based upon principles embodied in Scripture, the Declaration of Independence, the Constitution, and the Bill of Rights. It provides voter guidance and greater understanding of God, Scripture, and the laws that God created to govern men and nations. It will also challenge your understanding of the God-given purpose of your life.

<u>SPIRITUAL BATTLE, NOT POLITICAL BATTLE</u>. Franklin Graham said, "**<u>This is a spiritual battle, not a political battle</u>**." Rev. Al Sharpton said, "**<u>We wrestle not against flesh and blood, but against principalities, against powers</u>**" (Eph. 6:12). Both men stated a simple truth that most Americans fail to understand. The battle between Republicans and Democrats is first and foremost a spiritual battle, not a political battle.

However, these Christian leaders differ sharply in their understanding of where God stands in this battle. Sharpton said, "God is on our side!" Graham warned about the ungodly "progressive agenda" of Democrats. Who is right? Who is wrong? Why? This book will answer these questions.

From birth until death, life is spiritual warfare, with battles on all fronts. On the personal level, there is a battle for the heart and soul of every person. On the national level, there is a battle for the heart and soul of the nation.

PRIMARY ISSUES: This election is not first and foremost about the candidates or parties or any issue being debated by Americans. It is about God and the laws that He created to govern men and governments. Every vote is a vote for or against the God who created all men equal and endowed all men with certain inalienable rights, which include life, liberty, and the pursuit of happiness. Governments are instituted, as stated in the Declaration of Independence, to protect these God-given rights.

OBJECTIVES. The **primary objective of this book is obedience to the greatest commandment: "Thou shalt love the Lord thy God with all thy heart, and with all thy soul, and with all thy migh**t" (Deut. 6:5, KJV). The second objective is obedience to the second greatest commandment: "Thou shalt love thy neighbor as thyself" (Matt. 22:37-40, KJV). The third objective is to secure for our nation blessings that result from obedience to God's commandments. "Blessed is the nation whose God is the LORD." (Ps. 33:11, KJV). "Righteousness exalt[s] a nation: but sin is a reproach to any people" (Prov. 14:34, KJV). "If my people, which are called by my name, shall humble themselves, and pray, and seek my face, and turn from their wicked ways; then will I hear from heaven, and will forgive their sin, and will heal their land" (2 Chron 7:14, KJV).

APATHY. "All that is needed for evil to triumph is for good men to do nothing."[1] The Founding Fathers founded our

---

[1] "All that is necessary for the triumph of evil is that good men do nothing."

nation as "one nation under God." Today most Christians stand silently on the sidelines as God is removed from our schools, workplace, and government. During every national election, millions of Christians do not vote. Some do not vote because they do not like the candidates. By refusing to choose between the lesser of evils, they ensure that evil men govern our nation.

FOR SUCH A TIME AS THIS. The 2020 election will affect the direction of the United States for many years to come. The next president will nominate Supreme Court justices who will serve for life. The Senate will approve or disapprove of the President's nominees. The decisions of the president, Congress, and the Supreme Court will determine what laws we live under and whether we are "one nation under God." Accept this challenge and warning from the Lord.

> And Mordecai told them to answer Esther: "Do not think in your heart that you will escape in the king's palace any more than all the other Jews. For if you remain completely silent at this time, relief and deliverance will arise for the Jews from another place, but you and your father's house will perish. Yet who knows whether you have come to the kingdom for such a time as this?" (Esther 4:13-14, NKJV)[2]

All Christians have a duty, like Esther, to obey God's calling on their lives. All Christians have a duty to put on the

---

"This is probably the most quoted statement attributed to Burke, and an extraordinary number of variants of it exist, but all without any definite original source." "Edmund Burke," Wikiquote, http://en.wikiquote.org/wiki/Edmund_Burke.

[2] Holy Bible, New King James Version. Nashville: Thomas Nelson, Inc., 1982.

full armor of God and to do battle for the Lord and to be salt and light in all areas of life.

DEFINING CHRISTIAN. A Christian is not simply someone who believes in Christ or attends church. "**Faith without works is dead**" (James 2:20; 2:26, KJV). **Politics is faith in action**. Being a Christian requires living and voting Christian values. To make this book more concise, a chapter which defines what it means to be a Christian in much greater detail has been moved to Appendix A.

CHRISTIAN LEADERS. Why do so many Christian leaders fail to provide moral guidance to Christians in the area of politics, law, and government? First, some mistakenly believe their first priority should be obedience to the Great Commission, saving souls for Christ. Their first priority should be obedience to the Greatest Commandment, loving God with all their heart, mind, soul, and strength. Their lives should be God-centered, not man-centered. Second, they neglect part of Christ's command in the Great Commission: "teaching all that I have commanded you." Third, they fail to fully understand God, overemphasizing His love and neglecting His holiness, which cheapens Christ's death on the cross. Fourth, they try to be invitational, avoiding divisive issues, to welcome non-believers and to maintain peace within their congregations. As moral leaders with a duty to teach moral values, they should teach Scripture on decisive issues without taking sides between Republicans and Democrats.

SEPARATION OF CHURCH AND STATE. Today most Americans believe in separation of church and state in a way that would be anathema to God and the founding fathers. Christians who believe that God does not care about politics, law, or government or how we vote demonstrate amazing lack of understanding of God and Scripture. Many believe that God only cares about spiritual matters. They are wrong. Do they really believe that God cared about the righteousness of Nineveh and Sodom and Gomorrah, but not the righteousness of the United States, founded as "one nation under God?"

"**<u>Righteousness exalts a nation</u>**..." (Prov. 14:34, KJV). **<u>God cares more than we can possibly care about the moral state of our nation</u>** and whether we live and vote His values. First, God cares because He is the one true God, who created all the laws that govern men and nations. Second, God cares because he is love. He loves each of us more than we can possibly love ourselves. Third, God cares because He is holy. He cannot tolerate sin. He must judge and punish all sin. The holy, loving, God who created all things seen and unseen and the laws that govern men and nations cares more about what men and laws govern our nation than we can possibly care.

<u>IGNORANCE</u>. "Ignorance is not a virtue in politics or in life. It's not cool to not know what you are talking about...." Those very true words were spoken by President Obama in a commencement speech on May 21, 2016. **<u>Christ said, "Ye do err, not knowing the Scriptures</u>**, nor the power of God" (Matt. 22:28-30, KJV). During every national election, millions of Americans vote contrary to Christian values because they do not know the Scriptures.

<u>VOTER GUIDANCE</u>. So, how should Christians vote? First, they should vote based upon principles and laws revealed by God through scripture. Second, they should vote based upon principles and laws embodied in the Declaration of Independence, the Constitution, and the Bill of Rights. Third, they should vote for candidates who support Supreme Court justices who will uphold the Constitution. Where can

Christians look for voter guidance? First, Chapters 2 reviews guidance from Christian organizations. Second, the Conclusion to this book provides a summary of guidance in this book.

BOOK ORGANIZATION. This book is divided into chapters and subchapters. **Readers who do not have time to read the entire book should read the Conclusion, which provides a detailed, comprehensive summary of the book**.

Chapter 1 is the Introduction. Chapter 2 summarizes Christian voter guidance from Christian organizations. It is placed up front so readers can immediately get guidance on from Christian organizations whose expertise is the area of politics, law, and government. Chapter 3 lays the foundation for the book. It discusses basic principles of living and voting Christian values and the vital importance of scripture and biblical law to living and voting Christian values.

Chapter 4 discusses the War on Trump. Chapter 5 reviews the 2020 Democratic National Convention. Chapter 6 reviews the 2020 Republican National Convention. After the death of George Floyd, I reorganized this book, moving issues of the 2020 election from the rear to Chapter 7. These issues include jobs and the economy, global pandemic, Supreme Court, racism and police, national security, law and order, gun control, education, healthcare, immigration, environment, and voting by mail.

Chapter 8 reviews scripture on several issues (role of government, taxes, abortion, homosexuality and same-sex marriage). Chapter 9 shows what voting in accordance with the principles embodied in the Declaration of Independence, Constitution, and Bill of Rights requires. Chapter 10 discusses what voting for rights and freedoms requires (liberty, pursuit of happiness, freedom of speech, freedom of religion). Chapter 11 shows what voting for truth requires. Chapter 12, the Conclusion, provides a detailed, comprehensive summary of the book.

CHAPTER 2.0

CHRISTIAN VOTER GUIDANCE

<u>SECTION REVIEW</u>. This section contains Christian voter guidance developed by Christian organizations. The first chapter lists sources of Christian voter guidance. The second discusses congressional vote scorecards developed by Family Research Council Action and Family Policy Alliance (formerly CitizenLink). The third chapter reviews congressional vote scorecards developed by National Right to Life. The fourth chapter reviews the 2020 Party Platform Comparison of Family Research Council Action

<u>CHAPTERS</u>:
2.1 Sources of Christian Voter Guidance
2.2 Congressional Scorecards of Family Research
Council Action and Family Policy Alliance
2.3 Congressional Scorecards of National Right to Life
2.4 The 2020 Party Platform Comparison of
Family Research Council Action

SOURCES OF CHRISTIAN
VOTER GUIDANCE

Christians who need voter guidance may go to the websites of these Christian organizations.

FRC Action (Family Research Council Action) provides the most comprehensive Christian voter guidance. **Go to www.FRCaction.org. Click on "Voting Resources" for**: (1) **Voter Registration**. (2) **Voter Guide**. Enter zip code for voter information for your area or search by name for information on 80,000 candidates. (3) **Party Platforms**. Watch excellent 4-minute video on party platforms, then **read 2-page comparison of party platforms**. (4) **Scorecard. Click on "House" or "Senate"** to see how every member of Congress voted. Note extreme difference between Republicans and Democrats. **Most Republicans score 90%-100% for voting Christian values. Most Democrats score 0%.**

On the FRC Action website, www.FRCaction.org, you may also click on "Issues" for many articles on: (1) Life, (2) Marriage & Family, and (3) Religious Freedom.

Billy Graham Evangelistic Association (BGEA, www.billygraham.org, 877-247-2426). **Subscribe to Decision Magazine** or view online at www.DecisionMagazine.com. Decision Magazine provides **excellent spiritual guidance and voter guidance**. Current cost is only $15.95/year, a small donation to one of the best Christian organizations in the world. Its ministries include world evangelism, Christian teaching, humanitarian support, disaster relief, etc.

Family Policy Alliance (formerly CitizenLink, www.FamilyPolicyAlliance.com). Affiliate of Focus on the Family. Go to website. Click on "Issues" for information and Scripture related to Life, Family, Sexuality, and Religious Freedom. In the past, Family Policy Alliance developed congressional scorecards with FRC Action, which are reviewed in a following chapter.

American Family Association Action (www.afa.net). Their website now links you to FRC Action website for voter guidance.

National Right to Life (www.NRLC.org). Click on "Legislation" then "Congressional Scorecards 1997-Present," which show how members of Congress voted on life-related issues. Click on "Issues" for information on life-related issues.

The Heritage Foundation (www.Heritage.org). Click on "Explore Issues" for **detailed articles on about 50 topics**, to include the Constitution, courts, economy, federal budget, national debt, deficit, taxes, entitlements, health care, Medicare, social security, welfare, family, marriage, education, energy, environment, immigration, defense, terrorism, etc.

CONGRESSIONAL SCORECARDS
OF FRC ACTION AND
FAMILY POLICY ALLIANCE

INTRODUCTION. The best way to evaluate a candidate is not to look at what he said or promised when trying to get elected, but how he actually voted. Voting records reveal extreme differences between Republicans and Democrats. Most Republicans vote Christian values most of the time. Most Democrats vote against Christian values most of the time. The extreme degree to which this is true is almost beyond belief, but clearly proven by scorecards that show exactly how elected officials voted on issues that required the application of Christian values. To make this chapter more concise and easier to read, details about issues voted upon have been moved to Appendix D. The conclusion to this chapter provides a concise, detailed summary of the chapter.

Family Research Council Action (FRC Action) and Family Policy Alliance, an affiliate of Focus on the Family (formerly called Citizenlink), and American Family Association Action (AFA Action) produced "Vote Scorecards" that show how members of Congress voted on "the most clear-cut, pro-family votes." This chapter will review the scorecards published during two election years: 2008 and 2012. During 2008, FRC Action and CitizenLink published a scorecard for 100th Congress, First Session that covered votes cast during 2007.[3] During 2012, FRC Action and CitizenLink published a

---

[3] "Vote Scorecard, 110th Congress, 1st Session," FRC Action and Focus on the Family Action, http://www.frcaction.org, accessed July 9, 2008.

scorecard for 112th Congress, First Session that covered votes cast during 2011.[4] Go to www.frcaction.org to view scorecards and see exactly how every member of Congress voted.

2008 SENATE SCORECARD. The 2008 scorecard reveals extreme disparity between the voting records of Republicans and Democrats in the U.S. Senate. **Senators Obama, Biden, and Clinton all scored 0%.** Republicans scored an amazingly high average of 86%. Most Republicans scored 100% (58%; 29 of 50). They voted with Christian values, with FRC Action and CitizenLink, on all 7 issues. Ten Republicans (20%) scored 85-99%. Seven Republicans (14%) scored 57-71%. One Republican (2%) scored 42% (Senator McCain). Three Republicans (6%) scored 28% (Senators Collins and Snowe of Connecticut and Spector of Pennsylvania). No Republican scored lower than 28%. Democrats scored an average of only 8.02%, less than one-tenth the average score of Republicans.[5] See Appendix D for details on the issues voted upon.

2008 HOUSE OF REPRESENTATIVES SCORECARD. The 2008 scorecard also reveals extreme disparity between the voting records of Republicans and Democrats in the U.S. House of Representatives. Republicans scored an average of 87%. Congressman Pence scored 93% (100% in 2012). Most Republicans scored 100% (53%; 108 of 203). They voted Christian values, with the positions of FRC Action and CitizenLink, on all 11 issues. 54 Republicans (27%) scored 76-99%. 26 Republicans (13%) scored 51-75%. Nine Republicans (4.4%) scored 26-50%. Five Republicans

---

[4] "Vote Scorecard, 112th Congress, 1st Session," FRC Action and Citizenlink, http://www.frcaction.org, accessed February 17, 2012.
[5] "Vote Scorecard, 110th Congress, 1st Session," FRC Action and Focus on the Family Action, http://www.frcaction.org, accessed July 9, 2008.

(2%) scored 1-25% (Congressman Shays of Connecticut, Castle of Delaware, Kirk of Illinois, Gilchrest of Maryland, and Frelinghuysen of New Jersey). Only one Republican (0.5 %) scored 0% (Congressman Norwood of Georgia).[6]

Democrats scored an average of only 10%, about one-eighth the average score of Republicans. Almost half of the Democrats scored 0% (46%; 109 of 235). They always voted against Christian values, against the positions of FRC Action and CitizenLink. 72 Democrats (another 31%) scored only 6%, barely above 0. 29 Democrats (12%) scored 12-25%. 9 Democrats (4%) scored 26-50%. 9 Democrats (4%) scored 51-75%. Only 5 of 235 Democrats (2%) scored 76-99% (Congressman Marshall of Georgia, Ellsworth of Indiana, Peterson of Minnesota, and Taylor of Mississippi Lincoln Davis of Tennessee. Only 2 of 235 Democrats (1%) scored 100% (Congressmen McIntyre and Shuler of North Carolina).[7] See Appendix D for details on the issues voted upon.

2012 SENATE SCORECARD. The 2012 scorecard reveals extreme disparity between the voting records of Republicans and Democrats in the U.S. Senate. The average score for Republicans was 73%. The average score for Democrats was less than 2% (1.65%). No Democrat scored above 14%. 88% of Democrats scored an absolute 0%.[8] **Obama, Biden, and Clinton were not senators in 2012**. See Appendix D for details on the issues voted upon.

2012 HOUSE OF REPRESENTATIVES SCORECARD. The 2012 scorecard also reveals extreme

---

[6] Ibid.

[7] Ibid.

[8] "Vote Scorecard, 112th Congress, 1st Session," FRC Action and Citizenlink, http://www.frcaction.org, accessed February 17, 2012.

disparity between the voting records of Republicans and Democrats in the U.S. House of Representatives. The average score for Republicans was about 89%. The average score for Democrats was about 9%. 91% of Democrats scored 10% or less.[9] Congressman Pence, a Republican, scored 100%. See Appendix D for details on the issues voted upon

    <u>CONCLUSION</u>. The scorecards jointly produced by Family Research Council Action (FRC Action) and Citizenlink, an affiliate of Focus on the Family, show how members of Congress voted on "the most clear-cut, pro-family votes." **Senators Obama, Biden, and Clinton scored 0%.** Trump did not serve in Congress, so he is not on the scorecards. Senate Republicans scored an average of 86%. Most Republicans scored 100% (58%; 29 of 50). Senate Democrats scored an average of only 8.02%, less than one-tenth the average score of Republicans. Most Democrats scored 0% (67%; 33 of 49).

    In the House of Representatives, Republicans scored an average of 87%. Most Republicans scored 100% (53%; 108 of 203). Congressman Pence scored 93% (100% in 2012). Democrats scored an average of only 10%, about one-eighth the average score of Republicans. Almost half of the Democrats scored 0% (46%; 109 of 235). 72 Democrats (another 31%) scored only 6%, barely above 0. In other words, 77% of Democrats (181 if 235) scored either 0% or 6%.

    On the 2012 Senate scorecard, the average score for Republicans was 73%. The average score for Democrats was less than 2% (1.65%). No Democrat scored above 14%. 88% of Democrats scored an absolute 0%. In the House of Representatives, the average score for Republicans was about

---

[9] Ibid.

89%. The average score for Democrats was about 9%. 91% of Democrats scored 10% or less. **<u>Obama, Biden, and Clinton were not senators in 2012.</u>**

Knowing these facts raises a couple questions. How can anyone who calls himself a Christian vote for any Democrat knowing that Democrats are so united in voting against Christian values? How can any Christian do anything that would help put Democrats in power, knowing that they would govern totally contrary to simple, basic moral laws revealed by God through Scripture? Jesus said His food was to do the will of His Father. Voting for a Democrat or doing anything that would put Democrats in power is totally contrary to what it means to be a Christian.

CONGRESSIONAL SCORECARDS OF NATIONAL RIGHT TO LIFE

INTRODUCTION. National Right to Life produces "Vote Scorecards" similar to that of Family Research Council Action and Citizenlink (formerly Focus Action). They show how members of Congress voted on issues related to abortion, health care, etc. All voting results discussed within this chapter are from the National Right to Life Committee (NRLC) "Federal NRLC Scorecard" for 110th Congress and 112th Congress.[10] The author of this book calculated all percentages. Go to www.nrlc.org to view scorecards and see exactly how every member of Congress voted. The conclusion to this chapter provides a very detailed summary of the results of these scorecards, for those who do not wish to read the all the details regarding all the votes. To make this chapter more concise and easier to read, the lengthy details about issues voted upon have been moved to Appendix E.

2008 SENATE SCORECARD. The 2008 National Right to Life scorecard for 110th Congress reveals amazing disparity between the voting records of Republicans and Democrats in the U.S. Senate. Again, **Senators Obama, Biden, and Clinton scored 0%.** Senate Republicans scored an average of 88%. Most Republicans scored 100% (63%; 32 of 51). Eleven Republicans (22%) scored 83-85%. Five

---

[10] "Federal NRLC Scorecard-110th Congress, Combined Sessions," National Right to Life Committee, http://www.nrlc.org, accessed July 7, 2008; "Federal NRLC Scorecard-110th Congress, Combined Sessions," National Right to Life Committee, http://www.nrlc.org, accessed July 21, 2012.

Republicans (10%) scored 57-66%. Three Republicans (6%) scored only 14%. No Republican scored lower.[11]

In 2008 Senate Democrats scored an average of only 9%, about one-tenth the average score of Republicans. Most Democrats scored 0% (71%; 35 of 49). They voted against the position of NRLC, against Christian values, on all 7 issues. Six Democrats (12%) scored 14%. Five Democrats (10%) scored 28-33%. Two Democrats (4%) scored 57-66%. One Democrat (2%) scored 85% (Senator Nelson of Nebraska). No Democrat scored 100%.[12] See Appendix E for details on the issues voted upon.

<u>2008 HOUSE OF REPRESENTATIVES SCORECARD</u>. The 2008 National Right to Life Committee (NRLC) Scorecard also reveals great disparity between the voting records of Republicans and Democrats in the U.S. House of Representatives. House Republicans scored an average of 88%. A large majority of Republicans scored 100% (71%; 143 of 201). They voted on all 7 pro-family issues, and they always voted with the recommendation of NRLC. 20 Republicans (10%) scored 76-99%. 19 Republicans (9.5%) scored 51-75%. 11 Republicans (5.5%) scored 26-50%. Five Republicans (2.5%) scored 1-25%). Three Republicans (0.5 %) scored 0%.[13]

In 2008 House Democrats scored an average of only 7%, less than one-tenth the average score of Republicans. A very large majority of Democrats scored 0% (85%; 199 of

---

[11] "Federal NRLC Scorecard-110th Congress, Combined Sessions," National Right to Life Committee, http://www.nrlc.org, accessed July 7, 2008.
[12] Ibid.
[13] Ibid.

233). They always voted against the position of NRLC, against Christian values, on all issues. 10 Democrats (4%) scored 1-25%. 8 Democrats (3%) scored 26-50%. 8 Democrats (3%) scored 51-75%. 8 Democrats (3%) scored 76-99%. No Democrat scored 100%.[14] See Appendix E for details on the issues voted upon.

2012 SENATE SCORECARD. The 2012 National Right to Life Committee (NRLC) Scorecard reveals great disparity between the voting records of Republicans and Democrats in the U.S. Senate. Senators were evaluated on 5 issues. Senate Republicans scored an average of 97%. Most Republicans scored 100% (90%; 43 of 48). Only five Republicans (10%; 5 of 48) scored less than 100%. Senate Democrats scored an average of only 1%. Most Democrats scored 0% (94%; 48 of 51). They voted against the position of NRLC, against Christian values, on all issues. Only 3 Democrats (6%) scored higher than 0%.[15] **Obama, Biden, and Clinton were not senators in 2012.** See Appendix E for details on the issues voted upon.

2012 HOUSE OF REPRESENTATIVES SCORECARD. The 2012 National Right to Life Committee (NRLC) Scorecard reveals great disparity between the voting records of Republicans and Democrats in the House of Representatives. Members of the House of Representatives were evaluated on 5 issues. House Republicans scored an average of 98%. Most Republicans scored 100% (94%; 229 of 243). Only 14 Republicans (6%; 14 of 243) scored less than 100%. House Democrats scored an average of only 5%. Most

---

[14] Ibid.

[15] "Federal NRLC Scorecard-110th Congress, Combined Sessions," National Right to Life Committee, http://www.nrlc.org, accessed July 21, 2012.

Democrats scored 0% (88%; 171 of 194). They voted against the position of NRLC, against Christian values, on all issues. Only 23 Democrats (12%) scored higher than 0% (23 of 243).[16] See Appendix E for details on the issues voted upon.

CONCLUSION. The 2008 National Right to Life Committee (NRLC) "Vote Scorecard", like the Focus Action and Family Research Council Action "Vote Scorecard", reveals extreme differences between the voting records of Republicans and Democrats. **Senators Obama, Biden, and Clinton all scored 0%.** Trump did not serve in Congress, so he is not on the scorecards. Most Republicans scored 100% (63%; 32 of 51), voting Christian values every time that they voted on the right to life issues selected by NRLC. Most Democrats scored 0%. Republicans scored an average of 88%. Democrats scored an average of only 9%, about one-tenth the average score of Republicans. Most Democrats scored 0% (71%; 35 of 49), always voting against Christian values.

In the U.S. House of Representatives, Republicans scored an average of 88%. Congressman Pence scored 100%. Most Republicans scored 100% (71%; 143 of 201), always voting for Christian values. Democrats scored an average of only 7%, less than one-tenth the average score of Republicans. Most Democrats scored 0% (85%; 199 of 233), voting against Christian values every time that they voted.

The 2012 National Right to Life Committee (NRLC) Scorecard reveals the same great disparity between the voting records of Republicans and Democrats. Senate Republicans scored an average of 97%. Most Republicans scored 100% (90%; 43 of 48). Senate Democrats scored an average of only 1%. Most Democrats scored 0% (94%; 48 of 51). They voted

---

[16] Ibid.

against Christian values on all issues.[17] House Republicans scored an average of 98%. Most Republicans scored 100% (94%; 229 of 243). Most Democrats scored 0% (88%; 171 of 194). They voted against Christian values on all issues.[18] **Obama, Biden, and Clinton were not senators in 2012**.

Knowing these facts raises the same questions raised by the "Vote Scorecard" developed by Focus Action and Family Research Council Action. How can any Christian vote for any Democrat knowing that Democrats are so united in voting against Christian values? How can any Christian do anything that would help put Democrats in power, knowing that they would govern totally contrary to simple, basic moral laws revealed by God through Scripture? Voting for most Democrats or doing anything that would put Democrats is totally contrary to what it means to be a Christian.

---

[17] "Federal NRLC Scorecard-110th Congress, Combined Sessions," National Right to Life Committee, http://www.nrlc.org, accessed July 21, 2012.
[18] Ibid.

THE 2020 PARTY PLATFORM COMPARISON OF FAMILY RESEARCH COUNCIL ACTION

INTRODUCTION. Family Research Council Action published the 2020 Party Platform Comparison in September 2020. It is a very helpful 2-page document that summarizes the sharp differences between Republicans and Democrats. To view, go to **www.FRCaction.org,** click on "Voting Resources," then click on "Party Platform."

GOD AND GOVERNMENT. The Republican Platform mentions God 15 times. It states, "If God-given, natural, inalienable rights come in conflict with government, court, or human-granted rights, God-given, natural, inalienable rights always prevail." The Republican Platform supports display of the Ten Commandments "as a reflection of our history and our country's Judeo-Christian heritage."

The Democratic Platform mentions God one time; it is silent on the role of God in government and the source of human rights. It stresses the "paramount importance of maintaining the separation between church and state enshrined in our Constitution." **The U.S. Constitution never mentions separation of church and state.**

MARRIAGE. Republicans support marriage as the union of one man and one woman. They oppose same-sex marriage and the Supreme Court ruling in Obergefell v. Hodges that made it legal. The Democratic Platform is silent on marriage. Democrats support same-sex marriage.

ABORTION. Republicans support the right to life of all children before and after birth and oppose all infanticide. They support the Born-Alive Abortion Survivors Protection Act, which bans abortion at 20 weeks, dismemberment abortion, abortion based on sex or disability, human cloning, and sale of body parts. It also bans the "use of public funds to perform or promote abortion or to fund organizations, like Planned Parenthood." Republicans also oppose tax-payer funding of abortion overseas and would restore the Mexico City Policy to prevent use of federal money to "provide or promote abortion" overseas.

Democrats support "codifying" the right to abortion. They support repeal of the Hyde Amendment, which prevents government funding of abortion. In other words, Democrats, who call themselves pro-choice, want to force all Americans who believe that abortion is murder to pay for abortions with their taxpayer dollars. Democrats will repeal President Trump's changes to Title X programs which prevent use of federal family planning grants for abortion. They will fight to overturn all federal and state laws that create any barriers to abortion and what they call "reproductive health care services." Democrats oppose FDA safety restrictions on abortion pills.

RELIGIOUS LIBERTY. The Republican Platform states, "We strongly support the freedom of Americans to act in accordance with their religious beliefs, not only in their houses of worship, but also in their everyday lives.... We value the right of America's religious leaders to preach, and Americans to speak freely, according to their faith.... [The government] is prohibited from policing or censoring speech based on religious convictions or beliefs." It also recognizes that "ongoing efforts to compel individuals and institutions of faith to transgress their beliefs are part of a misguided effort to undermine religion and drive it from the public square."

The Democratic Platform emphasizes the "paramount importance of maintaining the separation between church and state." It states that Democrats will fight for the Equality Act. That would, according to FRC, "remove religious liberty protections and even force churches to violate the tenants of their faith." The Democratic Platform rejects "broad religious exemptions" for "businesses, medical providers, social service agencies, and others..." In other words, Democrats will enact legislation that will significantly restrict religious freedom.

THE COURTS. The Republican Platform states, "We support the appointment of judges who respect traditional family values and the sanctity of innocent human life." It states that it wants to "reverse the long line of activist decisions—including Roe, Obergefell, and the Obamacare cases."

The Democratic Platform states that they will appoint judges that uphold decisions like Roe v. Wade. It applauds the decision that redefined the word "sex" in Title VII to include sexual orientation and gender identity (Bostock v. Clayton County). In other words, it states that Americans should have the right to decide whatever sex they want to be.

EDUCATION. The Republican Platform recognizes that parents, not the government, "are a child's first and foremost educators." It supports homeschooling, private schools, vouchers, tuition tax credits, and teaching the Bible as an elective in public schools. It states that Republicans will fight for "school choice" and "local control." School choice would be most helpful to a family that could not afford to send its children to a private Christian school.

Democrats oppose school choice, vouchers for private schools, and anything else that takes tax-payer money from public schools. Our family was forced to pay many thousands of dollars in taxes to fund public schools which our children never attended, and never even received a tax deduction or tax credit for the many thousands of dollars we paid for our children to attend private Christian schools.

<u>CONSCIENCE IN HEALTHCARE</u>. The Republican Platform states, "America's healthcare professionals should not be forced to choose between following their faith and practicing their profession. We respect the rights of conscience of healthcare professionals, doctors, nurses, pharmacists, and organizations, especially the faith-based groups which provide a major portion of care for the nation and the needy." The Democrats object to religious or conscience protections for these healthcare professionals.

<u>LGBT AGENDA</u>. The Republican Platform states that "all Americans should be treated with dignity and respect." The Democratic Platform says, "We will restore the United States position of leadership on LGBTQ+ issues" and appoint "senior leaders directly responsible for driving...LGBTQ+ issues within the federal government." That agenda includes insurance coverage for sex changes, to include surgery and hormone therapy, government identification and use of restrooms for whatever sex a person chooses to be, and allowing biological men to play in women's sports if they claim to be transgender women. Democrats would also fight for the Equality Act, which FRC Action states would "alter our entire federal civil rights framework, gut religious liberty, and advance abortion."

CONCLUSION. The 2020 Party Platform Comparison by Family Research Council Action shows that Republicans strongly support Christian values and Democrats strongly oppose them. This 2-page document contains more information on each of the areas discussed in this chapter. It also contains sections which address International Religious Liberty, Sex Education, and Social Experimentation in the Military. To view, go to **www.FRCaction.org**, click on "Voting Resources," then click on "Party Platforms."

CHAPTER 3.0

LIVING AND VOTING
CHRISTIAN VALUES

<u>SECTION REVIEW</u>. This section lays the foundation for this book. It discusses basic principles of living and voting Christian values. Readers who want to skip this section and read information more specific to this election should go to Chapter 4, The War on Trump. To make this section shorter and more concise, a chapter which defines what it means to be a Christian has been moved to Appendix A.

Organization of this section is as follows. The first chapter discusses basic principles of living and voting Christian values. The second chapter reviews the vital importance of scripture as the foundation for living the Christian life. The third chapter discusses the vital importance of biblical law to living Christian values.

<u>CHAPTERS</u>:
3.1 Basic Principles of Living and Voting Christian Values
3.2 The Vital Importance of Scripture to Living Christian Values
3.3 The Vital Importance of Biblical Law to Living Christian Values

BASIC PRINCIPLES OF LIVING AND VOTING CHRISTIAN VALUES

LIVING CHRISTIAN VALUES. Being a Christian requires living and voting Christian values. Most Christian leaders teach that men are saved by faith not works. Few teach that "faith without works is dead" (James 2:20; 2:26). Few teach these words of Christ:

> Not everyone that saith unto me, "Lord, Lord," shall enter into the kingdom of heaven; but he that doeth the will of my Father which is in heaven. Many will say to me in that day, "Lord, Lord, have we not prophesied in thy name? and in thy name have cast out devils? and in thy name done many wonderful works?" And then will I profess unto them, I never knew you: depart from me, ye that work iniquity (Matt. 7:21-23, KJV).

In other words, on Judgment Day Christ will reject many who call themselves Christians because they did not "do the will of [the] Father;" they did not live Christian values.

DEFINING CHRISTIAN. A Christian is not simply someone who believes in Christ. A Christian is a follower of Christ, a repentant sinner who dies to self and lives for Christ, someone who can join the Apostle Paul in saying, "For to me to live is Christ, and to die is gain" (Phil. 1:20-22). See Appendix F for a detailed definition of what it means to be a Christian, with supporting Scripture.

LIVING BY FAITH. God has ordained that man must live by faith. "The fool hath said in his heart, 'There is no God'" (Ps. 14:1; 53:1, KJV). A college professor who claims that only weak people need belief in a God is a fool who deliberately ignores the self-evident truth that there is a God. There is infinitely more scientific evidence in support of God and creation than evolution. Romans teaches that spiritual blindness results from a decision to ignore clear evidence of God revealed through creation.

> The just shall live by faith. For the wrath of God is revealed from heaven against all ungodliness and unrighteousness of men, who hold the truth in unrighteousness; because that which may be known of God is manifest in them; for God hath shewed it unto them. For the invisible things of him from the creation of the world are clearly seen, being understood by the things that are made, even his eternal power and Godhead; so that they are without excuse: because that, when they knew God, they glorified him not as God, neither were thankful; but became vain in their imaginations, and their foolish heart was darkened. Professing themselves to be wise, they became fools (Rom. 1:17-22).

FAITH AND REASON FOR LIVING. I describe a man's faith or religion as his reason for living. Every man has a faith or religion, which is his reason for living. How a person lives says more about their true faith, their real reason for living, than whether they claim to be a Christian or attend church. A man who claims to be a Christian and attends church every week but lives totally contrary to scripture is not a Christian.

<u>POLITICS AS FAITH IN ACTION</u>. Politics is faith in action. Voting Christian values is part of living Christian values. How a man votes says more about his real faith, his real reason for living, than whether or not he claims to be a Christian or attends church.

<u>MISSION</u>. The primary God-given mission of Christians is not to win souls for Christ or to make disciples of all nations or to love their fellow man as they love themselves. The primary God-given mission of every man, woman, and child is to "love the Lord our God with all your heart, mind, soul, and strength" (Luke Mt. 22:37-40). Loving God requires obedience to God's will and God's commandments. Christ said, "My food is to do the will of Him who sent me." All Christians should have the exact same attitude. Their first and foremost desire should be to do God's will at all times, to include when voting.

<u>KING DAVID</u>. One of the most amazing verses in Scripture contains the words of King David after he was confronted by the prophet Nathan for committing adultery and murder. King David, the only man described in scripture as "a man after God's heart," said, "I have sinned against the Lord" (2 Sam. 12:13, KJV). He understood that every thought, word, and action is first and foremost a thought, word, or action for or against God, not for or against his fellow man. Likewise, every vote is first and foremost a vote for or against God.

<u>FREEDOM</u>. Most Americans have a totally different understanding of freedom than that given by God in scripture. Most believe that freedom is the right to do whatever is right in

your own eyes, so long as you do not harm another person. That is totally contrary to Scripture. The words, "Every man did that which was right in his own eyes" (Judges 17:5-7; 21:24-25) describe a period of lawlessness in Israel (See Deut. 12:7-9; Prov. 12:15; 21:2). God commanded the Israelites to not do whatever was right in their own eyes, but to obey His commandments. King David said, "I will walk at liberty: for I seek thy precepts" (Ps. 119:45). In other words, true freedom is found through submission to God and obedience to His laws, not through doing whatever is right in your own eyes.

ARMOR OF GOD. Christians are called by God to be salt and light in all areas of life, to put on the full armor of God and to do battle for the Lord in our schools, workplace, government, and all other areas of life. Our nation is greatly in need of more Christians willing to do battle for the Lord in politics, law, and government, and more Christians simply willing to go to the polls and vote Christian values.

CHAPTER 3.2

THE VITAL IMPORTANCE OF SCRIPTURE TO LIVING CHRISTIAN VALUES

INTRODUCTION: Being a Christian requires living and voting in accordance with principles and laws revealed by God through Scripture. Christ said, "Ye do err, not knowing the Scriptures, nor the power of God" (Matt. 22:28-30, KJV). Christ was talking about the Old Testament. The New Testament was written after Christ's death and resurrection. Living and voting Christian values requires living and voting in accordance with Scripture, which includes the Old Testament.

QUESTION. "What is the one thing that I want you to believe more than anything else?" I asked my three daughters. The answer, I explained, was not God or Christ, but Scripture. Why?

FIRST REASON. God reveals Himself to man through Scripture. Without Scripture every man must imagine God in his own mind, and everyone gets it wrong in so many ways. Why is knowledge of God so important? Understanding of God, the Creator of all things seen and unseen, is the foundation for understanding of the meaning and purpose of all things seen and unseen. Americans today, including Christians, are at an all-time low for understanding of God and the meaning and purpose of their own lives. On Judgment Day most Americans will face the wrath of a holy, righteous God, in part because they never understood God or what He requires of man.

SECOND REASON. Second, God uses Scripture to reveal Christ to man. It gives prophecy regarding Christ and tells the story of His birth, life, death, and resurrection. God uses Scripture not only to give facts about Christ, but also, by telling the story of the life of Christ, to give the perfect example of what it means to be a Christian, a follower of Christ. Christ also provides an example of someone who understood the importance of Old Testament Scripture and studied it so diligently that as a young boy He knew more than the priests in the temple. He quoted it throughout His ministry.

THIRD REASON. Third, Scripture reveals what is required to become a Christian, a follower of Christ, through the words of Christ, Matthew, Mark, Luke, John, Paul, Peter, and other authors of Scripture. The Apostle Paul refers to "the holy Scriptures, which are able to make thee wise unto salvation through faith which is in Christ Jesus" (2 Tim. 3:15, KJV). The chapter entitled "Defining Christian" discusses the elements of being a Christian.

FOURTH REASON. Fourth, God uses Scripture to give the facts regarding the history ("His story") of the world and of His workings with His people and others from creation to Christ's birth, life, death, and resurrection and to the time of Christ's return to earth in glory.

FIFTH REASON. Fifth, God gives Christians the guidance needed to live the Christian life through laws and principles revealed in Scripture, through the words of Moses, King David, King Solomon, the prophets, Christ, Paul, and other authors of Scripture. Paul said," All Scripture is given by inspiration of God, and is profitable for doctrine, for reproof, for correction, for instruction in righteousness" (2 Tim. 3:16, KJV).

Without Scripture, every man does whatever is right in his own eyes, and even the most intelligent get it so very wrong. The words, "Every man did that which was right in his own eyes" (Judges 17:5-7; 21:24-25) describe a period of lawlessness in Israel (See Deut. 12:7-9; Prov. 12:15; 21:2). Proverbs states, "The way of a fool is right in his own eyes: but he that hearken[s] unto counsel is wise" (Prov.12:14-16) and "there is a way which seem[s] right unto a man, but the end thereof are the ways of death (Prov. 14:12; 16:25). God spoke through Isaiah saying, "For my thoughts are not your thoughts, neither are your ways my ways, saith the LORD. For as the heavens are higher than the earth, so are my ways higher than your ways, and my thoughts than your thoughts (Isa. 55:8-10). Jesus said, "Ye do err, not knowing the Scriptures, nor the power of God" (Matt. 22:29, KJV). Often what seems right to even the most intelligent of men is totally contrary to God's ways, because God's ways are higher than man's ways. The perfect example was President Obama, a very intelligent man with the best of intentions who fought for policies totally contrary to God's laws.

CONCLUSION. Belief in Scripture is more important than belief in God or Christ because Scripture defines God, Christ, and what it means to be a Christian. Every law student, lawyer, and judge consider two things in every case: the facts and the law. God uses Scripture to give man the facts and the law needed for living the Christian life. Without Scripture even Christians have totally wrong and conflicting opinions of God, Christ, what it means to be a Christian, and what it means to live and vote Christian values.

Scripture is a very special gift of God to man, given because God knew man desperately needed written guidance

for godly living. Men seek freedom through rebellion against
God's law, through doing whatever is right in their own eyes.
But true freedom and blessings only come through obedience
to God's laws. That is why King David said, "Thy word is a
lamp unto my feet, and a light unto my path" (Psalms 119:105)
and "I will walk at liberty: for I seek thy precepts" (Psalms
119:45, KJV).

THE VITAL IMPORTANCE OF BIBLICAL LAW TO LIVING CHRISTIAN VALUES

REASON FOR CHAPTER. Being a Christian requires living and voting in accordance with Biblical law. A Christian is by definition a follower of Christ who wants to love and serve God by doing "the will of the Father" by being obedient to God's laws revealed through Scripture. In other words, Christians need Scripture to live the Christian life. That is why Christ said, "Ye do err, not knowing the Scriptures, nor the power of God" (Matt. 22:28-30, KJV). Christ said, "Think not that I am come to destroy the law, or the prophets: I am not come to destroy, but to fulfill...." " (Matt. 5:17-18, KJV). King David said, "Thy word is a lamp unto my feet, and a light unto my path" (Psalms 119:105) and "I will walk at liberty: for I seek thy precepts" (Psalms 119:45, KJV).

Many Christians and Christian leaders are surprisingly ignorant regarding basic principles of biblical law. There is little emphasis on biblical law in seminaries, and most men in the ministry have little interest in law, politics, business, jobs, the economy, etc. They live in a different world and fail to provide the guidance that God offers through Scripture regarding these areas. Many concentrate on the love of God and neglect His holiness and righteousness. They fail to properly challenge Americans who live in a fantasy world where a loving God would never punish "good" people. Christians and Christian leaders fail to realize that study of biblical law provides amazing, fascinating insight into the heart and mind of God in many areas of life where we desperately need His guidance.

    <u>OLD TESTAMENT LAW</u>. Some Christians say that Jesus showed that Old Testament law is no longer applicable when He forgave the woman caught in adultery. The Pharisees tried to trap Jesus, knowing that the law called for stoning. Jesus evaded their trap by writing in the sand until all of the woman's accusers left. Then He said "Neither do I condemn thee: go, and sin no more"(John 8:10-12, KJV). Jesus was not a government official with authority or responsibility to impose punishment. Even a judge would not have authority to render judgment and impose the death penalty without a trial. When Christ returns, he will judge everyone.

    Many Christians believe that Old Testament law is part of the Old Covenant that God had with the nation of Israel, and that it was replaced by the New Testament or New Covenant, which does not require obedience to Old Testament law. Some clergy point to verses that seem to imply that the law was just a tutor to point sinners to Christ. "So that the law is become our tutor to bring us unto Christ, that we might be justified by faith. But now faith that is come, we are no longer under a tutor" (Gal. 3:24-25, ASV). "No longer under a tutor" means no longer under the law. However, assuming that one can ignore the law is totally contrary to the teachings of Christ and Scripture. God cares just as much about obedience to His laws today as when he killed thousands of His own people for what many today would consider minor disobedience.

    Many Christians and religious leaders do not understand how Old Testament law applies to modern times. Christ said, "<u>Think not that I am come to destroy the law, or the prophets: I am not come to destroy, but to fulfill. For verily I say unto you, till heaven and earth pass, one jot or one tittle shall in no wise pass from the law, till all be fulfilled</u>"

(Matt. 5:17-18, KJV). The law and the prophets are the books of law and the prophets in the Old Testament. The "jot" and "tittle" are the smallest parts of the Hebrew alphabet, similar to the dot on an "i" and apostrophe in the English language. \

Christ made it clear that He did not come to destroy Old Testament law, but to fulfill it, and that not even the smallest part of the law would "pass" until it was "fulfilled." As one of my professors in graduate school said, God the Father was not converted by Christ the Son. Christ's coming did not do away with Old Testament law. It fulfilled Old Testament laws related to payment for sin, because He was the Lamb of God who gave His life as payment for sin, but all other laws remained in full effect.

LOVING GOD. As noted in the Introduction, the most important biblical law is the Greatest Commandment, first stated by Moses: "Thou shalt love the Lord thy God with all thy heart, and with all thy soul, and with all thy might" (Deut. 6:5, KJV). Christ said: "Thou shalt love the Lord thy God with all thy heart, and with all thy soul, and with all thy mind. This is the first and great commandment" (Matt. 22:37-38, KJV; see Luke 10:27).

Many Old and New Testament passages state that loving God requires obedience to his commandments. "For this is the love of God, that we keep his commandments: and his commandments are not grievous" (1 John 5:3, KJV). "If ye love me, keep my commandments" (John 14:15, KJV). "He that hath my commandments, and keepeth them, he it is that loveth me: and he that loveth me shall be loved of my Father, and I will love him, and will manifest myself to him" John 14:21 (KJV). "Therefore thou shalt love the LORD thy God, and keep his charge, and his statutes, and his judgments, and his commandments, always" (Deut. 11:1, KJV). "In that I command thee this day to love the LORD thy God, to walk in his ways, and to keep his commandments and his statutes and his judgments, that thou mayest live and multiply: and the LORD thy God shall bless thee in the land whither thou goest to possess it" (Deut. 30:16, KJV). "But take diligent heed to do the commandment and the law, which Moses the servant of the LORD charged you, to love the LORD your God, and to walk in all his ways, and to keep his commandments, and to cleave unto him, and to serve him with all your heart and with all your soul" (Joshua 22:5, KJV).

Four of the most important commandments that deal with loving God are the first four of the Ten Commandments:

> I am the LORD thy God, which brought thee out of the land of Egypt, from the house of bondage.
> [First Commandment] Thou shalt have none other gods before me.
> [Second Commandment] Thou shalt not make thee any graven …for I the LORD thy God am a jealous God, visiting the iniquity of the fathers upon the children unto the third and fourth generation of them that hate me, And shewing mercy unto thousands of them that love me and keep my commandments.
> [Third Commandment] Thou shalt not take the name of the LORD thy God in vain: for the LORD will not hold him guiltless that taketh his name in vain.
> [Fourth Commandment] Keep the sabbath day to sanctify it… (Deut. 5:6-15, KJV).

Note that God brings terrible judgment upon those who hate Him, "visiting the iniquity of the fathers upon the children unto the third and fourth generation of them that hate me," but shows great mercy toward those who love him, "shewing mercy unto thousands of them that love me and keep my commandments" (Deut. 5:9-10, KJV). Many passages state that God shows love and mercy to those who love Him and keep his commandments (Ex. 20:6; Deut. 5:10; 7:9; 11:1-2, 13-14, 22-23; 19:9; Josh. 22:5-6; Neh. 1:5; Dan. 9:4; John 14:21; 15:10). Deuteronomy 7:9 (KJV) states: "Know therefore that the LORD thy God, he is God, the faithful God, which keepeth covenant and mercy with them that love him and keep his commandments to a thousand generations."

LOVING MAN. After Christ quoted the greatest commandment, He added the second greatest commandment.

> "Thou shalt love the Lord thy God with all thy heart, and with all thy soul, and with all thy mind." This is the first and great commandment. And the second is like unto it, "Thou shalt love thy neighbor as thyself." On these two commandments hang all the law and the prophets (Matthew 22:37-40, KJV).

Note Christ's final words: "On these two commandments hang all the law and the prophets" (Matt. 22:40, KJV). The law and the prophets are the books of law and books of the prophets of the Old Testament, which contain Old Testament law. Thus, Christ affirmed that all Old Testament law, which remains in effect, "hangs" on these two commandments.

The primary means of loving one's neighbor is obedience to the many commandments given through Scripture related to treatment of others. "And this is love, that we walk after his commandments. This is the commandment, That, as ye have heard from the beginning, ye should walk in it" (2 John 1:6, KJV). "By this we know that we love the children of God, when we love God, and keep his commandments" (1 John 5:2, KJV). Examples commandment related to loving one's neighbor include the final six of the ten commandments.

[Fifth Commandment] Honor thy father and thy mother, as the LORD thy God hath commanded thee; that thy days may be prolonged, and that it may go well with thee, in the land which the LORD thy God giveth thee.
[Sixth Commandment] Thou shalt not kill.
[Seventh Commandment] Neither shalt thou commit adultery.
[Eighth Commandment] Neither shalt thou steal.
[Ninth Commandment] Neither shalt thou bear false witness against thy neighbor.
[Tenth Commandment] Neither shalt thou desire thy neigh[bor]s wife, neither shalt thou covet thy neigh[bor]'s house, his field, or his manservant, or his maidservant, his ox, or his ass, or anything that is thy neigh[bor]'s. (Deut. 5:16-21, KJV).

HIGHER STANDARD. After declaring that He came not to destroy Old Testament law, but to fulfill it, Christ introduced a higher standard. First, He clarified the importance of obedience to even the "least commandments."

Then he reviewed many points of Old Testament law, and
showed that he required even higher standards.

> Whosoever…shall break one of these least
> commandments, and shall teach men so, he shall
> be called the least in the kingdom of heaven: but
> whosoever shall do and teach them, the same shall
> be called great in the kingdom of heaven…. Ye
> have heard that it was said…Thou shalt not kill;
> and whosoever shall kill shall be in danger of the
> judgment: But I say unto you, that whosoever is
> angry with his brother without a cause shall be in
> danger of the judgment…. Ye have heard that it
> was said… Thou shalt not commit adultery: But I
> say unto you, That whosoever looketh on a woman
> to lust after her hath committed adultery with her
> already in his heart…. It hath been said,
> Whosoever shall put away his wife, let him give
> her a writing of divorcement: But I say unto you,
> That whosoever shall put away his wife, saving for
> the cause of fornication, causeth her to commit
> adultery: and whosoever shall marry her that is
> divorced commit[s] adultery. Again, ye have
> heard that it hath been said… Thou shalt not
> forswear thyself, but shalt perform unto the Lord
> thine oaths: But I say unto you, Swear not at all….
> But let your communication be, Yea, yea; Nay,
> nay: for whatsoever is more than these cometh of
> evil. Ye have heard that it hath been said, An eye
> for an eye, and a tooth for a tooth: But I say unto
> you, That ye resist not evil: but whosoever shall
> smite thee on thy right cheek, turn to him the other
> also…. Ye have heard that it hath been said, Thou
> shalt love thy neighbor, and hate thine enemy. But

I say unto you, Love your enemies, bless them that curse you, do good to them that hate you, and pray for them which despitefully use you, and persecute you; That ye may be the children of your Father which is in heaven …. Be ye therefore perfect, even as your Father which is in heaven is perfect (Matt. 5:17-49, KJV).

Christ established higher standards for murder, adultery, divorce, justice and mercy, and loving one's enemies. Then He gave the clincher, the bottom line, the principle that should govern the life of every Christian: "Be ye therefore perfect, even as your Father which is in heaven is perfect" (Matthew 5:49, KJV). In other words, Christians are called to be perfect not only through complete obedience to the letter of Old Testament law (every jot and title), but also through complete obedience to the much higher standard of the true spirit and intent of the law, as taught and lived by Christ. No Christian can be perfect like God the Father, but every Christian is commanded by Christ to strive for perfection. This means getting up after falling, repenting of wrongdoing, and continuing to run the race which Christians are called to run, striving for perfection.

CONCLUSION. So, what does all this have to do with politics and elections? God provides much needed guidance to man through biblical law revealed through Scripture. Without biblical law, man cannot properly discern right from wrong. Being a Christian requires more than just believing in Christ as Lord and Savior. It requires taking up one's cross and following Christ, dying to self and living for Christ, and being obedient to God's commandments. These commandments include all Old Testament and New Testament laws not fulfilled by the coming of Christ. Christ fulfilled laws regarding sacrifice, because He was the Lamb of God, the final, perfect sacrifice. Christ said that He did not come to abolish the law, but to fulfill it, and gave an even higher standard for obedience to biblical law revealed through the Old Testament, the only Scripture that existed at the time of Christ. Being a Christian requires voting for candidates that support God's laws revealed through Scripture.

CHAPTER 4.0

THE WAR ON PRESIDENT TRUMP

<u>INTRODUCTION</u>. All Americans should be honest enough to acknowledge that there has been an intense, unrelenting, full-time war against President Trump waged by Democrats and the media, a war which began before he took office. In 2016 some Democrats ran for office promising to impeach Trump before he was even sworn in as President.

<u>LIBERAL DEMOCRAT MEDIA</u>. Lawyers, judges, and juries consider two things in every case: the facts and the law. Attorneys for the prosecution and defense present two totally different, conflicting views of the facts. Juries hear the arguments of both sides and decide who is telling the truth. Ideally, the media would present arguments from both sides, and let voters decide who is telling the truth, but that is not what happens in America today.

About half of Americans voted for Trump. However, virtually all reporters, newscasters, and talk show hosts hired by the major television networks (NBC, ABC, CBS, CNN) and newspapers (New York Times, Washington Post, USA Today) are liberal Democrats. They do not hire conservative Republicans who support Trump, because they despise Trump, and because they do not believe that conservative Republicans are capable of discerning and reporting the truth. Therefore, they present one view, one perspective, one interpretation of the facts to voters, that of Democrats, not Republicans. Then, fighting for what they believe is truth and justice, they present their arguments to voters for Democrats, and continually attack and condemn Trump and Republicans.

44

Reporters and talk show hosts interview fellow reporters and other Democrats, asking for their opinions, their interpretation of the facts. Rarely do they interview a conservative Republican, and when they do so they usually ask the Republican to explain and condemn the actions of Trump and/or other Republicans. Then they interview someone who contradicts the Republican. No reporter or talk show host who works for the mainstream media can advance his or her career with any report that is favorable to Trump or Republicans. They advance their careers by proving that they can do the best job of attacking them.

Trump and Republicans are continually attacked on virtually every news program and political talk-show on national television and in all the major newspapers. Political talk shows include ABC's The View, hosted by Whoopi Goldberg, NBC's Meet the Press with Chuck Todd, and ABC's This Week with George Stephanopoulos. Stephanopoulos is a liberal Democrat who worked for President Clinton on his presidential campaign and in the White House.

The View, like other shows, only presents an anti-Trump view to Americans. Whoopi Goldberg, someone we loved so much as an actress, now hatefully refuses to acknowledge President Trump as the President, calling him "the new guy" or the "current resident" of the White House. Joyce Behar hates all Republicans with a passion; she said that 70% of Republicans are racist. Megan McCain, the only Republican, hates Trump.

The intense hatred displayed by the women on The View is actually exceeded by the hatred demonstrated by Jimmy

Kimmel on ABC's Jimmy Kimmel Live and Seth Meyers on their night shows. Jimmy Fallon on NBC's Tonight Show strongly opposes Trump, but is less hateful. NBC's Saturday Night Live berates and mocks every Republican President. The extreme political bias of the media gives Democrats a huge advantage over Republicans.

PRESIDENTIAL CAMPAIGN--F.B.I. SURVEILANCE OF TRUMP. The Obama Administration illegally spied on and wiretapped Trump during the 2016 presidential campaign. The effort to do so was initiated by the Hillary Clinton campaign, which hired a former British intelligence agent to develop the falsified document used to fraudulently obtain the warrant to surveil the Trump campaign. During the 2016 presidential campaign, former President Bill Clinton was seen talking to the Attorney General, who worked for President Obama, at an airport for about 30 minutes. There was some coordination between the Obama Administration and the Clinton campaign.

AFTER INAUGURATION--WOMEN'S MARCH. Before and after inauguration, demonstrators carried signs saying "Impeach Trump" and "Not my President". The day after he took office there was a huge "Women's March" in Washington, D.C., but not all women were welcome. Pro-life women had their signs torn up by other women. It was an anti-Trump march the day after he took office, not a women's march for all women. The Women's March was inspired by the "Me Too" movement against all men guilty of mistreatment of women. Democrats condemned Trump for distant past sexual misconduct.

However, that was in total contrast to the way they treated President Clinton when he was found guilty of telling lies under oath about sexual misconduct in the Oval Office with an intern while he was President and living in the White House with his wife. He was disbarred as an attorney by the Supreme Court of Arkansas because he lied under oath, but Democrats in Congress gathered at the White House for a photo with the President to show their support for him, and claimed that it was just a personal matter which did not affect his ability to serve as President.

When Senator Biden led the Senate Judiciary confirmation hearings for Supreme Court Justice Clarence Thomas, Justice Thomas said, "This is a high-tech lynching…." The standard of proof in criminal cases is "beyond any reasonable doubt." The standard of proof in civil cases is "preponderance of the evidence." The standard of proof in a lynching is "guilty regardless of the evidence." That standard was applied to Justice Thomas, Justice Kavanaugh, and President Trump. They were all high-tech lynching. Scripture states that the law is a good thing if it is used lawfully. These are all examples of the law being used unlawfully.

All Americans should be honest enough to acknowledge exactly what each of these men were accused of doing, and admit that Democrats would never apply the same standard or take the same action against any Democrat. Justice Thomas was accused of talking dirty to a woman. Justice Kavanaugh was accused, about forty years in the past, of laying fully clothed on top of a fully clothed woman for a few seconds. President Trump was accused of distant past sexual misconduct. President Clinton was found guilty of lying under oath about having sexual relations with an intern in the Oval Office when he was President and living in the White House with his wife.

MUELLER INVESTIGATION. Democrats in Congress and the Executive Branch, two of the three branches of the federal government, have made many valiant attempts to remove President Trump from office. Shortly after inauguration, James Comey, head of the Federal Bureau of Investigation, leaked false information through a friend to the press in an attempt to initiate an investigation that would get President Trump removed from office. The false information was based on a false report called the Steele Dossier. That started a two-year investigation, led by former FBI Director Mueller, into whether Trump colluded with the Russians to win the 2016 election.

IMPEACHMENT TRIAL. That attempt to remove the President failed, so the Democrat-led House of Representatives held impeachment hearings. President Trump was accused of asking the Ukrainians for information (the facts, the truth) about Biden wrongfully using his position as Vice-President to get his son-in-law Hunter Biden a job for which he was totally unqualified but very highly paid for doing virtually nothing. Democrats and the press were outraged that the President dared to ask for the facts, the truth, about the unethical conduct of Biden, but never demonstrated any concern whatsoever about the obvious, glaring unethical conduct of Biden. The House of Representatives voted to impeach President Trump, but their attempt to remove the President from office failed because the Republican-led Senate voted against impeachment. The Democrats never would have even considered trying to impeach a Democrat for the same conduct. Again, scripture states that the law is a good thing if it is used lawfully. This is another example of the law being used unlawfully.

"YOU'RE FIRED!" When President Trump fired Comey and other personnel in the Executive Branch who tried to get him removed from office or who attacked him or were disloyal to him, Democrats accused him of obstruction of justice. The President is the head of the Executive Branch of the federal government. Everyone in the federal government works for the President except those in Congress, the Supreme Court, and Federal Courts. The President can and should remove from office anyone in the Executive Branch who is disloyal to him, working against him, or trying to get him removed from office. He is their boss. Democrats would never accuse the President of obstruction of justice if he was a Democrat.

MAYORS AGAINST TRUMP. Many Democratic mayors joined the war against Trump, declaring their cities "sanctuary cities" for illegal immigrants. In 2020, when President Trump used federal police to protect federal courthouses from violent protestors trying to break into and damage or destroy them, Democratic mayors voiced their opposition to Trump and the use of federal forces to protect federal buildings in their cities. The Democratic mayor of Portland actually thanked protestors attacking the Federal Courthouse in Portland for coming out to show their opposition to the President. Demonstrators in many cities demanded defunding of the police, and the mayors of New York City and Seattle actually agreed to partial defunding of the police.

PRESIDENTIAL DEBATE. The first presidential debate took place on September 29, 2020, in Cleveland, Ohio. President Trump said that he was willing to condemn white supremacists, but failed to clearly do so, instead saying that it was not right-white supremacists but left-wing groups like ANTIFA that were responsible for violent, destructive protests. Biden refused to condemn ANTIFA, saying that it is an idea, not an organization. The opposite is true. ANTIFA is an organization; white supremacists is not an organization. After the debate, every major news network falsely implied that Trump was a racist because he failed to condemn white supremacists. Neither candidate was willing to criticize any group of voters, but only Trump was being asked to condemn a group that might vote for him.

During the debate, Biden falsely implied that President Trump was a hypocrite because he voted by mail but condemned fraud related to voting by mail. Trump said that he had no problem with solicited ballots, but expressed great concern about fraud with unsolicited ballots, which are automatically mailed to everyone on voter registration files, dead or alive. See chapter on Voting by Mail for explanation. Trump also complained about fraud related to handling of ballots, citing a true case of military ballots for Trump being thrown in a trash can in Philadelphia by a poll-worker who was then fired. The day after the debate the New York Times ran an article falsely accusing Trump of being the greatest threat to the election because he expressed concern about voter fraud and was unwilling to accept without question or investigation the results of the election.[19] It was Democrats and the media who never accepted the results of the 2016 election.

Before the debate, the New York Times released information on President Trump's taxes, stating that he had only paid $750 in federal income tax a couple years. Every major news network stated or implied that Trump was guilty of tax fraud. During the debate, Trump said that he paid many millions of dollars in other taxes. The New York Post ran an article which clearly implied that Trump was guilty of tax

---

[19] "Tuesday's Debate Made Clear the Gravest Threat to the Election: The President Himself," David E. Sanger, The New York Times, September 30, 2020.

fraud, and contrasted him with President Carter, who paid $6,000 more than he was required to pay one year.[20] No news network or President Trump ever mentioned that he would have paid far more in federal income taxes if he had not given up his $400,000/year salary as President. No president in the history of the United States has given so much back to the American government.

CONCLUSION. During the past four years, the intense, unrelenting, full-time war waged by Democrats and the media against the President Trump and Republicans has reached an unprecedented intensity. They have continually attacked Trump, tried to remove him from office, and are now doing their best to prevent his re-election. This war began long before Trump, will continue long after him. This is first and foremost a spiritual war, not a political war. The primary forces in this war are spiritual forces, not Trump, Republicans, or Democrats. Americans need to know where God stands in this war, and make sure that they are on God's side.

---

[20] "How Trump's Taxes Compare to Those of Other Presidents," The Washington Post, September 28, 2020.

THE 2020 DEMOCRATIC
NATIONAL CONVENTION

<u>INTRODUCTION</u>. The 2020 Democratic National Convention was scheduled to take place in Milwaukee, Wisconsin during the third week in August, 2020. Due to the global pandemic, most speeches were pre-recorded and aired on major television networks August 17-20, 2020. There were many speakers. This chapter will only cover a few. It ends with notes from Biden's acceptance speech, the last speech of the convention.

The primary concerns of both parties are the policies and objectives embodied in their party platforms. Each party has very different interpretations of the facts and the laws that should govern our nation, and very different understanding of the policies needed to help Americans realize the American dream and live out the ideals embodied in Declaration of Independence, Constitution, and Bill of Rights.

Therefore, one would expect that the 2020 Democratic Convention would concentrate on explaining that vision and those policies, goals, and ideals to American voters. That did not happen. The primary objective of the Convention and most speakers, to include President Obama, Michele Obama, and Vice-President Biden, was to attack the character and competence of President Trump.

In 1992 Bill Clinton used the words, "It's the economy, stupid," to belittle President Herbert W. Bush (father of President George W. Bush), and to convince voters that he would do a better job of restoring jobs and the economy. Clinton, as the Governor of Arkansas, was less qualified to deal with jobs and the economy than President Bush, who had years of experience as President. But Clinton's advisors knew that insulting and belittling the President would win the support of some American voters. Democrats have excelled at the politics of personal destruction for many years.

As an Army officer, I understand the simple truth that you cannot win a war by being on the defensive. That is why generals like Grant, Lee, Patton, and MacArthur all achieved great victories by constantly attacking their enemies. That is what Democrats and the media have done with President Trump, every day that he has been in office, and that is what Democrats did during the Democratic National Convention.

<u>MICHELE OBAMA</u>. Michele Obama gave the longest and most important speech of the first night. Her duty and mission were clear. In 2016 she became famous for saying, "When they go low, we go high." That was an absolute lie. She proved it again by spending most of her time attacking the character and competence of President Trump. She falsely accused Trump of fanning racist sentiments, having "a total and utter lack of empathy," and blamed him for the deaths of 170,000 Americans. She said, "So let me be as honest and clear as I possibly can. Donald Trump is the wrong president for our country. He has had more than enough time to prove that he can do the job, but he is clearly in over his head... It is what it is."[21] Everything she said about Trump was a lie. Everything. See chapter on Republican National Convention for Trump's very long list of accomplishments.

---

[21] "Democratic Convention Highlights: 6 Takeaways from Night 1," Eric Bradner, Gregory Krieg, and Dan Merica, CNN, August 18, 2020.

<u>SENATOR BERNIE SANDERS</u>. Bernie Sanders, an extreme far-left liberal, also spoke during the first night. He said, "Many of the ideas we fought for that just a few years ago were considered radical are now mainstream. But let us be clear. If Donald Trump is reelected, all the progress we have made will be in jeopardy."[22] Franklin Graham warned about the ungodly progressive agenda of Democrats.

<u>REPUBLICANS FOR BIDEN</u>: During the first night, three Republicans who hate Trump spoke, saying that they would vote for Biden. These included former Ohio Gov. <u>John Kasich</u>, "Meg Whitman, who ran for governor of California as a Republican in 2010 but backed Hillary Clinton in 2016; Susan Molinari, a former Republican congresswoman from New York; and Christine Todd Whitman, former Republican governor of New Jersey and EPA chief under George W. Bush."[23] Note that California, New York, and New Jersey are all very liberal states, and Ohio is a swing state. None of these were conservative Republicans.

<u>REP. OCASIO-CORTEZ</u>. New York Representative Alexandria Ocasio-Cortez was only given 95 seconds to speak during the second night. She talked about the aspirations of the progressive movement. She said this "<u>mass people's movement</u>," is <u>dedicated to addressing</u> the "the wounds of <u>racial injustice, colonization, misogyny, and homophobia</u>," and building "reimagined systems of immigration and foreign policy that turn away from the <u>violence and xenophobia of our past</u>." It is a movement "that realizes the <u>unsustainable brutality of an economy that rewards explosive inequalities of wealth for the few at the expense of long-term stability for the many</u>, and who organized a historic, <u>grassroots campaign to</u>

---

[22] Ibid.
[23] Ibid.

<u>reclaim our democracy</u>."[24] Her words reflect a total rejection of the founding fathers and the principles that the United States was founded upon. This book shows that they also reflect a total rejection of Christian values. Also, it is the Republicans, not the Democrats, who have a long history of fighting against racial injustice. See chapter on Racism and Police and chapter on Republican National Convention.

<u>FORMER PRESIDENT OBAMA</u>. Former President Obama joined the personal attacks on Trump. He said, "Donald Trump hasn't grown into the job because he can't, and the consequences of that failure are severe. 170,000 Americans dead. Millions of jobs gone. Our worst impulses unleashed, our proud reputation around the world badly diminished, and our democratic institutions threatened like never before."[25]

Everything Obama said was a lie except the number of dead Americans and lost jobs. The implication that President Trump does not care about Americans is an absolute lie. The implication that he did not do his best to fight the global pandemic is an absolute lie. See next chapter for what was done to fight the virus. President Obama presents an excellent example of how much Democrats hate Republicans and are willing to lie about and disparage the character and accomplishments of Republicans to win elections.

President Obama complimented Biden's character by saying, "What I quickly came to admire about Joe Biden is his resilience, born of too much struggle; his empathy, born of too

---

[24] "Democratic National Convention 2020: Day 2," Gregory Krieg, Melissa Macaya, <u>Kyle Blaine</u>, <u>Jessica Estepa</u>, CNN, August 19, 2020.
[25] "Democratic Convention Takeaways: Make History, Pound Trump," Associated Press, August 19, 2020.

much grief. Joe's a man who learned – early on – to treat every person he meets with respect and dignity, living by the words his parents taught him: "No one's better than you, Joe, but you're better than nobody."[26]

SENATOR KAMALA HARRIS. Senator Harris, making history as the first black woman on a major ticket, spoke on the third night as the vice-presidential nominee. She joined the long list of Democrats attacking the character and incompetence of President Trump. "Trump's failure of leadership has cost lives and livelihoods... The constant chaos leaves us adrift. The incompetence makes us feel afraid. The callousness makes us feel alone. It's a lot."[27] Everything she said about Trump was an absolute lie. See chapter on Republican National Convention for comments by people who know Trump much better than Harris.

VICE-PRESIDENT BIDEN. Vice-President Biden gave his acceptance speech from an auditorium in Milwaukee, Wisconsin. He framed the current status of the United States of America by saying, "And now history has delivered us to one of the most difficult moments America's ever faced. Four, four historic crises all at the same time: a perfect storm. The worst pandemic in over 100 years, the worst economic crisis since the great depression, the most compelling call for racial justice since the '60s and the...accelerating threats of climate change."[28]

He stressed the importance of this election by saying, "This is a life-changing election. This will determine what America's going to look like for a long, long time. Character is

---

[26] Ibid.
[27] Ibid.
[28] "Full Text: Joe Biden's 2020 Democratic National Convention Speech," ABC News, August 21, 2020.

on the ballot. Compassion is on the ballot. Decency, science, democracy. They're all on the ballot. Who we are as a nation, what we stand for, and most importantly, who we want to be, that's all on the ballot. And the choice could not be more clear."[29] All this sounds very good, except the real question is not whether Biden is a nice man, but whether he will fight for and support Christian values.

<u>BIDEN ACCOMPLISHMENTS</u>. Unlike President Trump, who listed almost 50 accomplishments during his convention speech, Vice President Biden did not list any accomplishments. He served in Washington D.C. for 47 years, which included 8 years as Vice President under President Obama. He helped implement the Affordable Care Act, known as Obamacare, but that is totally unconstitutional, for reasons explained in the chapter on Healthcare. He helped usher in same-sex marriage, but that is totally contrary to Scripture cited in this book.

<u>BIDEN GOALS</u>. During his acceptance speech at the Democratic National Convention, Vice President Biden listed his goals as follows:

1.   First: "get control of the virus."
2.   Develop and deploy rapid tests.
3.   Make medical supplies and protective equipment.
4.   Ensure schools have resources need.
5.   Implement national mandate to wear masks.
6.   Economic plan is to "build back better."
7.   Build modern roads, bridges, highways, broadband, ports and airports and pipes that transport clean water.
8.   Create 5 million new manufacturing and technology jobs.

---

[29] Ibid.

9.   Building on Affordable Care Act, create a health care system that lowers premiums, deductibles, drug prices.
10. Create an education system that trains people for "the best jobs."
11. Create a child care and elder care system.
12. Create an immigration system.
13. Empower labor unions.
14. Institute equal pay for women.
15. Pay essential workers.
16. "Deal with climate change."
17. Lead the world in clean energy and create millions of good paying jobs in the process.
18. Maintain social security for seniors.[30]

CONCLUSION. This is a very short chapter because the Democratic National Convention did not concentrate on their vision for America or on discussion of policies needed to help Americans realize the American dream and live out the ideals embodied in Declaration of Independence, Constitution, and Bill of Rights. The Associated Press stated, "There has been one persistent theme in the Democratic National Convention...to portray President Donald Trump in highly personal ways as one unsuited for the White House both in skills and temperament. And no one, not even former President Barack Obama, has been holding back."[31]

Democrats and the media excel at the politics of personal destruction. That is how they win elections, and that is their primary strategy for this election. Christians should ignore the lies and vote Christian values. Americans should not vote first based upon anything that any candidate or anyone else says

[30] Ibid.
[31] "Democratic Convention Takeaways: Make History, Pound Trump," Associated Press, August 19, 2020.

when trying to get elected, or anything they promise to do when in office. Americans should vote first based upon the actual voting record and actual accomplishments of the candidates. Chapter 2 shows that Biden scored an absolute zero for voting Christian values.

CHAPTER 6.0

THE 2020 REPUBLICAN NATIONAL CONVENTION

<u>INTRODUCTION</u>. The 2020 Republican National Convention was scheduled to take place in Charlotte, North Carolina during the fourth week of August, 2020. Due to the global pandemic, most speeches were pre-recorded and aired on television August 24-27, 2020. Most events of the final night took place on the grounds of the White House for the first time in history. There were over 50 speakers. This chapter will only cite a few. It ends with notes from Trump's acceptance speech, the last speech of the convention.

<u>HERSCHEL WALKER</u>. Herschel Walker, a 58-year old black man, was a top NFL football player and winner of the Heisman Trophy, the highest award given to football players. He was also a bobsledder, sprinter, and martial artist. In other words, he was an absolutely amazing man and athlete. He said, "I've seen racism up close. I know what it is. And, it isn't Donald Trump.... It hurt my soul to hear the terrible names that people called Donald. The worst one is racist... I take it as a personal insult that people would think I've had a 37-year friendship with a racist.... People who think that don't know what they're talking about."[32] Walker said that Trump was always a "fair and loving" person who displayed "tremendous family values." He ended by saying, "If you love America and want to make it better, Donald Trump is your president."[33]

---

[32] "Herschel Walker Defends Trump in Passionate Speech... He's Not A Racist!!!," TMZ Sports, www.tmz.com, 8/25/2020.
[33] Ibid.

60

     <u>DANIEL CAMERON</u>. Daniel Cameron is the first black attorney general in Kentucky. He said, "I also think about Joe Biden, who says, if you aren't voting for me, 'you ain't black.' Who argued that Republicans would put us 'back in chains.' Who says there is no 'diversity' of thought in the Black community? Mr. Vice President look at me, I am Black. We are not all the same, sir. I am not in chains. My mind is my own. And you can't tell me how to vote because of the color of my skin."[34]

     He warned about Biden. "Joe Biden is a backwards thinker in a world craving forward-looking leadership. There's no wisdom in his record or plan, just a trail of discredited ideas and offensive statements. Joe Biden would destroy jobs, raise our taxes, and throw away the lives of countless unborn children. And he is captive to the radical left, a movement committed to cancel culture and the destruction of public discourse. They believe your skin color must dictate your politics. And if you fail to conform while exercising your God given right to speak and think freely, they will cut you down. The politics of identity, cancellation, and mob rule are not acceptable to me. Republicans trust you to think for yourselves and to pursue your American dream however you see fit."[35]

     Then he compared Biden's record to Trump's record. "Let's be honest: no one is excited about Joe Biden. And so, I ask you to judge the record. On criminal justice reform, Joe Biden couldn't do it, but President Trump did. On the economy, Joe Biden couldn't do it, but President Trump did build an economy that worked for everyone, especially minorities, and he will do it again. And on immigration, Joe

---

[34] "Daniel Cameron, Kentucky A.G., Speaks at the R.N.C.: Full Transcript," Maggie Astor, August 25, 2020.
[35] Ibid.

Biden promises more to illegal immigrants than he does to you. But President Trump believes his highest duty is to the American worker. The choice is clear."[36]

CLARENCE HENDERSON. Clarence Henderson is a black civil rights activist and military veteran. He said, "Freedom of thought is a powerful thing. Joe Biden said if you don't vote for him you ain't black. If you vote for him, you don't know history."[37] Henderson stressed that the Republican Party and President Trump had done more for black Americans than the Democrat Party. "It was the Republican Party that passed the 13th Amendment abolishing slavery; it was the Republican Party that passed the 14th Amendment giving black men citizenship; and it was the Republican Party that passed the 15th Amendment giving Black men the right to vote."[38] He said that Trump gave "record funding to HBCUs (Historically-Black Colleges)... created a record amount of jobs for the black community, and passed criminal justice reform through the First Step Act where 91 percent of the inmates released were black."[39] He said, "These achievements demonstrate that Donald Trump truly cares about black lives. His policies show his heart. He has done more for black Americans in four years than Joe Biden has done in 50!"[40]

SENATOR TIM SCOTT. Senator Scott is a black Republican senator from South Carolina. He said, "Joe Biden

---

[36] Ibid.

[37] "Civil Rights Activist Clarence Henderson: If You Vote For Biden, You Don't Know History," Tyler Stone, www.realclearpolitics.com, August 26, 2020.

[38] "Civil Rights Leader Clarence Henderson: If You Vote for Biden 'You Don't Know History'," Katherine Rodriguez, www.Breitbart.com, 26 Aug 2020.

[39] Ibid.

[40] Ibid.

said if a black man didn't vote for him, he wasn't truly black. Joe Biden said black people are a monolithic community. Joe Biden said poor kids can be just as smart as white kids. And while his words are one thing, his actions take it to a whole new level."[41] He then explained how "in 1994, Biden led the charge on a crime bill that put millions of black Americans behind bars" but "President Trump's criminal justice reform law fixed many of the disparities Biden created and made our system more fair and just for all Americans."[42] He said, "Biden failed our nation's Historically Black Colleges and Universities" but "President Trump signed into law historically high funding for HBCUs, as well as a bill to give them permanent funding for the first time ever!"[43]

Senator Scott said this election is "about the promise of America. It's about you and me…our challenges and heartbreaks, hopes and dreams."[44] He asked, "Do we want a society that breeds success, or a culture that cancels everything it even slightly disagrees with? Our nation's arc always bends back towards fairness. We are not fully where we want to be…but thank God we are not where we used to be! We are always striving to be better...When we stumble, and we will, we pick ourselves back up and try again. We don't give into cancel-culture, or the radical--and factually baseless--belief that things are worse today than in the 1860s or the 1960s.We have work to do...but I believe in the goodness of America…the promise that all men, and all women are created equal."[45]

---

[41] "Republican Senator for South Carolina Tim Scott Speaks During the First Day of the Republican Convention at the Mellon Auditorium in Washington on Aug. 24, 2020," NBC News, updated Aug. 25, 2020.
[42] Ibid.
[43] Ibid.
[44] Ibid.
[45] Ibid.

JA'RON SMITH. Ja'Ron Smith, assistant to the president and one of the top black senior officials in the administration, spoke about Trump's empathy. He said, "In the wake of the murder of Ahmaud Arbery, George Floyd, and LeGend Taliferro, a moment of national racial consciousness, I have seen his true conscience. I just wish everyone could see the deep empathy he shows to families whose loved ones were killed in senseless violence."[46]

RUDY GIULIANI. Giuliani served as President Trump's attorney and confidant. He said, "Biden and his fellow Democrats were widely criticized for not speaking up about the out-of-control violence plaguing Democrat cities in our country.... They said nothing about the alarming growth of murder and riots and attempts to end policing.... Their silence was so deafening that it reveals an acceptance of this violence because they will accept anything they hope will defeat President Donald Trump."[47]

MIKE POMPEO. Secretary of State Mike Pompeo spoke from Jerusalem on the second night of the convention. He rightfully stated that "the primary constitutional function of the national government is ensuring that your family and mine are safe and ensuring the freedom to live, to work, to learn, and to worship as they choose."[48] He listed foreign policy accomplishments of President Trump: ending unfair trade

---

[46] "Ja'Ron Smith, One of the Top Black Officials in the White House, Touts Trump's Empathy," Dartunorro Clark, NBC News, August 28, 2020.
[47] "Giuliani Tells NBC News He Will Attack Biden on Police Brutality Protests," Allan Smith, NBC News, August 28, 2020.
[48] "Pompeo at 2020 RNC: Trump Has Held China Accountable for Covering Up the China Virus," Tim Hains, www.realclearpolitics.com, August 25, 2020.

agreements with China, improving relations with North Korea, ending their nuclear testing, giving defensive weapons to Ukraine, strengthening NATO, killing Iranian terrorist Qasem Soleimani, responsible for the deaths of hundreds of American soldiers and thousands of Christians, wiping out the ISIS caliphate and killing its leader Abu Bakr al-Baghdadi, terminating a disastrous nuclear deal with Iran, moving the U.S. embassy to Jerusalem, and brokering a historic peace agreement between Israel and the United Arab Emirates.[49] He finished by saying that "the way each of us can best ensure our freedoms [is] by electing leaders who don't just talk, but who deliver."[50]

DONALD TRUMP, JR. Donald Trump, Jr. gave one of the best speeches of the convention. First he said what President Trump achieved before the global pandemic: "The greatest prolonged economic expansion in American history. The lowest unemployment rate in nearly 50 years. The lowest unemployment rates ever for black Americans, Hispanic Americans, women...."[51] He said when the President shut down flights from China to fight the virus, Biden and Democrats called him a racist and a xenophobe.

He warned that "Biden's radical leftwing policies would stop our economic recovery cold...shutting the country down-- again."[52] He said Biden "supported the worst trade deals.... He voted for NAFTA...down the tubes went our auto industry. He pushed TPP. Goodbye manufacturing jobs."[53] He said the

---

[49] Ibid.

[50] Ibid.

[51] "Donald Trump Jr., Speaks as He Tapes His Speech for the First Day of the Republican National Convention from the Andrew W. Mellon Auditorium in Washington, on Aug. 24, 2020." Susan Walsh, Associated Press, Aug. 24, 2020, updated Aug. 25, 2020 by NBC News.

[52] Ibid.

Chinese Communist Party favors Biden. He said Biden wants to "bring in more illegal immigrants to take jobs from American citizens. His open border policies would drive wages down for Americans."[54] He said Biden promised to repeal Trump Tax Cuts, which were "rocket fuel to the economy."[55] He reminded Americans that President Trump built the greatest economy ever and that he would do it again.

Donald Trump, Jr. warned that Democrats were "attacking the very principles on which our Nation was founded: Freedom of thought. Freedom of speech. Freedom of religion. The rule of law." He said, "If Democrats really wanted to help minorities...they'd let parents choose what school is best for their kids. They'd limit immigration to protect American workers. They'd support the police who protect our neighborhoods. They'd...negotiate trade deals that prioritizes America's interests... They'd end the endless wars and quit sending our young people to solve problems in foreign lands. They'd cut taxes for families and workers. They'd create Opportunity Zones that drive investment into inner cities."[56]

Addressing racism, police, and the death of George Floyd, he said, "All men and women are created equal and must be treated equally under the law...we must put an end to racism, and...ensure that any police officer who abuses their power is held accountable."[57] He also reminded Americans that police are heroes who deserve the deepest appreciation. He ended by challenging Americans to imagine the life, the

---

[53] Ibid.
[54] Ibid.
[55] Ibid.
[56] Ibid.
[57] Ibid.

country, and the world that they want, and explained how that
was the dream of Donald Trump and Republicans.

ERIC TRUMP AND TIFFANY TRUMP. Eric Trump
and Tiffany Trump, son and daughter of President Trump, also
gave outstanding speeches. However, this chapter is already
too long, so I have not included them.

VICE-PRESIDENT PENCE. Vice-President Mike Pence
spoke from Fort McHenry, which survived bombardment by
the British 206 years ago and inspired the writing of our
national anthem. Unlike Democrats who attacked the character
of President Trump, Pence attacked the decisions and agenda
of Biden. He said that Bob Gates, Secretary of Defense under
President Obama, said Joe Biden had "been wrong on nearly
every major foreign policy and national security issue over the
past four decades."[58] He opposed the raids that killed three top
terrorists: Osama Bin Laden, responsible for the death of about
3,000 Americans on 9/11; the leader of ISIS; and Iran's top
general Qassem Soleimani, responsible for the deaths of
hundreds of American soldiers in Iraq and Afghanistan.[59] He
supported the invasion of Iraq. He severely criticized Trump's
suspension of flights from China when the virus which came
from China hit the United States.

Pence warned that Biden's plan for America will "raise
taxes by nearly $4 trillion...abolish fossil fuels, end fracking,
and impose...climate change regulations that would drastically
increase the cost of living...repeal all the tariffs that are
leveling the playing field for American workers, support open

---

[58] "Full Text: Pence Says 'The Choice in this Election is Whether America
Remains America' in RNC Speech," Melissa Quinn, Kathryn Watson, CBS
News, August 26, 2020.
[59] Ibid.

borders; sanctuary cities; and free lawyers and healthcare for illegal immigrants," and taxpayer funding of abortion, and end school choice.[60]

Pence said that Senator Bernie Sanders told his followers that "Biden could be the most liberal President of modern times" and said that "many of the ideas we fought for, that just a few years ago were considered radical, are now mainstream" in the Democratic Party."[61] Pence warned that Biden is a Trojan horse for the radical left. He said President Trump would "set our nation on a path to freedom and opportunity...but Joe Biden would set America on a path of socialism and decline."[62]

He said, "Economic recovery is on the ballot, law and order is on the ballot. But so are things far more fundamental and foundational to our country."[63] He cited "freedom, free markets, and the unalienable right to life and liberty."[64] He said, "It's not so much whether America will be more conservative or more liberal, more Republican or more Democrat. The choice...is whether America remains America."[65]

IVANKA TRUMP. Ivanka Trump, daughter of President Trump, spoke just before her father on the final night of the convention. She made one interesting comment about politics in Washington D.C. "I was shocked to see people leave major challenges unsolved, so they [could] blame the other side and campaign on the same issue in the next election."[66]

---

[60] Ibid.

[61] Ibid.

[62] Ibid.

[63] Ibid.

[64] Ibid.

[65] Ibid.

[66] "Full Text: Ivanka Trump's 2020 Republican National Convention

She made many insightful comments about her father. "Donald Trump did not come to Washington to win praise.... [He] came to Washington for one reason, and one reason alone: To Make America Great Again! My father has strong convictions. He knows what he believes, and says what he thinks. Whether you agree with him or not, you always know where he stands.... He is so unapologetic about his beliefs that he has caused me and countless Americans to take a hard look at our own convictions, and ask ourselves, what do we stand for? Later she added, "The word "impossible" -- it only motivates him. Donald Trump...believes that nothing is beyond our reach, and the best is yet to come.... My dad believes in the potential of each individual."[67]

She made a couple comments that revealed the compassionate side of her father. "I've been with my father and seen the pain in his eyes when he receives updates on the lives that have been stolen by this plague." "I've stood by my father's side at Dover Air Force Base as he has received our fallen heroes, and each time it steeled his resolve to finally stop the endless foreign wars." She quoted him saying, "Don't let down those dairy farmers I met in Wisconsin. ... I don't want them to like this deal, I want them to love it!"[68]

She challenged Americans to ask: "What kind of America do we want to leave for our children?" She answered by saying, "We want a future where our kids can believe in American greatness...where every child can live in a safe community and go to a great school of their choice. We want a culture where differences of opinions and debate are

---

Speech," ABC News, August 27, 2020.
[67] Ibid.
[68] Ibid.

encouraged, not canceled; where law enforcement is respected; where our country's rich diversity is celebrated; and where people of all backgrounds, races, genders and creeds have the chance to achieve their God-given potential. This is the future that my father is working to build each day. You are the reason my father fights with all his heart and all his might."[69]

She discussed many accomplishments of her father. I will only cite a few, because he listed many in his acceptance speech. She said he was that he was "absolutely correct to take on trade when he did -- and bring our jobs, factories, and life-saving medicines back to the USA." She watched him "take the strongest, most inclusive economy in our lifetime; the lowest unemployment in half a century, and the highest wage increase for working families in decades -- and close it down to save American lives." Then he "rapidly mobilized the full force of government and the private sector to produce ventilators within weeks -- to build the most robust testing system in the world -- and to develop safe and effective treatments, and very soon a vaccine."[70]

<u>PRESIDENT TRUMP</u>. President Trump delivered his acceptance speech from the grounds of the White House on the final night of the Republican National Convention. He said this election will decide: (1) "whether we SAVE the American Dream, or whether we allow a socialist agenda to DEMOLISH our cherished destiny;" (2) "whether we rapidly create millions of high paying jobs, or whether we crush our industries and send millions of these jobs overseas, as has foolishly been done for many decades;" (3) "whether we protect law abiding Americans, or whether we give free reign to violent anarchists, agitators, and criminals who threaten our citizens;" and (4)

---

[69] Ibid.
[70] Ibid.

"whether we will defend the American Way of Life, or whether we allow a radical movement to completely dismantle and destroy it."[71] After saying what Democrats would do, he said, "But in this country, we don't look to career politicians for salvation. In America...we put our faith in Almighty God."[72]

Later Trump noted that, "During the Democrat Convention, the words "Under God" were removed from the Pledge of Allegiance – not once, but twice. The fact is, this is where they are coming from."[73] That reminds me of being shocked to hear loud demands, on the floor of the 2012 Democratic National Convention, for removal of all references to God and Israel from the 2012 Democratic Platform, the document that summarizes the positions, policies, agenda, and goals of the Democratic Party. Trump warned that the 2020 Democratic Platform, which he called the Biden-Bernie Manifesto, "calls for abolishing cash bail, immediately releasing 400,000 criminals onto your streets...."[74] As usual, Trump gave a very long speech, talking about the many negative results of electing Biden. This chapter is already too long, so I will just list Trump's goals and actual accomplishments.

<u>TRUMP'S ACCOMPLISHMENTS</u>. It is absolutely amazing what President Trump accomplished during less than 4 years in office, while under constant attack and investigation by Democrats and the media. He said, "I have done nothing but fight for YOU" and "I KEPT MY PROMISES."[75] He cited his accomplishments as follows:

---

[71] "Trump Accepts Republican Nomination for President at the 2020 RNC," NBC News, Aug. 28, 2020.
[72] Ibid.
[73] Ibid.
[74] Ibid.

1.   Before global pandemic hit, produced best unemployment numbers ever recorded for African-Americans, Hispanic-Americans, and Asian-Americans.
2.   Built the strongest economy in the history of the world.
3.   Passed record-setting tax and regulation cuts.
4.   Achieved, for first time, American Energy Independence.
5.   When Covid-19 virus hit, launched largest national mobilization since World War II, invoking Defense Production Act, and produced world's largest supply of ventilators. No American has been denied a ventilator.
6.   Shipped hundreds of millions of masks, gloves and gowns to front line healthcare workers.
7.   Rushed supplies, testing kits, and personnel to nursing homes and long-term care facilities.
8.   Had Army Corps of Engineers build field hospitals and Navy deploy hospital ships.
9.   Developed largest, most advanced testing system in the world. America has tested more than all Europe and more than every nation in the Western Hemisphere combined.
10. Developed a wide array of effective treatments, including a powerful anti-body treatment known as Convalescent Plasma that will save thousands of lives.
11. Reduced fatality rate by 80 percent since April. European Union's fatality rate is nearly three times higher.
12. After global pandemic hit, achieved smallest economic contraction of any major western nation, and recovering much faster.
13. Enacted largest package of financial relief in American history.
14. Saved or supported more than 50 million American jobs with Paycheck Protection Program.

---

[75] Ibid.

15. Gained over 9 million jobs over past three months, a new record.
16. Will have approved more than 300 federal judges, including two great new Supreme Court Justices.
17. Passed historic criminal justice reform, prison reform, opportunity zones, and long-term funding of black colleges.
18. Did more for African-American community than any president since Abraham Lincoln, first Republican president.
19. Have done more in three years for the black community than Joe Biden has done in 47 years.
20. Signed orders to massively lower cost of prescription drugs and give critically ill patients access to lifesaving cures.
21. Passed the decades long-awaited Right-to-Try legislation.
22. Spent nearly $2.5 trillion on completely rebuilding our military, which was very badly depleted.
23. Gave three separate pay raises to our great warriors.
24. Passed VA Accountability and VA Choice.
25. Obliterated 100 percent of ISIS Caliphate and killed its founder and leader Abu Bakr al-Baghdadi.
26. Eliminated world's number one terrorist, Iranian General Qasem Soleimani (responsible for killing or wounding hundreds of American soldiers with Iranian-made Improvised Explosive Devices, etc.).
27. Kept America out of new wars, and our troops are coming home.
28. Launched Space Force, first new branch of United States military since Air Force was created almost 75 years ago.[76]
29. Got NATO partners to pay $130 billion more per year. Will rise to $400 billion.
30. Achieved first Middle East peace deal in 25 years.
31. Kept my promise, recognized Israel's true capital, and moved our Embassy to Jerusalem for less than $500,000.
32. Recognized Israeli sovereignty over Golan Heights.

---

[76] Ibid.

33. Withdrew from terrible, one-sided Iran Nuclear Deal.

34. Withdrew from job-killing Trans Pacific Partnership.

35. Ended the NAFTA nightmare and signed new U.S. Mexico Canada Agreement.

36. Took toughest, boldest, strongest, hardest hitting action against China in American history.

37. Approved Keystone XL and Dakota Access Pipelines.

38. Ended unfair and costly Paris Climate Accord.

39. Removed Chairman of Board of Tennessee Valley Authority and foreign workers, so American workers were re-hired and are again providing power to Georgia, Alabama, Tennessee, Kentucky, Mississippi, North Carolina, and Virginia.

40. Secured America's borders more than ever before.

41. Built 300 miles of border wall, are adding 10 miles/week, and wall will soon be complete.

42. Ended catch-and-release and stopped asylum fraud.

43. Took down human traffickers who prey on women and children.

44. Deported 20,000 gang members and 500,000 criminal aliens.

TRUMP'S GOALS. President Trump listed his goals for his second term. He would also continue to work on many areas listed as accomplishments.

1. Expand charter schools and provide SCHOOL CHOICE to every family in America.

2. Support GOD-GIVEN RIGHT TO LIFE of all children, born and unborn,

3. When there is police misconduct, hold wrongdoers fully and completely accountable.

4.   Never allow mob rule like rioting, arson, violence in Democrat-run cities (Kenosha, Minneapolis, Portland, Chicago, New York).

5.   Maintain law and order. All federal crimes investigated, prosecuted, and punished to fullest extent of the law.

6.   Reclaim our independence from the left's repressive mandates. Resist cancel culture.

7.   Make America into the Manufacturing Superpower of the World.

8.   Expand Opportunity Zones, bring home our medical supply chains, and end our reliance on China.

9.   Continue to reduce taxes and regulations at levels not seen before.

10. Create 10 million jobs in the next 10 months.

11. Hire MORE police, increase penalties for assaults on law enforcement, and surge federal prosecutors in high-crime communities.

12. BAN deadly Sanctuary Cities.

13. Ensure that federal healthcare is protected for American Citizens, not illegal aliens.

14. Have strong borders, strike down terrorists, and keep America out of endless and costly foreign wars.

15. Appoint prosecutors, judges, and justices who believe in enforcing the law, not their political agenda.

16. Ensure equal justice for citizens of every race, religion, color and creed.

17. Uphold religious liberty, and defend Second Amendment right to keep and bear arms.

18. Protect Medicare and Social Security.

19. Protect patients with pre-existing conditions; that is a pledge from the entire Republican Party.

20. END surprise medical billing, require price transparency, and further reduce cost of prescription drugs and health insurance premiums.

21. Greatly expand energy development, continuing to remain number one in the world, and keep America Energy Independent.
22. Win the race to 5G. Build the world's best cyber and missile defense.
23. Fully restore patriotic education to our schools, and always protect free speech on college campuses.
24. Launch a new age of American Ambition in Space. Land first woman on the moon, and be the first nation to plant its flag on Mars.
25. Make America safer, stronger, prouder, and make America GREATER than ever before![77]

CONCLUSION. All Americans should have watched both conventions. Everyone should ask why the Democrats concentrated on attacking the character and competence of President Trump and talked so little about their agenda or Biden's actual accomplishments. I listened to both conventions. It is absolutely amazing what President Trump accomplished in his first term. I do not know what Biden accomplished after 47 years in Washington, D.C.

Christians should vote first based on Christian values embodied in Scripture, the Declaration of Independence, the Constitution, and the Bill of Rights. Christians should not vote based on what candidates promise when trying to get elected. They should vote based on how candidates actually voted and what they actually accomplished when in office and how these reflect Christian values. Chapter 2 shows that Biden scored zero for voting Christian values. This chapter and book show that President Trump scores very high for fighting for laws and policies that reflect Christian values and for choosing federal

---

[77] Ibid.

judges and Supreme Court justices who support Christian values.

CHAPTER 7.0

ISSUES OF THE 2020 ELECTION

<u>SECTION REVIEW</u>. Christians should NOT vote first based on issues discussed in this section. They should vote based on principles embodied in scripture, the Declaration of Independence, the Constitution, and the Bill of Rights.

The first chapter addresses jobs and the economy because it is the issue of greatest concern to most Americans. The second chapter discusses the 2020 global pandemic (Covid-19), because it greatly impacted jobs, the economy, and life in general for most people throughout the world.

The most important issue in every election is the Supreme Court (Chapter 3), because the President nominates justices who serve for life and because the Supreme Court affects so many issues (racism/civil rights, abortion, same-sex marriage, healthcare, education, immigration, etc.). The death of Justice Ginsburg makes the choice of President and senators who confirm Supreme Court justices even more critical.

The death of George Floyd at the hands of police made racism and police (Chapter 4, the longest chapter) the hottest political issue of the year. All Christians should be in total agreement on this issue. It should not be something that divides Republicans and Democrats.

National defense (Chapter 5) is important because the primary duty of the President is to protect Americans from all enemies, foreign and domestic. Law and order (Chapter 6) became a hot political issue when violent protests erupted in many cities after the death of George Floyd. Gun control is an important issue, because there have been so many mass shootings in schools and other locations.

The Constitution does NOT give the federal government authority to institute national healthcare or education programs (Chapters 8 and 9), and the Supreme Court cannot give this authority. No candidate for federal office should try to bribe voters with promises of healthcare or education benefits. The final three chapters (Chapters 10-12) address immigration, the environment, and voting by mail.

<u>CHAPTERS</u>:
7.1 Jobs and the Economy
7.2 Global Pandemic (Covid-19)
7.3 Supreme Court
7.4 Racism and Police
7.5 National Defense
7.6 Law and Order
7.7 Gun Control
7.8 Healthcare
7.9 Education
7.10 Immigration
7.11 Environment
7.12 Voting by Mail

JOBS AND THE ECONOMY

INTRODUCTION. Under President Trump, from 2016 to 2020, US markets hit record highs and unemployment hit record lows. Democrats claimed that the economic boom only benefited the wealthy, but that is totally false. Unemployment hit record lows for blacks, Hispanics, and all other Americans.

All that changed with the arrival of the global pandemic, which devasted the economies of most nations. Markets crashed and unemployment hit record lows. In the United States, markets have recovered most of their losses, but unemployment remains high. Full recovery may take years.

The big question in 2020 is who would do the best job as president in restoring jobs and the economy. President Trump has already proven that he excels in this area more than any other president. The Constitution gives the President limited power to influence jobs and the economy. His primary job is to protect the rights, freedom, and security of Americans to enable jobs and the economy to prosper. However, President Trump has proven an amazing ability to accomplish all of these tasks i.e. protecting the rights, freedom, and security of Americans and greatly improving jobs and economy at the same time.

ACCOMPLISHMENTS OF PRESIDENT—BEFORE GLOBAL PANDEMIC. During the Republican National Convention, President Trump listed his financial accomplishments before the global pandemic as follows.

1. Produced best unemployment numbers ever recorded for African-Americans, Hispanic-Americans, Asian-Americans.
2. Built the strongest economy in the history of the world.
3. Passed record-setting tax and regulation cuts.
4. Achieved, for first time, American Energy Independence.
5. Approved Keystone XL and Dakota Access Pipelines.
6. Withdrew from job-killing Trans Pacific Partnership.
7. Ended the NAFTA nightmare and signed new U.S. Mexico Canada Agreement.
8. Took toughest, boldest, strongest, hardest hitting action against China in American history.
9. Ended unfair and costly Paris Climate Accord. [78]

ACCOMPLISHMENTS OF PRESIDENT—AFTER GLOBAL PANDEMIC. President Trump listed his financial accomplishments after the global pandemic as follows:

1. Enacted largest package of financial relief in American history.
2. Saved or supported more than 50 million American jobs with Paycheck Protection Program.
3. Achieved smallest economic contraction of any major western nation, and recovering much faster.
4. Gained over 9 million jobs over past three months, a new record. [79]

"IT'S THE ECONOMY STUPID": In 1992 Bill Clinton used the words, "It's the economy, stupid," to belittle President Herbert W. Bush (father of President George W. Bush), and to convince voters that he would do a better job of restoring jobs and the economy. Clinton, as the Governor of

---

[78] "Trump Accepts Republican Nomination for President at the 2020 RNC," NBC News, Aug. 28, 2020.
[79] Ibid.

Arkansas, was less qualified to deal with jobs and the economy than President Bush, who had years of experience as President. But Clinton's advisors knew that insulting and belittling the President would win the support of American voters.

<u>2018 ELECTIONS</u>: So, what did Democrats claim was the most important issue during the 2018 elections, when markets were hitting record highs and unemployment record lows under a Republican President? Did they say, "It's the economy stupid." No—they said healthcare was the most important issue, and most Americans believed them. There is absolutely no part of the Constitution that discusses and gives the federal government jurisdiction regarding healthcare. See chapter on healthcare.

<u>BIDEN</u>: Biden served in Washington, D.C. for 47 years. He served as a senator for most of those years, and as Vice President for 8 years. He never had any experience in the business world, and he had virtually no influence on the economy during the 47 years that he served in Washington.

<u>TRUMP</u>. Trump has an academic degree from a top business school, almost 4 years of service as President, and many years of experience in the business world, far more than any other president in the history of the United States. He is the most knowledgeable and most experienced President when it comes to business, jobs, and the economy.

Trump knows the rules and laws that govern business, and has used them to become extremely wealthy. He is a billionaire. He has applied that same knowledge, experience, and expertise to improve jobs and the economy for all Americans, to include women and all minorities.

Americans who want to more fully understand the business expertise and experience of Donald Trump can read any of his books. These include (1) "Great Again: How to Fix our Crippled America" (2016), (2) "Time to Get Tough: Make America Great Again" (2015), (3) Crippled America: How to Make America Great Again" (2015), (4) "Trump: The Art of the Deal" (2015), (5) "Midas Touch: Why Some Entrepreneurs Get Rich and Why Most Don't" (2012), and (6) "Think Like a Champion: An Informal Education in Business and Life" (2010), (7) "Think Big: Make it Happen in Business and in Life" (2008), and (8) "Trump: How to Get Rich " (2004).

CONCLUSION. Donald Trump is infinitely more qualified to deal with jobs and the economy than Joe Biden. Indeed, he is more qualified than any other President in the history of the United States. Under President Trump, markets hit record highs and unemployment hit record lows. Under President Trump, jobs and economy can and will recover infinitely better than they would under Biden.

CHAPTER 7.2

THE GLOBAL PANDEMIC
(COVID-19)

<u>INTRODUCTION</u>. The Covid-19 global pandemic was the most significant world event of 2020. The last global pandemic to greatly impact the United States was the 1917-1918 Spanish Flu, over 100 years ago. The United States was just one of many nations to be surprised and dramatically impacted by the Covid-19 global pandemic.

No Christian should vote based upon anything related to the global pandemic. Christians should vote based upon principles and laws embodied in scripture, the Declaration of Independence, Constitution, and Bill of Rights. In other words, Christians should vote based upon the Christian values that they have before and after the global pandemic.

<u>CURRENT STATUS, CURRENT BATTLE</u>. At the time of this writing, over 200,000 Americans have died from the Covid-19 virus, and that number may rise to over 400,000. Democrats will do their best to say that President Trump and his administration failed to do everything possible to prevent these deaths. They will, as always, falsely accuse President Trump and Republicans of not caring about their fellow Americans. These lies are already being told by politicians, reporters, and the hosts of late-night shows. Former President Obama implied that President Trump did not know what he was doing and did not even pretend to be in charge. No American should believe these lies.

<u>ACTIONS OF PRESIDENT</u>. During the Republican National Convention, President Trump said, "I have done nothing but fight for YOU."[80] He listed actions to combat the Covid-19 virus as follows:

1. When Covid-19 virus hit, launched largest national mobilization since World War II, invoking Defense Production Act, and produced world's largest supply of ventilators. No American has been denied a ventilator.
2. Shipped hundreds of millions of masks, gloves and gowns to front line healthcare workers.
3. Rushed supplies, testing kits, and personnel to nursing homes and long-term care facilities.
4. Had Army Corps of Engineers build field hospitals and Navy deploy hospital ships.
5. Developed largest, most advanced testing system in the world. America has tested more than all Europe and more than every nation in the Western Hemisphere combined.
6. Developed a wide array of effective treatments, including a powerful anti-body treatment known as Convalescent Plasma that will save thousands of lives.
7. Reduced fatality rate by 80 percent since April. European Union's fatality rate is nearly three times higher.[81]

<u>JURISDICTION—UNITED STATES</u>. The United States is called the United States for a reason. It is not a dictatorship or monarchy. When the President tried to impose rules on states to combat Covid-19, governors rightfully objected. The Constitution maximizes the freedom of Americans by minimizing the power of the federal government. The tenth amendment states that "powers not

---

[80] "Trump Accepts Republican Nomination for President at the 2020 RNC," NBC News, Aug. 28, 2020.
[81] Ibid.

delegated to the United States by the Constitution, nor prohibited by it to the States, are reserved to the States respectively, or to the people." [82]

Vice President Biden has falsely claimed that Trump has failed Americans by not instituting a national mask mandate. Exactly how would Biden enforce that mandate? With federal troops? With the small number of federal police in each state?

JURISDICTION—STATE AND LOCAL. States and local governments bear primary responsibility for management of response to and recovery from the global pandemic. Each state is different. Some have very few cases. Some have very large numbers of cases in some areas (in some cities, meat-packing plants, etc.). Governors and mayors must take whatever action is best for their state or city.

The governor of Ohio, for example, has rightfully instituted stricter guidelines for red counties—counties that have higher numbers of cases of Covid-19. When the counties turn orange, he relaxes restrictions.

However, the power of governors is limited and can be challenged. How would a governor enforce a mask mandate in a red county? Would he use state police or the National Guard? Both are impossible. Enforcement must come at city and county level, from city police, county sheriffs, and county health departments.

Also, governors and presidents do not make laws. Legislatures legislate. They make the laws, and the executive

---

[82] See Appendix D for Bill of Rights and 10th Amendment.

branch enforces the laws, at all levels of government i.e. city, county, state, and nation.

 "<u>THIS TOO WILL PASS</u>." Democrats and the media constantly criticize the President for saying that the Covid-19 virus "is what it is" and that it will pass. But that is true. Behind the scenes, he has Vice President Pence, medical and military personnel, and others talking to governors every day and doing everything possible to help them fight the virus. But he is a businessman acutely aware that the Covid-19 virus has devastated countless small and large businesses and corporations. Some will be forced out of business. Others will take years to recover. He wants to do everything possible to help the nation recover and prosper.

CHAPTER 7.3

SUPREME COURT

INTRODUCTION. The most important issue in every election is the Supreme Court because Presidents appoint Supreme Court justices who serve for life. A president may serve only four years. His decisions may be reversed by the next president. A Supreme Court Justice may serve 20 to 30 years, and his or her rulings dramatically affect the lives of Americans for many years after the President leaves office. Also, the Supreme Court makes rulings on countless vitally important issues (abortion, same-sex marriage, racism/civil rights, healthcare, education, immigration, national defense, law and order, gun control, etc.).

The death of Justice Ruth Bader Ginsburg on September 18, 2020 made the choice of President and senators who confirm Supreme Court justices even more critical. Mordecai said: "Yet who knows whether you have come...for such a time as this?" (Esther 4:13-14, NKJV)[83] President Trump and Republican senators are called by God "for such a time as this." As Christian soldiers, they are called to put their lives and careers on the line for the Lord, to be willing to sacrifice everything for this.

Biden said voters should elect the President, and the President should choose the next Supreme Court Justice. Voters did elect President Trump and a Republican majority in the Senate. In the words of President Trump and Michelle

---

[83] Holy Bible, New King James Version. Nashville: Thomas Nelson, Inc., 1982.

88

Obama, "It is what it is." Thank God. Praise the Lord. What an amazing gift from God.

There have been 29 Supreme Court vacancies during Presidential election years. During 19 of those 29 years, the President and the Senate majority were the same party. During 17 of those 19 years, the President nominated and Senate confirmed a new Supreme Court justice. "It is what it is." The only individuals that can derail the appointment of a new Supreme Court justice are a few extremely blind, foolish, unprincipled senators like Collins and Murkowski, who want to delay a vote until after the election. Republicans can only lose 4 votes. Vice-President Pence can break a tie.

Republicans and President Trump, in total contrast to Democrats and Biden, support the appointment of federal judges and Supreme Court Justices who uphold the Constitution and do not try to legislate from the bench.[84] Legislation, making law, is the duty of elected members of the legislature, which at the federal level is Congress (Senate and House of Representatives).

No Democrat will appoint a Supreme Court justice who will uphold the Constitution, because doing so would be totally contrary to deeply-rooted values of Democrats. The primary purpose of the Constitution is to define the limits of power of the federal government. Democrats only support justices who ignore those limits of power, granting totally unconstitutional education, healthcare, and other benefits. The Supreme Court justices they appoint will use the interstate commerce clause, taxation clause (Obamacare), and other parts of the Constitution to justify actions by Congress that are totally

---

[84] "2012 Values Voter Presidential Voter Guide," Family Research Council Action, http://www.frcaction.org, accessed August 3, 2012.

contrary to the Constitution. See chapters on Constitution, Democratic Platform, and Biblical Role of Government.

APPOINTMENTS OF PRESIDENT TRUMP. In total contrast to President Obama, President Trump appointed two conservative justices to the Supreme Court: Neil Gorsuch and Brett Kavanaugh. However, they have proven to be very different justices, only voting with each other about 70% of the time, less than any two justices appointed by the same president since John F. Kennedy. "In contrast, Justices Sonia Sotomayor and Elena Kagan, appointed by President Barack Obama, agreed more than 96% of the time. Chief Justice John Roberts agreed with Justice Samuel Alito, a fellow George W. Bush appointee, more than 90% of the time."[85]

In December 2018, Kavanaugh actually "sided with Roberts and the court's liberals to reject a case involving two states seeking to bar Planned Parenthood from receiving Medicaid funding. Gorsuch sided with the conservatives." In other words, Kavanaugh actually voted to force all Americans who believe that abortion is murder to fund abortion through payment of federal taxes.

APPOINTMENTS OF PRESIDENT OBAMA. Biden would appoint Supreme Court justices like those appointed by President Obama. Few Presidents in the history of the United States appointed Supreme Court justices who rule so contrary to Scripture and the Constitution as President Obama. During his first two years in office, President Obama replaced 2 of the 9 Supreme Court Justices, as many as President George W. Bush replaced in 8 years. Obama's advisors were "preparing for the possibility of a third vacancy, which could make his

[85] "Trump's Two Supreme Court Justices Kavanaugh and Gorsuch Split in First Term Together," Tucker Higgins, CNBC, Jun 29 2019.

imprint even more indelible."[86]

In 2009 President Obama appointed Sonia Sotomayor to the Supreme Court. Sotomayor helped direct litigation of a private organization that filed many pro-abortion lawsuits, to include challenges to parental notification requirements.[87] Tony Perkins, President of Family Research Council, said:

> President Obama has chosen a nominee with a compelling personal story over a judicial pick with a solid judicial philosophy…. Judge Sotomayor's failure to premise her decisions on the text of the Constitution has resulted in an extremely high rate of reversal before the high court to which she has been nominated…. Judge Sotomayor appears to subscribe to a very liberal judicial philosophy that considers it appropriate for judges to impose their personal views from the bench. President Obama promised us a jurist committed to the "rule of law," but, instead, he appears to have nominated a legislator to the Supreme Court.... In a 2005 panel discussion at the Duke University Law School… the judge stated that the U.S. Court of Appeals is "where policy is made" …. Our constitution states otherwise and public surveys indicate that the American public understands this constitutional principle and wants judges who interpret the law and do not act as life-tenured judicially empowered social workers. [88]

---

[86] "Where Do the Candidates Stand on Life: Mitt Romney, Barack Obama," National Right to Life, http://www.nrlc.org.

[87] "The Presidential Record on Life: President Barack Obama 2009-present," National Right to Life, http://www.nrlc.org.

[88] "Sotomayor: A Policy Maker or a Jurist?", Family Research Council

In other words, Judge Sotomayor is an extremely liberal judge who believes in making policy and legislating from the bench, totally contrary to her duty to interpret and apply the law to the facts of each case. Legislation, making law, is the duty of <u>elected</u> members of the legislature, which at the federal level is Congress (Senate and House of Representatives).

On May 11, 2010, the Washington Post announced President Obama's appointment of Elena Kagan, a woman who never served as a judge at any level and only a short time as Solicitor General. As former Dean of Harvard Law School, Kagan barred Armed Forces recruiters from the Law School's Office of Career Services in protest of the "Don't ask, don't tell" policy regarding homosexuals serving in the Armed Forces.[89] As a key political aide to President Clinton, Kagan helped direct a political strategy that would nullify a ban on partial-birth abortions during the Clinton Administration.[90]

Tony Perkins, President of Family Research Council, said:

> Throughout her career, Ms. Kagan has supported
> the promotion of abortion, even if it includes
> funding with American tax dollars. She publicly
> disagreed with the decision in Rust v. Sullivan that
> gave the government the right to deny taxpayer

Action, http://www.frcaction.org, May 26, 2009.

[89] Jonathan Blakely, "One Top GOP Line of Attack: Kagan's Opposition to Military Recruitment at Harvard Law School's Office of Career Services," ABC News, http://abcnews.go.com/blogs/politics/2010/05/one-top-gop-line-of-attack-kagans-opposition-to-military-recruitment-at-harvard-law-schools-office-of-career-services/.

[90] "The Presidential Record on Life: President Barack Obama 2009-present," National Right to Life, http://www.nrlc.org.

funds to groups that perform or promote abortions.
A large majority of Americans disagree with her
on that point, as did the Supreme Court…. Ms.
Kagan's memo to President Bill Clinton in 1997…
advised the President to support a "compromise"
allowing for "health exceptions" to the ban on the
gruesome and cruel procedure of partial birth
abortion… a blatant attempt to create a giant
loophole rendering the bill meaningless.[91]

In other words, Elena Kagan is a woman who never
served as a judge and is a very strong supporter of partial birth
abortion, taxpayer funding of abortion, and the homosexual
lifestyle. She is absolutely, without any question whatsoever,
the Supreme Court Justice who is least qualified to be on the
U.S. Supreme Court.

A Washington Post article discussing the significance of
the Kagan appointment stated:

With his second Supreme Court nomination...
President Obama has laid down clear markers of
his vision for the court, one that could prove to be
among his most enduring legacies. Together with
Justice Sonia Sotomayor, Elena Kagan's
confirmation would represent a shift toward a
younger, changing court, one that values
experiences outside the courtroom and emphasizes
personal interactions as much as deep knowledge
of the law. Kagan, 50, the solicitor general named
to replace outgoing liberal Justice John Paul

---

[91] "FRC Action: Elena Kagan's Pro-Abortion Record is Far Outside the
Mainstream," Family Research Council Action, http://www.frcaction.org,
May 19, 2010.

Stevens, would…provide a <u>lasting, liberal presence</u>, and administration officials hope she would, in the words of one, "<u>start to move the court into a different posture and profile</u>."[92]

Advisers said that President Obama believed that "although Kagan has never been a judge, she would be able to play an 'outsize role' on the bench by swaying her colleagues when opinion is divided."[93] Richard Garnett, law professor and associate dean of the University of Notre Dame Law School and former law clerk for Chief Justice Rehnquist, said Obama was "poised to make a lasting impact on the court."

The notion that he is just replacing one member of the so-called liberal wing with another, I think, is superficial… President Obama has a chance to <u>entrench his view of the Constitution for many years to come</u>.[94]

Why would President Obama appoint someone who never served as a judge on any court at any level to the highest court in the nation? Simply put, his objective was not to pick someone who would simply do the job of a judge, to interpret and apply the law to the facts of each case. His goal was to choose someone who could influence others to legislate from the bench and implement his policies.

---

[92] Anne E. Kornblut and Robert Barnes, "Kagan Would Emphasize Supreme Court Moving in New Direction," <u>The Washington Post</u>, <u>http://www.washingtonpost.com/wp-dyn/content/article</u> <u>/2010/05/10/AR2010051001116.html</u>, May 11, 2010.
[93] Ibid.
[94] Ibid.

<u>CONCLUSION</u>. Presidents appoint Supreme Court justices who serve for life. President Trump appointed two conservative justices who will continue to greatly influence the direction of our nation for many years after he is no longer in office. He will soon appoint a third. Biden would, like President Obama, appoint extremely liberal justices.

What are the consequences of appointment of liberal justices? Why should Americans care? First, liberal Supreme Court justices approve totally unconstitutional decisions of the President and Congress. These decisions increase taxes and reduce the freedom of religion and freedom of speech of Christians. Americans are forced to pay greater taxes to pay the education and healthcare bills of other Americans. Christians are forced to pay for abortions, abortive drugs, sterilization, contraceptives, and support homosexual couples by paying for their healthcare. Also, when Democrats have a majority in the Senate, they chair the Senate Judiciary Committee and block the nomination of pro-life, conservative Christians as federal judges and Supreme Court justices.

CHAPTER 7.4

RACISM AND POLICE

<u>INTRODUCTION</u>: Different races are like different colors of the rainbow. Each reflects the glory of the God equally, because God created all men equal. All Americans, especially Christians, should be in total agreement with this simple truth. It should not be an issue that divides Republicans and Democrats. However, it has sharply divided Republicans and Democrats for over 200 years. Few Americans understand the history of this conflict. This chapter discusses America before and after the death of George Floyd, systemic racism and police (facts and figures), defunding the police, and the history of Republicans, Democrats, and racism.

<u>AMERICA BEFORE THE DEATH OF GEORGE FLOYD--ACTIONS OF PRESIDENT</u>. During the Republican National Convention, President Trump listed his actions to help black Americans and other minorities as follows:

1. Before global pandemic hit, produced best unemployment numbers ever recorded for African-Americans, Hispanic-Americans, and Asian-Americans.
2. Passed historic criminal justice reform, prison reform, opportunity zones, and long-term funding of black colleges.
3. Did more for African-American community than any president since Abraham Lincoln, first Republican president.
4. Have done more in three years for the black community than Joe Biden has done in 47 years.[95]

---

[95] "Trump Accepts Republican Nomination for President at the 2020 RNC," NBC News, Aug. 28, 2020.

This is not a complete list of everything President Trump did for black Americans and other minorities. When Trump said, "I have done nothing but fight for YOU!",[96] he meant ALL Americans. Everything on his very long list of accomplishments was done for ALL Americans. See end of chapter on Republican National Convention for complete list of almost 50 accomplishments.

After Charlottesville, one of President Trump's sons said, "My father only sees green." In other words, Trump is a businessman who thinks first and foremost about jobs and the economy for all Americans. That is his absolute, resolute focus. Unlike many black and white Democrats, he does not think in terms of or discriminate based upon race. He does his very best to fight for ALL Americans and provide the very best jobs and economy for ALL Americans.

<u>AMERICA AFTER THE DEATH OF GEORGE FLOYD</u>. One of the most important, nation-changing events of 2020 was the death of George Floyd, a black man, at the hands of police in Minneapolis, and the national and international protests that followed. Thousands of white Americans joined black Americans in demonstrations in many cities across the United States, demanding justice, police reform, and police defunding. George Floyd was not the only black American to die at the hands of police in 2020, but seeing the video of him slowly being killed by a policeman who had a knee on his neck for over 8 minutes rightly provoked national and international outrage.

<u>SYSTEMIC RACISM FACTS AND FIGURES</u>: After the death of George Floyd, many demonstrators, politicians, and news networks said there is a major problem with systemic

---

[96] Ibid.

racism in police throughout the United States, which has resulted in police killing large numbers of unarmed black men. Democratic Senator Kamala Harris of California said, "A black person in America…has never been treated as fully human…. America has never fully addressed the systemic racism…in our country."[97] Democratic Senator Cory Booker of New Jersey said, "This is the story of life every single day. And we have so many…African-American men, mostly unarmed, being murdered by police officers and no way of holding them accountable."[98] The Floyd family attorney called this killing of black men a "genocide" and racism a national "pandemic." [99]

Sometimes it is helpful to check the facts regarding an issue, and to try to look at both sides. Since 2015, The Washington Post has kept records on shootings. In 2018 there were 7,407 black homicide victims.[100] Most were black men killed by other black men, not by police. Little or nothing is said about this, because it is not a racial issue. In 2019, police killed 1,004 people. Most were armed. Race is only known for 802 cases: 371 were white, 236 were black.

Of the 1,004 people killed by police in 2019, only 19 were unarmed whites, and only 9 were unarmed blacks. That is not genocide. Also, "a police officer is 18½ times more likely to be killed by a black male than an unarmed black male is to be killed by a police officer."[101] In other words, for every 9

---

[97] C. Douglas Golden, "Tucker Carlson Does the Math on Police Shootings, Says This Is 'Not Even Close to Genocide'," The Western Journal, June 5, 2020.
[98] Ibid.
[99] Ibid.
[100] Ibid.
[101] Ibid.

unarmed black men that are killed by police, about 166 police are killed by black men.

Only about 13% of the population of the United States is black, so black men are only 6%-7% of the population. But black men kill about 40% of the police officers killed in the line of duty each year. But it is not a newsworthy event when a policeman is killed by a black man, because it is not considered a racial incident. We need to care about all black lives and all blue lives. All lives are precious and of equal value, because God created all men equal and precious. None of these facts excuse the murder of George Floyd.

Why, when an unarmed black man is killed by a white policeman, is that policeman and all other white policemen presumed to be guilty of racism? Isn't that racism? Love begets love; hate begets hate; and racism begets racism. Perceived love begets actual love; perceived hate begets actual hate; and perceived racism begets actual racism.

If about 166 policemen are killed in the line of duty by black men for every 9 unarmed black men that are killed by policemen, and if about 40% of all policemen killed in the line of duty are killed by black men even though black men are only 6% to 7% of the population, isn't it equally logical to conclude that black men have an even greater problem with systemic racism toward police? Isn't it equally wrong, racist, and prejudicial to assume that these black men are motivated by hatred and racism in their hearts and minds? Doesn't the higher moral standard of Dr. Martin Luther King, Jr. require us to judge each person individually not based upon the color of their skin but based upon the content of their character and their actions?

"Say her name." Protestors carried signs with these words to remind everyone that Breonna Taylor was a precious human being killed by police during a botched police raid in Louisville, Kentucky. Can you imagine if we had a sign with the names of all black Americans killed by police? It would be a long list. Now can you imagine holding a sign next to that sign with the names of all policemen killed by black men? It would be a much longer list. Many were husbands who left widows and fathers who left fatherless children. Shouldn't we be equally concerned about them? Why is nothing said about them? Why is it politically correct to say the names of all black Americans killed by police, but politically incorrect to mention the name of any policeman killed by a black man? Does it have anything to do with the agenda of Democrats or the presidential election?

<u>DEFUNDING OF POLICE</u>: Many young Americans protesting the death of George Floyd demanded defunding of the police. The mayors and/or city councils of New York City, Seattle, and other cities agreed to partial defunding of their police. I have lived in black urban neighborhoods on the east coast and west coast. I know they need police protection more than other neighborhoods. I know the people who live in these neighborhoods want police protection. The last thing they need is defunding of police. They need police trained in de-escalation, proper use of deadly force (only as a last resort), and better, closer relationships with the men, women, and children that they police. They are there to protect and serve, not simply to enforce the law.

Every American should read the Black Lives Matter website. It states, "We know that police don't keep us safe—and as long as we continue to pump money into our corrupt criminal justice system at the expense of housing, health, and education investments—we will never be truly safe."[102] Everything in that statement is false.

First, thousands of policemen, mostly white, put their lives on the line every day to protect black Americans. About 40% who are killed in the line of duty are killed by black men, although black men are only 6% to 7% of the population.

Whenever police reduce their presence in black urban neighborhoods, the murder rate soars. On the weekend of July 4, 2020, about 670 Americans were killed. Most were black men shot by black men in black urban neighborhoods with illegally acquired weapons. A very small black girl was killed in Atlanta when bullets ripped through her family's car. The black mayor of Atlanta said, "We are killing ourselves."

Second, the Constitution of the United States gives the federal government absolutely no authority to fund housing, healthcare, or education. The tenth amendment states that "powers not delegated to the United States by the Constitution, nor prohibited by it to the States, are reserved to the States respectively, or to the people."[103] The Constitution does not even mention or give any branch of the federal government any authority with respect to housing, healthcare, or education. Supreme Court decisions, always changing and often 5-4, cannot give this authority.

Do Americans really believe that the federal government had authority and responsibility to provide housing, healthcare, and education to all Americans, but failed to do so for over 200 years? Exactly what gives the

---

[102] "What Defunding the Police Really Means," www.blacklivesmatter .com, July 6, 2020, downloaded August 2, 2020.
[103] Ibid.

government the right to take lawfully earned income from one person and give it to another? Doesn't that violate the God-given rights to freedom and the pursuit of happiness?

<u>STATUTES, FLAWED HUMANS, IMPERFECT NATION</u>: After the death of George Floyd, protestors started tearing down statutes of Confederate soldiers. Then they started tearing down statutes of the founding fathers. They even wanted to tear down a statute of Abraham Lincoln, the president who fought to free black Americans from slavery. George Washington and Thomas Jefferson owned slaves. They were great men who founded our nation on belief in God and the laws that He created to govern men and governments, but they, like we, were very flawed men.

If I asked black Americans who first enslaved their ancestors, most would say white men, but that would be wrong. They were first captured and sold into slavery by African men from other tribes. One of the songs that all Christians love to sing is Amazing Grace. It was written by a former Captain of a slave ship, who was amazed that God could forgive even him for his sins against his fellow man. We all very flawed humans greatly in need of forgiveness.

Jesus told us to take the log out of our own eye before trying to take the speck out of another man's eye (Matt. 7:4-5; Luke 6:42). It is always easier for us to see the faults in someone else, than it is for us to see our own faults. We all have many faults, many shortcomings, many blind spots. "For now, we see in a mirror dimly, but then face to face. Now I know in part; then I shall know fully, even as I have been fully known." 1 Cor. 13:12).

President Obama, speaking at the funeral of Congressman John Lewis, said that words "to form a more perfect union" are an admission to the simple truth that we have an imperfect union. He said that the duty of each generation is to make it a more perfect union. I agree. We live in the greatest nation in the world, founded as one nation under God. The God-given duty, mission, and calling of each generation is put on the full armor of God and fight to make is a more perfect union.

HISTORY OF BLACK AMERICANS: The history of black Americans has some parallels to the history of the people of Israel. God allowed His chosen people to be captured and enslaved for hundreds of years by the Egyptians. Then He sent Moses to bring them out of slavery and into the promised land. God allowed black Americans to be enslaved in the southern states in the United States of America. Then He sent Abraham Lincoln, Dr. Martin Luther King, Jr., Congressman John Lewis, and others to fight for their freedom and bring them out of slavery.

God is a master at taking what Satan means for evil and using it for good. The best example is the cross. Satan rejoiced at the torture and death of Christ, but God used it to show the immeasurable depth of His love for us, to save us from our sins and from living for ourselves, and to restore our relationship with Him, our Creator, Savior, Redeemer.

What black Americans fail to fully understand or fully embrace is the dream of freedom of the founding fathers of this nation. President Obama's pastor said, "We didn't land on Plymouth Rock; Plymouth Rock landed on us." Many black Americans seem to think that they are victims of the founding fathers, not beneficiaries.

Patrick Henry said, "Give me liberty or give me death." The founding fathers never would have traded their precious freedom for government benefits, but that is precisely what Democrats want to do. They promise government benefits paid for only by the wealthy few, but that is a lie. God warned the Israelites about reliance on a king and government. He warned them that the king would demand 10% in taxes. Today Americans pay far more than 10% (federal, state, and local income tax, sales tax, fuel tax, real estate tax, etc.). Americans spend much of each year just working to pay their taxes. See chapters on Role of Government and Taxation.

<u>AMERICAN CIVIL WAR, REPUBLICANS, DEMOCRATS</u>: Most Americans do not understand American history regarding the American Civil War, how black Americans were freed from slavery, and what happened after they were given the right to vote. Before the Civil War, only white men were allowed to vote. Most voted for Abraham Lincoln because he and the Republican Party strongly opposed slavery. After Lincoln was elected, Democrats in southern states formed the Confederate States and started the American Civil War to protect slavery in their states. More American soldiers died in the American Civil War than in all other wars combined (640,000 to 700,000).[104] Most were white men fighting for the Union, fighting against slavery.

Dr. Martin Luther King, Jr. gave his "I Have a Dream" speech from the steps of Lincoln Memorial in Washington, D.C., because it was President Lincoln, a Republican President, who fought and won the American Civil War and freed black slaves. After losing the Civil War, Confederate

---

[104] "Casualties Numbers and Battle Death Statistics For the American Civil War," www.historynet.com, downloaded June 3, 2020.

officers formed the KKK (Ku Klux Klan). The KKK lynched many black men and assassinated white Republican congressmen who opposed slavery. It used murder and terror to force Americans living in the south to vote for Democrats.[105]

Congressman John Lewis was the youngest speaker on the steps of Lincoln Memorial. He joined forces with Rev. Martin Luther King, Jr. as a teenager. He helped plan and lead the freedom march over the Edmund Pettus bridge in Selma. The bridge may be renamed after him, because Edmund Pettus was an extreme racist, general in the Confederate Army, Grand Dragon of the KKK, and a Democratic senator.

After the American Civil War, "it was the Republican Party that passed the 13th Amendment abolishing slavery...the 14th Amendment giving black men citizenship; and...the 15th Amendment giving Black men the right to vote."[106] However, today over 90% of black Americans vote as Democrats, and any black man who fails to do so is considered a traitor.

I will never forget one black pastor, who was also a graduate of Harvard Law School, saying that another black pastor told him, "You're not black enough." He was darker than most black Americans. He was "not black enough" because he voted Republican. Today most black Americans vote with the Democrats and Confederate soldiers who fought to keep their ancestors enslaved, formed the Ku Klux Klan, and lynched many black men. They vote with Edmund Pettus,

---

[105] "Ku Klux Klan," www.history.com, October 29, 2009; updated February 21, 2020; downloaded August 8, 2020. "Ku Klux Klan," www.wikipedia.com, downloaded June 4, 2020.
[106] "Civil Rights Leader Clarence Henderson: If You Vote for Biden 'You Don't Know History'," Katherine Rodriguez, www.Breitbart.com, 26 Aug 2020.

a Confederate general, Grand Dragon of the Ku Klux Klan, and Democratic senator.

<u>SPIRITUAL WARFARE—REPUBLICANS AND DEMOCRATS</u>: Again, the battle between Republicans and Democrats is first and foremost a spiritual battle, not a political battle. Christian leaders differ in their understanding of God's position on this battle. Franklin Graham and other Christian leaders have warned about the ungodly "progressive agenda" of Democrats. In 2016 and 2020 Rev. Al Sharpton said, "We wrestle not against flesh and blood, but against principalities and powers" (Eph. 6:12). In 2016 he said, "God is on our side!" So, was God on the side of Republicans before, during, and after the American Civil War, but is He now on the side of Democrats? Why do firmly committed, totally devoted Christian leaders differ so greatly on this issue?

One of the blind spots of Christian leaders is their lack of understanding of how biblical law applies to men and governments today. They understand the gospel of love and the absolute need to love one's fellow man. They understand that God created laws of math and science that govern the physical world (law of gravity, law of momentum). But they do not understand how Old Testament laws apply to the purpose, role, and jurisdiction of government. The founding fathers understood some of these principles, and they are embodied in the Declaration of Independence and Constitution, but they are not taught in colleges or seminaries today.

In 1963, during the March on Washington, D.C., Dr. Martin Luther King, Jr. said, "I have a dream that one day this nation will rise up and live out the true meaning of its creed: 'We hold these truths to be self-evident; that all men are created equal.'" He said, "I have a dream that my four little children will one day live in a nation where they will not be judged by the color of their skin but by the content of their character."[107] Most Republicans, from 1800 to present date, have believed in and fought for this moral standard of no discrimination on the basis of race. Most Democrats have not, until the 1960's, when it became politically expedient for them to do so.

USING RACISM TO WIN ELECTIONS: White supremacists try to use race to gain advantage over others. Is it racist for a Republican but not racist for a Democrat to use race to gain advantage or to try to win elections? White Republicans do not use race, because if they did, they would immediately be called racist and rejected by both Republicans and Democrats. However, since 1960 black and white Democrats have used race to try to win elections.

In 1960, during the presidential election, Dr. Martin Luther King was wrongfully jailed after demonstrating against desegregation at a lunch counter in an Atlanta department store. President Eisenhower failed to intervene. Presidential candidate John F. Kennedy voiced his opposition, which led to King's release and helped Kennedy win the presidential election 8 days later.[108] President Kennedy and President B. Lyndon Johnson, who became President when Kennedy was assassinated, won the votes of black Americans by supporting the civil rights movement. President Johnson personally confronted and threatened racist southern Democrats in Congress, doing his best to force them to vote for the Civil

---

[107] "I Have a Dream Speech," www.History.com, Nov. 30, 2017, updated Jan. 15, 2020, downloaded July 29, 2020.
[108] "Martin Luther King, Jr., American Religious Leader and Civil-Rights Activist," David L. Lewis, www.britannica.com, downloaded July 29, 2020.

Rights Act of 1964, telling them that Democrats would win the votes of black Americans "for 100 years." This is clearly portrayed in the movie "L.B.J."

Since 1960, Democrats have called every Republican president a racist. In the movie Created Equal: Clarence Thomas in his Own Words, Supreme Court Justice Thomas explains that even President Reagan was called a racist, and how he as a black man was considered a traitor to other black Americans because he served in the Reagan Administration. The NAACP ran a television add against President George W. Bush, clearly implying that he was a racist. After Hurricane Katrina hit New Orleans, Democrats said that he did not care about black Americans. Now he is good friends with President Obama and his wife, and spoke at the funeral of Congressman John Lewis. If he was still President, he would be called a racist.

During the 2019 Democratic Presidential Debates, Senator Harris surged in the polls when she called former Vice President Biden a racist. I watched both funeral services for George Floyd. He was honored as a wonderful Christian man greatly loved by friends and family. I greatly enjoyed the Christian worship. The black Americans praising the Lord were my brothers and sisters in Christ. I totally agreed with almost everything that was said by most of the pastors who spoke. However, Rev. Al Sharpton turned both funerals into political events, repeatedly attacking and berating President Trump, and promising to use the family of George Floyd and the mothers of other victims of police to motivate Americans to register to vote for Democrats to replace President Trump and Republicans at the federal and state level.

I also watched the funeral of Congressman John Lewis. First President Obama falsely accused President Trump of sending federal troops into cities to tear gas peaceful demonstrators. Then he used the funeral to challenge Americans to vote for Democrats.

When Attorney General Barr was testifying before Congress in July 2020, a black Congressman accused him of systematic racism because he did not bring any black attorneys to the office with him. Barr probably did not know a single black conservative Republican attorney in the Department of Justice. There is a racist presumption of racism where there is no racism. Like white supremacists many black Americans want discrimination based upon race, in favor of their race.

WHITE MEN CAN'T JUMP: Every black man who has played basketball with white men knows that "White Men Can't Jump." There is actually a movie by that title. If we assume that is true, then to have a fair game, shouldn't black men give white men a few points before the start of each game? I don't know of any black men or white men who would want that. Fairness dictates that everyone must earn every point they get. Also, that would violate Rev. Martin Luther King's dream and ideal of no discrimination on the basis of race.

Actually, there is real, systematic racial discrimination built into American law, and the Supreme Court approved of that discrimination, with Justice Thomas dissenting. Any white man who tries to apply to college, medical school, or law school is at a great disadvantage compared to a black man or any other minority, because the law allows racial discrimination against white Americans and in favor of minorities to enhance the "diversity" of schools.

<u>BLACK LIVES MATTER WEBSITE</u>: Part of the Black Lives Matter website states the goals of BLM.

> BLM's #WhatMatters2020 is a campaign aimed to maximize the impact of the BLM movement by galvanizing BLM supporters and allies to the polls in the 2020 U.S Presidential Election to build collective power and ensure candidates are held accountable for the issues that systematically and disproportionately impact Black and under-served communities across the nation.
>
> BLM's #WhatMatters2020 will focus on issues concerning racial injustice, police brutality, criminal justice reform, Black immigration, economic injustice, LGBTQIA+ and human rights, environmental injustice, access to healthcare, access to quality education, and voting rights and suppression.[109]

Many of these are noble objectives. However, BLM seeks to achieve these goals though the election of Democrats, who would, as explained throughout this book, have objectives and employ means that are totally contrary to principles embodied in Scripture, the Declaration of Independence, and the Constitution. Some BLM protestors carried signs saying, "No Justice, No Peace." Like all Democrats, they believe that the end justifies the means. It never does.

---

[109] "BLM's #WhatMatters2020," www.blacklivesmatter.com, downloaded August 2, 2020.

On October 3, 2020, I was given a handout from www.PolicePledge.com which contrasts the values of Black Lives Matter, Inc. with American values. BLM values include: (1) Defund police. (2) Conform to the mob or be cancelled. (3) Riots and violence are acceptable tactics to enact a leftist agenda. (4) Erase American history: rewrite the past so our children forget America's founding principles. (5) Founded by Marxists who believe in total government ownership and control. (6) Rejects nuclear family and need for fathers.

American values, in total contrast, include: (1) Police make communities safer. (2) Free speech and intellectual debate are needed for a diverse society. (3) Peaceful demonstrations and democratic process bring meaningful change. (4) Teach American history: learn from the past to create a brighter future. (5) Uphold individual liberty and right of workers to benefit from their labor. (6) Strong families create a healthy society.

<u>MODERN LYNCH MOBS</u>: Today, when a black man or woman is killed by police, many black and white Americans assume a lynch mob mentality toward the policemen. They are presumed guilty of murder regardless of the facts or the law. Even if they are assaulted by the victim (Michal Brown case) or fired upon (Breona Taylor case), and there are loud demands for murder charges against the police and violent protests if they do not get the justice that they demand. Oprah actually paid for 17 billboards demanding justice for Breona Taylor, long before the results of the grand jury were even known.

Also, there is repeatedly a problem with extreme dishonesty regarding the facts of these cases. Whoopi Goldberg described Trayvon Martin simply as a small, young innocent man who with Skittles in his pocket because he simply went to a store for some candy. She failed to mention that at the time that he was killed he was a bigger, stronger young man on top of and giving a severe beating to George Zimmerman. President Obama, running for re-election, said, "He could have been my son," just because the color of his skin was black. Michael Brown stole a bag of chips, assaulted a store clerk, refused orders to not walk down the middle of the street, and assaulted the police officer who shot him. Protestors shouted, "Hands up, don't shoot!", but that was a lie, and they burned down the store where he stole the chips and assaulted the store clerk who tried to stop him. There is a strong pattern of dishonesty in many but not all of these cases.

<u>FAMILY HISTORY</u>: I am grateful for my family history regarding racism. If my Norwegian ancestors had moved to the United States before the American Civil War, they would have fought with Union Army, against the slavery of the south. In 1951, years before anyone knew Rosa Parks, Dr. Martin Luther King, Jr., or Congressman John Lewis, my mother was working as a nurse at a Veteran's Administration hospital in Mississippi, during the height of Jim Crow laws. She was called into her supervisor's office and told to stop calling black World War II veterans "Sir." She refused to obey her supervisor. As a Christian, she knew that God created all men equal.

From the 1950's until age 90 in 2018, my father served as a pastor, missionary to Brazil, state prison chaplain, and hospital chaplain. He always treated all Americans and Brazilians, of all races, with the utmost of respect, as his brothers and sisters in Christ, because they were. My father, mother, and I are Christians first and foremost, and Republicans only because we are Christians.

CONCLUSION: Black lives matter. All lives matter equally because God created and continues to create all men equal. The life of every black man killed by police is precious beyond measure, but so is the life of every policeman. Black men are only 6% to 7% of the U.S. population, but black men kill about 40% of all policemen killed in the line of duty. About 18.5 policemen are killed for every unarmed black man killed by police, but you will not hear these facts on the news, because that is not a politically correct message and not helpful to Democrats or the media, especially during a presidential election.

After the American Civil War, black Americans voted Republican because Republicans fought the war, freed the slaves, and gave them the right to vote. After the war, Democrats (former Confederate officers), formed the KKK, lynched black men, and killed white Republicans who opposed slavery.[110] Today over 90% of black Americans vote as Democrats. They vote with the Confederate officers who formed the KKK and with Edmund Pettus, the man the Selma bridge is named after. He was a Confederate general, Grand Dragon of the KKK, and Democratic Senator.

The American Civil War of the 1860's was a spiritual battle, not a political battle. Every Confederate soldier fought against the God who created all men equal. The American Civil War of the 2020's is a spiritual battle, not a political battle. Every vote is for or against the God who created the laws that govern men and governments.

---

[110] "Ku Klux Klan," www.history.com, October 29, 2009; updated February 21, 2020; downloaded August 8, 2020. "Ku Klux Klan," www.wikipedia.com, downloaded June 4, 2020.

Why, in the 1860's, did hundreds of thousands of Confederate soldiers fight to their deaths against God without fear of God? Fear of God is the beginning of wisdom. They displayed extreme foolishness which led to eternal separation from God. And why, today, do Americans who support abortion and same-sex marriage not fear the wrath of the holy God who created man, woman, and marriage? And why do Americans put more faith in man and government than God, and want to trade their precious freedom as Americans for greater dependence on government?

The simple answer is spiritual blindness. Romans 1 states that God gives those who fail to acknowledge Him over to vain thinking. After committing adultery and murder, King David, the only man called a man after God's heart, told God, "Against thee and thee only have I sinned." He understood that every thought, word, and action is first and foremost for or against the God who created and sustains all life. He understood that His first and foremost duty was not to love his fellow man, but to love God with all his heart, mind, soul, and strength. Accordingly, every vote is first and foremost for or against God.

Today black Christians and black Christian leaders are just as spiritually blind as white Christians and white Christian leaders, but in a very different way. Their primary concern is not abortion or the murder of millions of unborn black or white children. It is not homosexuality or same-sex marriage. The United States could embrace the morality of Sodom and Gomorrah and they would not care. They see themselves as victims, not as "more than conquerors" with Christ. Their primary concerns are racism and social justice, and they look to man and government for justice and salvation, not to God. I challenge black Christians to tell me if I am wrong. You are my brothers and sisters in Christ, and that should be a much stronger bond than race. We are all children of the one true God, the Creator of all things seen and not seen.

CHAPTER 7.5

NATIONAL DEFENSE

INTRODUCTION. The primary and most important constitutional duty of the President is to serve as Commander in Chief of all armed forces of the United States and to defend Americans from "all enemies, foreign and domestic." This chapter discusses national defense in general, and the current threat of domestic and international terrorism.

ACCOMPLISHMENTS OF PRESIDENT. During the Republican National Convention, President Trump listed his national defense accomplishments as follows.

1.   Spent nearly $2.5 trillion on completely rebuilding our military, which was very badly depleted.
1.   Gave three separate pay raises to our great warriors.
2.   Passed VA Accountability and VA Choice.
3.   Obliterated 100 percent of ISIS Caliphate and killed its founder and leader Abu Bakr al-Baghdadi.
4.   Eliminated world's number one terrorist, Iranian General Qasem Soleimani (responsible for killing or wounding hundreds of American soldiers with Iranian-made Improvised Explosive Devices, etc.).
5.   Kept America out of new wars, and our troops are coming home.
6.   Launched Space Force, first new branch of United States military since Air Force was created almost 75 years ago.[111]
7.   Got NATO partners to pay $130 billion more per year. Will rise to $400 billion.
8.   Achieved first Middle East peace deal in 25 years.

---

[111] Ibid.

9. Kept my promise, recognized Israel's true capital, and moved our Embassy to Jerusalem for less than $500,000.
10. Recognized Israeli sovereignty over Golan Heights.
11. Withdrew from terrible, one-sided Iran Nuclear Deal.[112]

NATIONAL DEFENSE—TOP PRIORITY. Most Republicans and Democrats running for president claim they will do the best job of defending America. So, who is more truthful? Who can be trusted to do the best job of protecting Americans? Most Americans know that the top priority of Republican presidents is to serve as Commander in Chief and to defend America from all enemies foreign and domestic. The top priority of Democrats is not national defense, but taking care of Americans through totally unconstitutional costly healthcare, education, and other programs. That is why funding for the military declined sharply under President Obama, but greatly increased under President Trump. See chapters on Education, Healthcare, and Democratic Platform.

TERRORISM—ISIS/ISIL. One of the greatest threats to the United State is domestic and international terrorism. The greatest terrorist threat to the United States and Europe in 2016 was posed by ISIS/ISIL. What are these groups and what is the difference between ISIS and ISIL?

> The two acronyms refer to the same group. ISIS stands for Islamic State in Iraq and Syria because the group's territory straddles the border between the two counties. ISIL stands for Islamic State in Iraq and the Levant. The Levant is the historic name given to the entire region east of the Mediterranean from Egypt, east to Iran and to

---

[112] "Trump Accepts Republican Nomination for President at the 2020 RNC," NBC News, Aug. 28, 2020.

Turkey. U.S. officials use ISIL instead of ISIS to emphasize the group's goal to expand its influence beyond the borders of Syria and Iraq. The group began as a splinter from the terrorist group al Qaeda. The goal of ISIS is to create an Islamic state in Middle Eastern and African countries."[113]

Donald Trump has demonstrated much greater concern for and dedication to defeating ISIS/ISIL overseas, in Syria, Iraq, etc. Biden gives higher priority to a host of domestic issues for which the president has no constitutional authority.

DOMESTIC TERRORISM. During the past decade, domestic terrorism has repeatedly posed a threat to Americans. President Obama said the terrorist threat has "evolved into a new phase" of attacks hatched at home by extremists "poisoning the minds" of killers already on American soil.[114] Many Americans have been killed or injured on American soil by fellow Americans inspired by foreign terrorists. Trump demonstrated much greater concern and dedication to defeating terrorism on American soil. He has also promised to build a better wall between Mexico and the United States, which will more effectively prevent foreign terrorists from entering the United States.

CONCLUSION. Biden, like other Democrats, cannot be trusted to make national security or funding of the armed forces of the United States his top priority. His top priority is taking care of Americans through costly, unconstitutional social programs outlined in the Democratic Platform (education, healthcare, etc.). Only Trump can be trusted to

---

[113] "ISIS vs ISIL—what's the difference?" Kacie Yearout, USA Today Network, December 29, 2015.
[114] Ibid.

make national defense his top priority, to restore military strength, and to properly defend Americans from all enemies, foreign and domestic. As President, he has already proven this.

CHAPTER 7.6

LAW AND ORDER

<u>INTRODUCTION</u>. During the past few years, law and order have become a major issue and problem in more ways than most Americans realize. The most obvious are protests following the murder of George Floyd. Others include F.B.I. surveillance of Trump before he took office, all attempts to remove the president from office, the nomination of Supreme Court Justice Kavanaugh, sanctuary cities, etc.

<u>PROTESTS AFTER THE DEATH OF GEORGE FLOYD</u>. After the death of George Floyd, there were protests in many large cities throughout the United States. Most daytime protests were peaceful. Some protestors broke store windows and looted stores, but most were peaceful. However, many night-time protests turned violent. Some protestors came equipped for violent confrontation with police, wearing helmets and armed with bricks, rocks, frozen water bottles, fireworks, and other incendiary devices, which they threw at police. Many police officers were injured; a few were shot and killed. Some protestors used lasers to blind police. In Portland, 113 federal officers suffered eye injuries before the end of August, 2020. Some demonstrators used Molotov cocktails and other incendiary devices to destroy police cars and buildings.

President Obama, Nancy Pelosi, and other Democrats falsely accused President Trump of sending federal troops into cities to tear gas peaceful demonstrators. That was an absolute lie. Nancy Pelosi actually called them storm troopers, trying to make Trump look like Hitler, a dictator, a fascist. The federal police, part of the Department of Homeland Security, were protecting federal buildings from violent demonstrators who

120

were trying to break down protective barriers around the buildings so they could attack and damage or destroy the buildings.

Democratic mayors voiced their opposition to Trump and the use of federal forces to protect federal buildings in their cities. The Democratic mayor of Portland was filmed thanking protestors attacking the Federal Courthouse in Portland for coming out to show their opposition to Trump. His feelings about those protestors may have changed after they targeted his home. Demonstrators in many cities demanded defunding of the police. The mayors or city councils of New York City, Seattle, and Minneapolis actually agreed to partial defunding of the police.

Democrats speaking during the Democratic National Convention failed to speak out against or condemn the rioting, looting, attacks on police, or destruction of buildings and police cars. Republicans speaking during the Republican National Convention condemned their silence and called for law and order. Biden never spoke out when police officers were killed. After three demonstrators were shot and killed, he finally spoke up and condemned the violence.

SANCTUARY CITIES. When Trump became President, the Democratic mayors of many large cities declared their cities "sanctuary cities" for illegal immigrants. They were not fighting to protect legal immigration; they were fighting to protect illegal immigration. They refused to obey or help enforce federal immigration laws enacted by Congress long before President Trump became President. Governors remained silent, refusing to condemn the lawlessness in their cities.

THE WAR ON PRESIDENT TRUMP. The entire chapter entitled "The War on President Trump" describes the intense, unrelenting, full-time, lawless war against President Trump waged by Democrats and the media, a war which began before he even took office. In 2016 some Democrats ran for office promising to impeach Trump before he was even sworn in as President. During the 2016 presidential election, the Obama Administration illegally spied on and wiretapped the Trump campaign.

After President Trump took office, James Comey, head of the Federal Bureau of Investigation, a man who works for the President, leaked false information to the press through a friend to initiate an investigation to try to get President Trump removed from office. After that attempt failed, the House of Representatives held impeachment hearings and voted to impeach the president.

HIGH-TECH LYNCHINGS. As stated in the chapter on The War on Trump, when Senator Biden led the Senate Judiciary confirmation hearings for Supreme Court Justice Clarence Thomas, Justice Thomas said, "This is a high-tech lynching…." The standard of proof in a lynching is "guilty regardless of the evidence." That standard was applied to Justice Thomas, Justice Kavanaugh, and President Trump. They were all high-tech lynchings. Senator Harris was one of the meanest, most aggressive, and most lawless leaders in the high-tech lynching of Justice Kavanaugh. That same lynch-mob mentality is now being applied to any white officers who kill any black man or woman, even if the police officers are fired upon and returning fire to try to save their own lives so they can go home to their families at the end of the day.

GOD'S WORD ON LAW AND ORDER. The words "and everyone did what is right in his own eyes" (Judges 17:5-7; 21:24-25) describe a period of lawlessness in Israel. That is why God commanded the Israelites to not do what was right in their own eyes, but to obey his commandments (Deut. 12:8; Judges 17:5-7; 21:24-25). There is an unprecedented level of lawlessness in American today; the words "and everyone did what is right in his own eyes" describe Americans today more than ever before.

CONCLUSION. All Americans should support peaceful protests but condemn the violence, rioting, looting, attacks on police, and destruction of buildings and police cars by lawless, violent protestors. They should be arrested and prosecuted to the fullest extent of the law.

Scripture states that government officials are ministers of God. In the eyes of God, the President of the United States is the highest minister of God in the American government. Scripture states that the law is a good thing, if used lawfully. From 2016 to 2020, Democrats have used the law unlawfully in many ways to try to get rid of President Trump and to block his nomination of Justice Kavanagh.

This entire book shows that President Trump is fighting to uphold laws and principles embodied in Scripture, the Declaration of Independence, the Constitution, and the Bill of Rights. Democrats and the media are waging war against God and the laws and principles that this nation was founded upon.

The intense, unrelenting, full-time war waged by Democrats and the media against the President Trump has reached an unprecedented intensity. They have continually attacked Trump, tried to remove him from office, and are now doing their best to prevent his re-election.

This war began long before Trump, will continue long after him. This is first and foremost a spiritual war, not a political war. The primary forces in this war are spiritual forces, not Trump, Republicans, or Democrats. Americans need to know where God stands in this war, and make sure that they are on God's side.

CHAPTER 7.7

GUN CONTROL

INTRODUCTION. Americans are sharply divided on gun control and the right to bear arms. Virtually all Americans agree that there is a constitutional right to bear arms, but they sharply disagree on what type of weapons are justified by the Constitution. Some Democrats have made remarks like, "You don't need an assault weapon to hunt deer." Many Democrats want to ban ownership of all "assault weapons." They need to read the Declaration of Independence and Second Amendment.

SECOND AMENDMENT. The Second Amendment grants the right to bear arms. It states: "A well-regulated Militia, being necessary to the security of a free State, the right of the people to keep and bear Arms, shall not be infringed."[115] Note that the absolute "right of the people to keep and bear Arms" which "shall not be infringed" is linked to the need for a "well-regulated Militia" for defense of the government. The primary need for the arms, is not for hunting or self-defense, but for defense of "a free state." Therefore, the type of weapons justified by the Second Amendment are not for hunting or self-defense, but for defense of the government.

DECLARATION OF INDEPENDENCE. The entire Declaration of Independence is an argument for the right of the people to bear arms and to use those arms to overthrow any government which violates their God-given rights to life, liberty, and the pursuit of happiness. See Appendix B for full text of Declaration of Independence.

---

[115] Ibid.

       <u>MASS SHOOTINGS</u>. During the past 71 years, since 1949, there have been 28 mass shootings in the United States with 10 or more fatalities. 13 occurred during the past decade. Handguns were used in 23 of 28 shootings, rifles in 15, and shotguns in 6. Only handguns were used in 12 of the 28 shootings, and only rifles in 6 shootings. All other shootings involved a combination of handguns, rifles, and/or shotguns.

       There was no great demand for stricter gun-control laws after 26 Christians were killed in 2017 at Sutherland Springs Church in Sutherland Springs, Texas. However, there were great demands for stricter gun-control laws after 27 students and teachers were killed in 2012 at Sandy Hook Elementary School in Newtown, Connecticut and after 17 students and teachers were killed in 2018 at Stoneman Douglas High School in Parkland, Florida. Demands included better background checks and a ban on assault weapons.

       Assault rifles were used in the shootings at Newtown and Parkland. However, only pistols were used in the deadliest school shooting, where 32 students and teachers were killed at Virginia Tech in Blacksburg, Virginia in 2007.

       Most Americans do not realize that semi-automatic pistols can be more deadly than assault rifles in school shootings. First, several pistols can be hidden in a small bag or backpack. Second, pistol clips can hold many rounds, and clips can be changed very quickly. Third, pistols can be aimed and fired faster than rifles, and there is no need for a long-range weapon in a school shooting. Therefore, instituting a ban on assault rifles could result in greater use of semi-automatic pistols, which may be even more deadly.

ASSAULT RIFLES. Neither Republicans nor Democrats would allow general public ownership of fully automatic weapons like those used by our armed forces. The primary issue is whether Americans should be allowed to own assault rifles.

As an Army officer, I fired and qualified many times on the .45 caliber pistol, 9mm pistol, and M-16 rifle. I fired many other weapons, to include the AK-47 rifle, 7.62mm and .50 caliber machine guns, 40mm grenade launcher, and 20mm anti-aircraft cannon. I also served on crews for firing the M60A1 tank and 105mm artillery.

The AR-15, a semi-automatic rifle which looks like the fully-automatic M-16 rifle, is the most popular "assault weapon" in the United States. It functions exactly the same as all other semi-automatic rifles. You simply pull the trigger for each shot. It is actually less powerful than many hunting rifles. The bullets are very small (.223 caliber, 5.56 mm), and the cartridges have less gunpowder than many rifle cartridges.

It would be ridiculous to ban "assault weapons" just because they look like military weapons, and it would be impossible to ban all semi-automatic rifles. I would only use a semi-automatic rifle for hunting, because a bolt-action, lever-action, or pump-action weapon force you to lose your sight picture to chamber each round. Magazine capacity is another issue.

BACKGROUND CHECKS. Republicans and Democrats should be able to agree upon reasonable background checks. All Americans understand the need to pass a driving test before being given a driving license. All Americans should also understand the need to pass a background test before buying a weapon. Americans with mental illness, Americans on a do-not-fly terror watch-list, and Americans who have been convicted of certain violent crimes should not be permitted to buy weapons. Republicans and Democrats should ignore demands of the NRA and come to reasonable agreement regarding background checks. However, this issue should not be a deciding factor in any election, because there are so many other issues which are far more important in the eyes of God.

CONCLUSION. Voting with the Constitution and Declaration of Independence requires voting Republican because Republicans better support the right to bear arms. Both founding documents provide justification for the right to bear arms not for hunting or self-defense, but for defense of good government or overthrow of a government that denies the God-given rights of life, liberty, and the pursuit of happiness. Millions of Americans own assault rifles. Instituting a ban on assault rifles could result in greater use of semi-automatic pistols, which may be even more deadly in school shootings. However, Republicans and Democrats should agree to reasonable background checks and reasonable restrictions on who should be denied the right to bear arms.

CHAPTER 7.8

HEALTHCARE

<u>INTRODUCTION</u>. What part of the Constitution gives the federal government authority to legislate national healthcare? Answer: no part. The federal government of the United States is a government of enumerated powers. Each branch of government only has the powers granted to it by the Constitution. All other powers are reserved to the people and the states. Healthcare is not even mentioned in the Constitution. The federal government has absolutely no authority to enact national healthcare. The Supreme Court does not have the power or authority to change that.

What part of the Constitution is wrongfully used to justify legislation regarding many subject areas not even mentioned in the Constitution? Answer: Interstate Commerce Clause. Article 1, Section 8, states: "The Congress shall have Power…To regulate Commerce with foreign Nations, and among the several States, and with the Indian Tribes."[116]

I used the nation's most popular bar-preparation materials to prepare for the bar examination that enabled me to practice law. The law professor advising law school graduates throughout the United States said, "If you have any question about whether or not the Interstate Commerce Clause authorizes the federal government to do something, the answer is: 'Yes!'" In other words, the federal government wrongfully

---

[116] "Constitution of the United States," U.S. National Archives & Records Administration, 8601 Adelphi Road, College Park, MD, 20740-6001, • 1-86-NARA-NARA • 1-866-272-6272; http://www.archives.gov/exhibits/charters/constitution.html.

129

uses the Interstate Commerce Clause to justify legislation in many areas not authorized by the Constitution.

OBAMACARE. On March 23, 2010, President Obama "signed the Patient Protection and Affordable Care Act (Obamacare) into law, which provided federal funding for health plans that pay for abortion on demand and lead to large-scale rationing of lifesaving medical treatments."[117]

Governor Romney said, "Obamacare will violate that crucial first principle of medicine" 'Do no harm.'"[118] He believed that the Obama health care law, which would open the door to federal subsidies for abortion coverage and rationing of lifesaving medical care, should be repealed.[119]

RESULTS OF OBAMACARE. Exactly what are the results or consequences of Obamacare for Christians?

1. ABORTION. "Obamacare is a massive expansion of taxpayer-subsidized abortion.[120] In other words, American taxpayers who believe that abortion is murder are forced to pay higher taxes to fund millions of abortions. After describing in great detail President Obama's lengthy and "abysmal record on life,"[121] Carol Tobias, President of National Right to Life, said,

---

[117] "National Right to Life Endorses Governor Mitt Romney," "Where Do the Candidates Stand on Life: Mitt Romney, Barack Obama," "Statement by Carol Tobias, National Right to Life President," Carol Tobias, National Right to Life, Committee, http://www.nrlc.org, April 12, 2012.
[118] Ibid.
[119] Ibid.
[120] Bruce Hausknecht, "Obamacare Decision Next Week: What's at Stake?" Citizenlink, http://www.citizenlink.com/2012/10/29/pro-life-group-proves-that-obamacare-subsidizes-abortion/, June 22, 2012.
[121] Carol Tobias, "Statement by Carol Tobias, National Right to Life President."

But even more far-reaching than all of this, is how President Obama impacted our health care system. In 2012, Congress passed and President Obama signed into law, the Patient Protection and Affordable Care Act, also known as ObamaCare. Today, every fifth child dies from abortion, and that percentage will rise because of ObamaCare. This program will enshrine abortion and rationing of health care in our society for generations to come.[122]

2. <u>RELIGIOUS FREEDOM</u>. The mandate from the Health and Human Services (different from individual mandate to buy insurance), a byproduct of Obamacare, "requires most religious organizations and their private employers to provide employee healthcare coverage for drugs, medical procedures and other services against their deeply held religious beliefs."[123] These drugs and medical procedures may include abortion, abortion inducing drugs, contraceptives, sterilization, reproductive counseling, etc.[124] Andy Newland, Vice President of Hercules Industries, said the mandate requires business owners to compromise their beliefs.

> We never imagined the federal government would order our family business to provide insurance for drugs we object to covering. If you put yourself back to when the Founders founded America, it seems so contradictory to

---

[122] Ibid.

[123] Bruce Hausknecht, "Obamacare Decision Next Week: What's at Stake?"

[124] Bethany Monk, "HHS Contraception Mandate Deadline Falls Wednesday," http://www.citizenlink.com, July 31, 2012; "President Obama to Freedom of Religion: Nertz to You!", Family Research Council Action, http://www.frcaction.org, August 6, 2012.

their intention that Americans be free to live out their beliefs in a country that was created for freedom from religious persecution.[125]

Newland said the mandate prevents families from bringing their moral and principles into their business. "What ethical and moral principles do you use to run your business? We'll end up with no ethical or moral principals at all."[126]

Emily Hardman, Communications Director for Becket Fund for Religious Liberty, said that the mandate is "a violation of those individuals with religious beliefs… People don't have to give up their faith when they enter their business."[127]

The only organizations exempted from the mandate are seminaries and churches that only employ and serve members of their own faith (and plans "grandfathered" under the rule). Catholic universities and hospitals are not exempt.[128] They are forced to violate their deeply held religious beliefs.

Fines for non-compliance can be as much as $100 per day per employee, an amount that can bankrupt a business.[129] In other words, to survive in the United States, Christian businesses or organizations will be forced by the government to violate their deeply held moral and religious beliefs.

3. <u>LIMITS ON GOVERNMENT</u>. The "individual mandate" of Obamacare (different from mandate of Health and

---

[125] Ibid.

[126] Ibid.

[127] Ibid.

[128] Ibid.

[129] "President Obama to Freedom of Religion: Nertz to You!"

Human Services) requires all Americans to buy health insurance or pay a penalty.[130] This mandate is totally contrary to the U.S. Constitution, the highest law of our nation, as explained below.

4. <u>COST TO TAXPAYERS</u>. The incredibly high cost of Obamacare to U.S. taxpayers will continue to rise dramatically. In 2010 the Congressional Budget Office estimated the ten-year cost of Obamacare to be $944 billion. In 2011 it estimated $1,442 billion. In 2012 it estimated $1,856 billion. See Forbes Magazine article at footnote.[131]

5. <u>COST TO STATES</u>. Obamacare requires states to demand "massive dollars" from taxpayers to fund Obamacare. States must raise $33.5 billion from 2014 to 2020.[132]

6. <u>REDISTRIBUTION OF WEALTH</u>. Obamacare is a massive, monumental federal redistribution of wealth program that any good socialist or communist would take great pride in having created. Totally contrary to the Constitution, it forces American taxpayers to pay the healthcare bills of other Americans. How massive is the redistribution? The Los Angeles Times reports that California will receive about $15 billion from American taxpayers.[133] How would you feel if the government forced you to pay for all the healthcare bills of your neighbors? How can any elected or appointed government official be so incredibly blind and foolish to think that healthcare is a right, and that the government has the right to

---

[130] Bruce Hausknecht, "Obamacare Decision Next Week: What's at Stake?"
[131] Avik Roy, "CBO: Obamacare Will Spend More, Tax More, and Reduce the Deficit Less Than We Previously Thought," http://www.forbes.com, August 27, 2012.
[132] Bruce Hausknecht, "Obamacare Decision Next Week: What's at Stake?"
[133] Ibid.

force any American to pay the healthcare bills of other Americans? What about the food bills, the rent or mortgage bills, the home heating bills, the college education bills, the legal bills, etc. Exactly where do you draw the line and why?

SUPREME COURT RULING. On June 28, 2012 the United States Supreme Court ruled Obamacare to be constitutional. Justice Kennedy was expected to be the deciding vote between liberals and conservatives. However, in a shocking turn of events that surprised experts, Chief Justice Roberts, a conservative appointed by President George W. Bush, joined four liberal justices in ruling Obamacare constitutional. Neither Justice Kennedy nor the conservative justices were able to convince Chief Justice Roberts to rejoin conservatives in ruling Obamacare unconstitutional. To see entire text of 193-page majority opinion, go to reference in footnote.[134]

SCOTUS stands for Supreme Court of the United States. SCOTUSblog is sponsored by Bloomberg Law. SCOTUSblog summarized the majority opinion of the Affordable Care Act in one paragraph.

In Plain English: The Affordable Care Act, including its individual mandate that virtually all Americans buy health insurance, is constitutional. There were not five votes to uphold it on the ground that Congress could use its power to regulate commerce between the states to require everyone to buy health insurance. However, five Justices agreed that the penalty that someone must

---

[134] "The Supreme Court's Obamacare Decision: Full Text," The Atlantic, http://www.theatlantic.com/politics/archive/2012/06/the-supreme-courts-obamacare-decision-full-text/259102/, June 28, 2012.

pay if he refuses to buy insurance is a kind of tax that Congress can impose using its taxing power. That is all that matters. Because the mandate survives, the Court did not need to decide what other parts of the statute were constitutional, except for a provision that required states to comply with new eligibility requirements for Medicaid or risk losing their funding. On that question, the Court held that the provision is constitutional as long as states would only lose new funds if they didn't comply with the new requirements, rather than all of their funding.[135]

In an article titled "Roberts: Our Decision Isn't About Whether Obamacare Is Sound Policy," Chief Justice Roberts explained the ruling upholding the Affordable Care Act:

We do not consider whether the Act embodies sound policies. That judgment is entrusted to the Nation's elected leaders. We ask only whether Congress has the power under the Constitution to enact the challenged provisions. In this case we must again determine whether the Constitution grants Congress powers it now asserts, but which many States and individuals believe it does not possess. Resolving this controversy requires us to examine both the limits of the Government's power, and our own limited role in policing those boundaries. [136]

---

[135] Derek Thompson, "The Health Care Decision Explained in 1 Paragraph on SCOTUSblog," The Atlantic, http://www.theatlantic.com/business/archive/2012/06/the-health-care-decision-explained-in-1-paragraph-on-scotusblog/259097/, June 28, 2012.
[136] Chief Justice Roberts, "Roberts: Our Decision Isn't About Whether

In other words, Chief Justice Roberts first and foremost made it abundantly clear that his decision did not mean that he approved of the legislation by Congress as good policy for the nation. That was the responsibility of elected members of Congress. The question remains: Why did Chief Justice John Roberts decide to join liberal justices in ruling Obamacare constitutional? The Catholic World News explained his decision as follows:

> The US Supreme Court has upheld the constitutionality of President Obama's sweeping health-care reform legislation. Writing for the majority in a hotly contested 5-4 decision, Chief Justice John Roberts said that the individual mandate—the requirement that every citizen must purchase health insurance—was in effect a tax. "Because the Constitution permits such a tax, it is not our role to forbid it, or to pass upon its wisdom or fairness," he wrote.
> The June 28 ruling does not affect the lawsuits brought by Catholic institutions to challenge the law's requirement that all health-care insurance programs must include coverage for contraception. Those suits will continue to move forward. The US bishops' conference responded to the Supreme Court decision by urging Congress to change the law, saying that it should be amended to eliminate funding for abortion, ensure conscience rights, and provide protection for immigrants. The statement noted that the US bishops have not sought to

Obamacare Is Sound Policy," <u>Talking Points Memo Livewire</u>, <u>http://livewire.talkingpointsmemo.com/entries/roberts-our-decision-isnt-about-whether-obamacare-is</u>, June 28, 2012.

overturn the legislation entirely.[137]

Chief Justice Roberts ruled that Obamacare (The Affordable Care Act) was constitutional because "the requirement that every citizen must purchase health insurance—was in effect a tax" and "the Constitution permits such a tax." In other words, he ruled Obamacare constitutional because the Constitution gives Congress the power to levy taxes.

As noted in the same quote from the Catholic World News, the dissenting justices, in a joint opinion, said: "In our view, the act before us is invalid in its entirety."[138] To view the minority opinion in its entirety, see reference at footnote.[139] For more information on the ruling, see "ObamaCare and the Power to Tax" from the Wall Street Journal,[140] "Obamacare: Dissenting Justices Opinion" from the Lorinov's Blog,[141] "Obamacare Dissenting Opinion the Original Majority Opinion?" from the Kansas Citian.[142]

---

[137] "Supreme Court Upholds Obama Health-care Reform," Catholic World News, http://www.catholicculture.org/news/headlines/ index.cfm ?storyid=14767, June 28, 2012.

[138] Ibid.

[139] "SCOTUS Obamacare Ruling: The Dissenting Opinion in It's Entirety," Patriots for America, http://patriotsforamerica.ning.com/forum/topics/ scotus-obamacare-ruling-the-dissenting-opinion-in-it-s-entirety, June 28, 2012.

[140] "ObamaCare and the Power to Tax," Wall Street Journal, http://online.wsj.com/article/SB10001424052702303561504577495242473 319890.html, June 28, 2012.

[141] Rob Lorinov, "Obamacare: Dissenting Justices Opinion," Lorinov's Blog, http://roblorinov.wordpress.com/2012/06/28/obamacare-dissenting-justices-opinion/, June 28, 2012.

[142] Ed Whelan, "Obamacare Dissenting Opinion the Original Majority Opinion?," Kansas Citian, http://thekansascitian.blogspot.com /2012/06/obamacare-dissenting-opinion-original.html, June 28, 2012.

CONCLUSION. Was Chief Justice Roberts correct in ruling that Obamacare (The Affordable Care Act) was constitutional because the Constitution grants Congress the power to levy taxes? Absolutely not! He was wrong because the Constitution does not grant Congress the power to force Americans to pay taxes for any purpose not authorized by the Constitution. The Constitution does not grant any branch of the federal government authority to levy taxes for healthcare. Congress cannot forcefully take money from one American to pay the healthcare bills of another American.

The minority opinion held that Obamacare (The Affordable Care Act) was "invalid in its entirety." Was the minority opinion correct? Absolutely, because the federal government of the United States is a government of enumerated powers. Each branch of government only has the powers granted to it by the Constitution. Healthcare is not even mentioned in the Constitution. The federal government has absolutely no authority to enact national healthcare. Trying to use the Interstate Commerce Clause or the taxing clauses of the Constitution to justify legislation of national healthcare totally violates the intent of the Founding Fathers to establish a government of limited, enumerated powers and renders the reservation of all other powers to the states quite meaningless.

Also, President Trump eliminate the "penalty tax" imposed by Obamacare, the "tax" that Chief Justice Roberts recommended to make Obamacare legal. In other words, if Obamacare went before the Supreme Court today, it would be declared unconstitutional because Justice Ginsburg is gone and because the primary reason that Chief Justice Roberts declared it constitutional has been eliminated.

So, what are the consequences of Obamacare for Christians? First, Christians are forced to pay higher federal and state taxes to pay the healthcare bills of other Americans and to fund the killing of millions of unborn or partially born American children. Second, Christians are forced to buy health insurance or be fined. Third, Christian organizations are forced, against their deeply held moral and religious beliefs, to perform or support abortions, abortive drugs, sterilization, contraceptives, etc. Organizations that fail to comply may be fined and forced into bankruptcy.

CHAPTER 7.9

EDUCATION

INTRODUCTION. No American should vote for any candidate based upon any promise of educational benefits. It is illegal and unethical for any candidate for federal office to promise educational benefits to voters.

DECEPTION TO WIN VOTES. To win votes, Democrats promise generous but totally unconstitutional educational benefits not paid for not by them. First, Democrats lie by telling Americans that they have the right to education benefits from the federal government. Each branch of the federal government only has those powers specifically granted to it by the Constitution. The Constitution does not give the president or any other part of the federal government any authority to grant educational benefits to Americans.

Second, Democrats try to convince voters that they have the right to education benefits paid for by other taxpayers. The federal government has no moral or legal authority to forcefully take lawfully earned income from one taxpayer and use it to pay the education bills of another taxpayer. See chapters on Constitution and Bill of Rights.

2016 ELECTION. During the 2016 election, Hillary Clinton and Democrats offered free college education to all families who earn less than $125,000/year (83% of all families) and debt free education to all others. Clinton promised to pay for all this by only increasing taxes on the richest Americans and on corporations. She falsely claimed that rich were not paying their fair share. The rich are already paying virtually all federal income taxes. The top 1% pays about 27% of all federal income taxes. Our College debt already exceeds credit card debt in the United States. Obama doubled the national debt without giving free college. There is no way that Democrats can pay for all the educational benefits that they promise to voters, but they know that they can win votes with the false promises.

    <u>CONCLUSION</u>. No American should vote for any Democrat who promises unconstitutional federal educational benefits. It is illegal and immoral to forcefully take money from some taxpayers and give it to others in the form of educational benefits. It is also impossible for Democrats to pay for the generous educational benefits that they have promised to voters. Every 4 years, during every presidential election, Democrats promise educational benefits, but they never fulfill their promise.

CHAPTER 7.10

IMMIGRATION

<u>INTRODUCTION</u>. Christians should not vote first on immigration. Again, they should vote first based upon God's laws and principles revealed through scripture and second based on American laws and principles embodied in the Declaration of Independence, Constitution, and Bill of Rights.

<u>LAWLESSNESS OF DEMOCRATS</u>. The lawlessness of Democrats on the subject of immigration is absolutely shocking. All Americans should support legal immigration and oppose illegal immigration.

First, the federal government should cut federal funding to sanctuary cities that shield illegal immigrants from federal immigration agents. Second, US laws should be changed so that no one who enters the US illegally is rewarded with an asylum hearing. They should apply for asylum through the US embassy in their country, and only travel to the United States after their request for asylum has been approved.

Our family has good Christian friends who entered the United States legally working for a business, but had to fight for many years to get green cards allowing them to stay. The father runs a business that employs Americans. Why should illegal immigrants get more favorable treatment?

<u>TRUMP VS. BIDEN</u>. There are sharp differences between Trump and Biden on immigration. Everyone should know that Trump would do a better job of protecting Americans from: (1) immigration of terrorists, (2) drug traffic

142

from Mexico, and (3) illegal immigration. Biden would place far fewer restrictions on immigration, and is far more likely to legalize millions of illegal immigrants.

ACCOMPLISHMENTS OF PRESIDENT. During the Republican National Convention, President Trump listed his accomplishments related to borders and immigration as follows.

1. Secured America's borders more than ever before.
2. Built 300 miles of border wall, are adding 10 miles/week, and wall will soon be complete.
3. Ended catch-and-release and stopped asylum fraud.
4. Took down human traffickers who prey on women and children.
5. Deported 20,000 gang members and 500,000 criminal aliens.[143]

IMMIGRATION AND TERRORISM. Most immigrants from South America want to live and work in the United States and be law-abiding citizens. Most are Catholics who pose no threat of terrorism. The same cannot be said for all Muslims. ISIS/ISIL terrorists strongly desire to infiltrate immigrants fleeing Syria and other Arab nations and commit acts of terror in the United States and Europe. It would be terrorist malpractice to not try to do so.

Democrats claim that we should allow properly vetted immigrants from war-torn Muslim nations into the United States. However, it is impossible to properly vet many of these immigrants. When I had to get a top-secret clearance in the Army, the Army gathered information on every place that I

---

[143] "Trump Accepts Republican Nomination for President at the 2020 RNC," NBC News, Aug. 28, 2020.

had lived, worked, and attended school. It is impossible to properly investigate individuals fleeing war-torn areas. There is no one to call and no way to verify their information or whether or not they pose a threat to the United States.

The Christian values of freedom of speech and freedom of religion are vital parts of the Constitution. The Koran does not permit freedom of religion or freedom of speech. Christians in Egypt pay higher taxes because the Koran requires higher taxes from non-Muslims. Authors in Europe were killed for criticizing Islam. Non-Muslims who try to share their faith in a Muslim nation may be imprisoned. The Bible commands Christians to love their enemies. The Koran offers great rewards for killing non-Muslims.

In some Muslim communities in Europe and the United States, Muslims have tried to implement and enforce their laws, which may be totally contrary to state and federal laws. After Germany accepted many thousands of Syrian refugees, crime rates for theft and rape skyrocketed, and Germans set records for the purchase of tasers and other self-defense weapons. There are about 25 Muslim Arab nations. Some are very wealthy. Arab Muslim refugees should flee to Muslin nations who speak their language and practice their religion.

<u>CONCLUSION</u>. The presidential candidates sharply differ on immigration. Americans who want more protection from immigration of terrorists, illegal drug traffic, and illegal immigration should vote for Trump. Americans who want fewer restrictions on immigration and the legalization of millions of illegal immigrants should vote for Biden.

CHAPTER 7.11

ENVIRONMENT

<u>INTRODUCTION</u>. Climate change is one of the very few areas where many Democrats are right more than many Republicans. However, any American who believes that climate change justifies voting for any Democrat is greatly mistaken. Doing so would be contrary to Christian values, for reasons stated in this chapter and throughout this book.

<u>WINNING VOTES DISHONESTLY</u>. During every election, Democrats use arguments about the environment, climate change, and global warming to win votes dishonestly. They talk about non-polluting renewable energy resources like solar power, wind power, etc. However, use of these energy sources is not economically feasible for most Americans. How many Democrats drive cars powered by solar cells or fuel cells? How is the electricity generated for the few that drive electric cars? Is it generated by a coal plant or nuclear plant? How many Democrats live in a solar, wind, or geothermal heated/cooled homes? Most Americans cannot afford these non-polluting energy sources because they are too costly. However, Democrats talk about them to win votes.

President Obama promised much greater use of renewable energy resources, but after eight years in office there are no changes for most Americans. Most Americans will continue to drive gas-powered cars and live in homes heated by gas or electricity from coal or nuclear-powered plants. The false claims of Democrats win votes but do little to change energy use by Americans.

BIDEN'S PLANS. Bidens plans for the next four years reflect the same pattern of totally dishonest promises to change the energy use of Americans. During the first presidential debate, the moderator, Chris Wallace repeatedly, asked Biden how he would pay for extremely expensive plans to remodel millions of homes to make them more energy efficient. Biden claimed that his plans would generate many jobs, but repeatedly failed to say how he would pay for these jobs or for the labor and materials to needed to remodel millions of homes.

TRUMP'S ACCOMPLISHMENTS. President Trump's accomplishments related to environment include the following: (1) signed largest public land bill in a decade; (2) signed Save Our Seas Act to clean oceans; (3) rebuilding of rural water infrastructure in 23 states; (4) signed bipartisan wildlife conservation legislation; (5) improved Endangered Species Act.[144] While global carbon dioxide emissions have greatly increased during the past few decades, since 2005 the United States reduced emissions more than any other nation, and they continue to decline.[145]

Democrats and the media strongly condemned President Trump for withdrawing the United States from the Paris Climate Accord. It imposed costly regulations on American energy producers, gave other nations subsidies paid by the United States, and gave China a free pass to pollute for over 10 years. It would cost the United States $3 trillion and 6.5 million jobs by 2040. That would cripple the United States economy. [146]

---

[144] "President Trump's Accomplishments," Ohio Battleground Alliance, Ohio Women for Liberty, downloaded September 30, 2020.
[145] "President Trump is Right to Get Us Out of the Bad Paris Climate Accord: Senator Barrasso," John Barrasso, USA Today, November 5, 2019.

Biden has promised to rejoin the Paris Climate Accord. Biden's other plans, discussed above, would cripple the U.S. economy even more than the Paris Climate Accord. However, the Green New Deal that many Democrats are fighting for would totally devastate the U.S. economy even more than Biden's plans or the Paris Climate Accord. Can you imagine flying in battery-powered, propeller-driven commercial aircraft which are not permitted to use jet fuel? Where does the energy come from needed to charge billions of electric cars, trucks, and trains and heat and cool billions of homes and office buildings? Does it come from coal or nuclear power plants? Why are Democrats so strongly compelled to lie about and deceive Americans on every single issue?

DOMINION MANDATE. When God created man, He gave the Dominion Mandate: "Be fruitful, and multiply, and replenish the earth, and subdue it: and have dominion over the fish of the sea, and over the fowl of the air, and over every living thing that moveth upon the earth (Gen 1:28, KJV). The Dominion Mandate gives man the duty to care for the earth and use its resources in a responsible manner.

Some Republicans, in the face of overwhelming scientific evidence, deny climate change. I have visited many national parks, and I have seen the evidence of the incredible acceleration in the decline of glaciers. Many shows on the Public Broadcasting Station show scientists researching the results of increasing water temperatures at the poles. Polar bears in Canada and penguins and other wildlife at the poles are losing their ice fields and food supply.

---

[146] Ibid.

<u>WORSHIP CREATION MORE THAN CREATOR</u>. As a Christian attorney I had to ask myself why Democrats are so very wrong on virtually every topic except climate change. Then I remembered the words of Romans 1.

> For the wrath of God is revealed from heaven against all ungodliness and unrighteousness of men…because that which may be known of God is manifest in them; for God hath shewed it unto them. For <u>the invisible things of him from the creation of the world are clearly seen, being understood by the things that are made, even his eternal power and Godhead</u>; so that they are without excuse: Because that, when they <u>knew God, they glorified him not as God</u>, neither were thankful; but became vain in their imaginations, and their foolish heart was darkened. Professing themselves to be wise, they became fools.... Wherefore God also gave them up…. Who changed the truth of God into a lie, and <u>worshipped and served the creature more than the Creator</u>, who is blessed forever, Amen (Romans 1:18-25, KJV).

God has revealed His existence and wonder and majesty through creation, but some Democrats have chosen to worship creation more than the Creator, as proven by the policies that they support.

<u>CONCLUSION</u>. All Americans should care about the environment, and do their part to improve it by recycling, etc. However, any American who chooses to vote with Democrats because of concerns about the environment or climate change is choosing to serve "the creature more than the Creator." It is

as simple as that. Also, Americans should not be deceived by dishonest promises of change or action designed to win votes, promises which can never be kept.

CHAPTER 7.12

VOTING BY MAIL

<u>INTRODUCTION</u>. Due to the global pandemic, voting by mail will be more important during the 2020 election. I have voted by mail for many years, and served as a Presiding Judge, which simply means poll manager, at a polling location in Ohio for many years. President Obama falsely accused President Trump of "kneecapping the post office" before the election. Contrary to what many Democrats have claimed, mail service should not be a major factor in this election, for reasons stated herein.

<u>VOTING BY MAIL VERSUS UNIVERSAL MAIL-IN-VOTING (UNSOLICITED BALLOTS)</u>. Most Americans do not know the difference between regular voting by mail and "universal" mail-in-voting. The key word that makes all the difference is "universal." On September 30, 2020, during the first Presidential debate, President Trump said that he had no problem with solicited ballots, but expressed concern about fraud with unsolicited ballots.[147] The words "unsolicited ballots" are simply different words used to describe the same thing i.e. universal mail-in-voting.

President Trump has, with good reason, complained about possible fraud with universal mail-in-voting (unsolicited ballots). If Ohio had it, I would automatically receive 5 actual ballots in the mail, for me, my wife, and our 3 daughters. My wife and I could complete and mail all 5 ballots, although our

---

[147] "Tuesday's Debate Made Clear the Gravest Threat to the Election: The President Himself," David E. Sanger, The New York Times, September 30, 2020.

150

daughters no longer live at home. Our daughters could also vote where they live. Ballots may also be mailed to people who have been dead for years, but not removed from the voter rolls, and someone else could complete them if they had the information needed to do so.

For regular voting by mail, I mail a Vote by Mail Application, also called a request for an absentee ballot, to my county Board of Elections 1-4 months before the election. This year all voters received a Vote by Mail Application around the first week of September, two months before the election. I received 5 application for me, my wife, and our three daughters. The applications must be received by the Board of Elections by noon on the Saturday before Election Day.

I receive my ballot in the mail 3-4 weeks before the election. I can immediately complete and mail the ballot. It takes 1-2 days for my ballot to get from my home or post office to my county Board of Elections. Mail is never an issue. As stated by Governor Christie on Meet the Press in August 2020, the problem is not with the mail, but with the Board of Elections, which must verify all signatures and personal information and scan all the ballots. Ohio has machines which can scan ballots and record all votes very quickly, so the one thing that takes significant time is having a Republican and Democrat verify signatures and personal information before the ballots are scanned. That is what can really delay getting election results, especially in a state where tons of mail-in-ballots cannot be opened and scanned until election day.

However, even with regular voting by mail, I could cheat the system by mailing Vote by Mail Applications for all 5 family members to my county Board of Elections. I would receive 5 ballots in the mail. My wife and I could complete, sign, and mail all 5 ballots. No one would know that 2 voters had submitted 5 ballots. Nevertheless, it is less likely that this kind of voter fraud would happen with regular mail in voting than with universal mail-in-voting because you must submit a request for each absentee ballot and provide all the required information and signatures just to get the ballots.

VOTER FRAUD. As the Presiding Judge at my polling location, I handled all provisional voters. I remember a young man whose name was not in the signature book deciding not to vote when I informed him that his vote would not be counted until the Board of Elections verified all information on the provisional voter form that he had to complete. I believe that he was trying to vote illegally, but found out that he could not do it at our polling place. Voter fraud is rare at in-person voting locations in Ohio, because everyone must vote in their precinct, provide identification, and sign next to their name in the poll signature book.

However, there may be much more extensive voter fraud with mail-in-voting. Trump complained about fraud related to handling of ballots, citing a true case of military ballots for Trump being thrown in a trash can in Philadelphia by a poll-worker who was then fired. Voter fraud of this nature may be widespread, but rarely detected.

CONCLUSION. Voter fraud is rare when voting is in-person at the precincts in which voters reside. Mail will not be a major issue and voter fraud is rare but still very possible with regular voting by mail. However, universal-mail-in voting could result in greater problems with voter fraud, because each Board of Elections will have to quickly process massive numbers of mail-in ballots, and it cannot not quickly verify with absolute certainty who actually received, completed, signed, and mailed each ballot. Also, many ballots will be rejected because signatures or personal information do no match or the ballots are mailed without the inner envelope with the signatures and personal information needed to verify the identity of the voter.

CHAPTER 8.0

VOTING SCRIPTURE

<u>SECTION REVIEW</u>. This section discusses scripture on several key issues. The first chapter shows that God's ideal is not a government which does more to care for its people or discriminates based upon wealth or other factors. The second chapter shows that God's ideal is the same tithe rate or "tax rate" for rich and poor, without discrimination based upon wealth or economic class. The third chapter shows that abortion is murder in the eyes of God. The fourth chapter shows that homosexuality and same-sex marriage are extreme perversions of God's design for man, woman, and marriage.

<u>CHAPTERS</u>:
8.1 Scripture on Role of Government
8.2 Scripture on Taxes
8.3 Scripture on Abortion
8.4 Scripture on Homosexuality and
Same-Sex Marriage

SCRIPTURE ON ROLE OF GOVERNMENT

INTRODUCTION. "I believe that I am my brother's keeper." During the 2008 election, Senator Obama often used these words to explain what he believed to be the proper role of government, caring for its people. No other subject divides Christians between Republicans and Democrats more than the proper role of government. Most Democrats want a government that does more to take care of the people, especially the poor and the middle class. Most Republicans want a smaller federal government, which does less to care for its people. So, who is right and who is wrong?

SCRIPTURE ON GOVERNMENT. What does God prefer, a government that does more to care for its people, or a government that does less? Does Scripture give any hint about God's ideal for government? First, consider 1 Samuel 8:4-22.

SCRIPTURE: 1 Samuel 8:4-22 (KJV):

Then all the elders of Israel gathered themselves together, and came to Samuel unto Ramah, and said unto him, "Behold, thou art old, and thy sons walk not in thy ways: now make us a king to judge us like all the nations." But the thing displeased Samuel, when they said, "Give us a king to judge us." And Samuel prayed unto the LORD. And the LORD said unto Samuel, "Hearken unto the voice of the people in all that they say unto thee: for they have not rejected thee, but they have rejected me, that I should not reign over them. According to all the works which they have done since the day that I brought them up out of Egypt even unto this day, wherewith they have forsaken me, and served other gods, so do they also unto thee. Now therefore hearken unto their voice: howbeit yet protest solemnly unto them, and shew them the manner of the king that shall reign over them." And Samuel told all the words of the LORD unto the people that asked of him a king. And he said, "This will be the manner of the king that shall reign over you: He will take your sons, and appoint them for himself, for his chariots, and to be his horsemen; and some shall run before his chariots. And he will appoint him captains over thousands, and captains over fifties; and will set them to ear his ground, and to reap his harvest, and to make his instruments of war, and instruments of his chariots. And he will take your daughters to be confectionaries, and to be cooks, and to be bakers. And he will take your fields, and your vineyards, and your olive yards, even the best of them, and give them to his servants. And he will take the tenth of your seed, and of your vineyards, and give to his officers, and to his servants. And he will take your menservants, and your maidservants, and your goodliest young men, and your asses, and put them to his work. He will take the tenth of your sheep: and ye shall be his servants. And ye shall cry out in that day because of your king which ye shall have chosen you; and the LORD will not hear you in that day." Nevertheless, the

people refused to obey the voice of Samuel; and
they said, "Nay; but we will have a king over
us; that we also may be like all the nations; and
that our king may judge us, and go out before
us, and fight our battles." And Samuel heard all
the words of the people, and he rehearsed them
in the ears of the LORD. And the LORD said to
Samuel, "Hearken unto their voice, and make
them a king."

COMMENTARY: 1 Samuel 8:4-22 tells the story
about when the elders of Israel told Samuel that the people
wanted a king "like all other nations." God told Samuel to
warn them how much a king would take i.e. their sons,
daughters, best young men, menservants, maidservants, fields,
vineyards, and taxes. In other words, God was not just warning
them about the king. He was warning them about having a
government that would demand so much from them. The
Israelites would also have less freedom to spend their own
money as they chose, because a greater portion of their income
would be taken from them to pay taxes to support the
government. Taxes would be 10%, the exact same amount due
in tithes to God. That is extremely low compared to all the
taxes paid by Americans (federal, state, and local income
taxes, sales tax, fuel tax, real estate tax, etc.).

SCRIPTURE: Genesis 4:9 (KJV): "And the LORD
said unto Cain, Where is Abel thy brother? And he said, I
know not: Am I my brother's keeper?"

COMMENTARY: These are not words used by Christ,
but words used by Cain immediately after he killed his brother
Abel. They have absolutely nothing to do with the role of
government.

<u>SCRIPTURE</u>: Matthew 22:37-40 (KJV):

Jesus said unto him, "Thou shalt love the Lord thy God with all thy heart, and with all thy soul, and with all thy mind. This is the first and great commandment. And the second is like unto it, thou shalt love thy neighbor as thyself. On these two commandments hang all the law and the prophets."

<u>COMMENTARY</u>:   Christ declared the second greatest commandment to be, "Thou shalt love thy neighbor as thyself." During the 2008 election, Senator Obama probably intended to refer to this concept, the duty to love one's fellow man as oneself, when he used the words, "I am my brother's keeper." However, he completely failed to understand that this is a command given by God to individuals and does not describe the purpose of government or grant any authority to government. More specifically, it does not give government authority to take money by force from those who have lawfully earned that money and give it to the poor in the form of benefits. That is not love. Love is by definition an act of the will. Christ's command gives individuals a duty to love one's fellow man as oneself, and this is an act of the will of the individual who chooses to be obedient to the command and to love his fellow man as he loves himself.

<u>SCRIPTURE</u>: Exodus 23:1-3 (TNIV): "Do not show favoritism to the poor in a lawsuit."[148]

---

[148] <u>Holy Bible</u>, Today's New International Version, 2001, 2005, <u>International Bible Society</u>.

<u>COMMENTARY</u>: Exodus 23:3 states that the government must ensure equal justice for the rich and the poor, and this also means it should not make judgments in favor of the poor just because they are poor. The government should show impartiality not partiality toward the poor, because the government does not have authority, responsibility, or jurisdiction to favor or care for the poor.

<u>SCRIPTURE</u>: Leviticus 19:15 (KJV): "Ye shall do no unrighteousness in judgment: thou shalt not respect the person of the poor, nor honor the person of the mighty: but in righteousness shalt thou judge thy neighbor."

<u>COMMENTARY</u>: Leviticus 19 contains laws, which God directed Moses to give to the Israelites. Leviticus 19:15 states that one should not "respect" (favor) the poor in judgments. In other words, this verse also states that the government must ensure equal justice for the poor, and not make judgments in favor of the poor. Government should show impartiality not partiality toward the poor, because the government does not have authority, responsibility, or jurisdiction to favor or care for the poor.

<u>SCRIPTURE</u>: Romans 13:1-7 (New KJV):

Let every soul be subject to the governing authorities. For there <u>is no authority except from God, and the authorities that exist are appointed by God. Therefore, whoever resists the authority resists the ordinance of God, and those who resist will bring judgment on themselves</u>. For rulers are not a terror to good works, but to evil. Do you want to be unafraid of the authority? Do what is good, and you will have praise from the same. <u>For he is God's minister to you for good. But if you do evil, be afraid; for he does not bear the sword in vain; for he is God's minister, an avenger to execute wrath on him who practices evil.</u> Therefore, you must be subject, not only because of wrath but also for conscience' sake. <u>For because of this you also pay taxes, for they are God's ministers attending continually to this very thing. Render therefore to all their due: taxes to whom taxes are due, customs to whom customs, fear to whom fear, honor to whom honor.</u>

<u>COMMENTARY</u>: Romans 13:1-7 is one of the most important passages in Scripture about government. First, Paul states the command that everyone must "be subject to the governing authorities." Second, he states the reasons for this command, that "there is <u>no authority except from God</u>" and that all "authorities that exist are appointed by God." Third, he draws a conclusion based upon this rule, that anyone who resists authority resists God's law and "bring[s] judgment on themselves." This general rule and conclusion apply to "all authorities that exist" (parents, employers, etc.), but Paul's concentration in this passage is on government authorities. Fourth, Paul states that Rulers are "God's ministers" for good, but they do "not bear the sword in vain" because they are God's "avenger to execute wrath" on those who do evil. Fifth, Paul concludes that one must be subject to government authorities, not just for fear of their "wrath," but for "conscience' sake" (because it is the right thing to do). Sixth, Paul makes one final conclusion, that one should therefore give taxes, customs, fear, and honor to the authorities as is due to them.

All authorities are "appointed by God" and are "God's ministers." If God wants everyone to fear and honor government authorities, then what does God think about how some Americans treat elected officials? Governor Clinton won a presidential election with the phrase, "It's the economy, stupid." The word stupid was used to belittle the first President Bush, a man of great honor and dignity. Many Democrats, talk show hosts, and others mocked the second President Bush, in complete disobedience to this Scriptural directive.

CONCLUSION. Scripture discusses the role of government. Romans 13:1-7 states that all "authorities that exist are appointed by God," and that anyone who resists the authorities resists God's law and brings "judgment on themselves." Rulers are "God's ministers" for good. They do "not bear the sword in vain" because they are God's "avenger to execute wrath" on evildoers. One must be subject to government authorities not just for fear of their "wrath," but because it is the right thing to do. All citizens must pay taxes and give proper respect to government officials.

During the 2008 election, Senator Obama often quoted the words "I am my brother's keeper" to explain what motivates him to government service. However, these are not words used by Christ, but words used by Cain after killing his brother Abel (Gen. 4:9). They have nothing to do with government.

Exactly what part of Scripture gives government any responsibility or authority to care for the poor or the middle class or anyone else? Answer: No part. In "Matthew 22:37-40 Christ gives the command to "love thy neighbor as thyself." This commandment is given to individuals; it does not grant any authority to government. Obedience requires a very personal act of the will of the individual who chooses to love his neighbor. The purpose of government is not to provide or care for citizens, but to protect life and liberty and thereby enable the pursuit of happiness.

Exodus 23:3 and Leviticus 19:15 both direct governments to ensure equal justice for the poor, and not make judgments in favor of the poor. Government should show impartiality not partiality toward the poor, because the government does not have authority, responsibility, or jurisdiction to favor the poor.

In 1 Samuel 8:8-20 God told Samuel to warn the people that a king would take their sons, daughters, fields, vineyards, menservants, maidservants, best young men, and 10% in taxes, the same amount due in tithes to God. God clearly recommends the smallest possible government, which gives the people the greatest possible freedom to keep and spend their own earnings. The founding fathers of the United States understood God's ideal, which is embodied in the U.S. Constitution, of smaller government, lower taxes, and greater personal freedom and responsibility for all citizens. They were fiercely independent men who greatly treasured their freedom and would not trade it for government benefits.

SCRIPTURE ON TAXES

INTRODUCTION. Again, "fairness" in taxation is one of the primary themes of Democrats. Democrats always claim that the "wealthy few" do not pay their fair share of taxes and that the middle class pay more than their fair share. The chapter on Truth in Taxes proved this totally false, showing that about half of Americans, mostly middle and lower class, do not pay any federal taxes, and that the rich pay much higher taxes than the poor or middle class. So, what is the heart and mind of God on taxes? Does Scripture give any hint about where God stands on this hot political issue?

SCRIPTURE. First, consider God's command through Moses in Leviticus:

> And all the tithe of the land, whether of the seed of the land, or of the fruit of the tree, is the Lord's: it is holy unto the Lord. And if a man will at all redeem ought of his tithes, he shall add thereto the fifth part thereof. And concerning the tithe of the herd, or of the flock, even of whatsoever passeth under the rod, the tenth shall be holy unto the Lord (Leviticus 27:30-32).

Note that the God's tithe or "tax rate" was a tenth (10%) for everyone, both the rich and the poor. See also Deut. 12:5-11; 14:22-28; Num. 18:24-28; Mal. 3:8-10; Heb. 7:1-4.

Second, consider 1 Samuel 8:8-20. See prior chapter for more complete quote (1 Samuel 8:4-22).

> And Samuel told all the words of the LORD unto the people that asked of him a king. And he said, "This will be the manner of the king that shall reign over you: He will take your sons, and appoint them for himself, for his chariots, and to be his horsemen; and some shall run before his chariots. And he will appoint him captains over thousands, and captains over fifties; and will set them to ear his ground, and to reap his harvest, and to make his instruments of war, and instruments of his chariots. And he will take your daughters to be confectionaries, and to be cooks, and to be bakers. And he will take your fields, and your vineyards, and your oliveyards, even the best of them, and give them to his servants. And he will take the tenth of your seed, and of your vineyards, and give to his officers, and to his servants. And he will take your menservants, and your maidservants, and your goodliest young men, and your asses, and put them to his work. He will take the tenth of your sheep: and ye shall be his servants. And ye shall cry out in that day because of your king which ye shall have chosen you; and the LORD will not hear you in that day."

Note that God tells Samuel to warn the people that a king would take their sons, daughters, fields, vineyards, menservants, maidservants, best young men, and taxes. Taxes would be 10%, the same amount due in tithes to God.

CONCLUSION. So where does God stand on taxes for the rich and the poor? First, God's "tax rate" for tithes is exactly the same rate for the rich and the poor: 10%. Second, God warned that a king would charge exactly the same rate for the rich and the poor: 10%. Thus, it would seem that in the eyes of God a flat tax rate that is exactly the same for both the rich and the poor would be the "fairest" rate.

God warned the Israelites about the heavy burden that a king would impose, when the tax rate would be only 10%, which is far less than most Americans pay today. It seems quite clear from a careful reading of 1 Samuel 8:8-20 that God would strongly recommend the smallest possible federal government as envisioned by the founding fathers of our nation and as required by the highest law of the land, the Constitution.

What does scripture say about different treatment of different economic classes? Exodus 23:3 and Leviticus 19:15, quoted in the prior chapter, direct government to ensure equal justice for the poor, and not make judgments in favor of the poor. In other words, government should show impartiality not partiality toward the poor, because the government does not have authority, responsibility, or jurisdiction to favor the poor.

SCRIPTURE ON ABORTION

<u>INTRODUCTION</u>. Life is the first, most basic, most fundamental, most important inalienable right mentioned in the Declaration of Independence. Without life, all other rights are meaningless, because no one can exercise any rights without life.

A candidate's position on abortion should be a deciding factor for Christians. Scripture reveals the heart and mind of God and His laws, which are rooted in His unchanging character. A candidate's position on abortion reveals the heart and mind of the candidate in relation to the heart and mind of God and His laws.

Is abortion a woman's right to choose to control her own body, or is it murder of an innocent, completely helpless child? Most Republicans are pro-life. They believe abortion is murder of an innocent, completely helpless child. Most Democrats are pro-abortion. They believe that a woman has a right to terminate the life of her unborn child before birth. See Congressional voting scorecards.

Most Democrats in Congress voted to support all pro-abortion policies supported by President Obama, except the after-birth killing of a child that survives abortion. When Democrats have a majority in Congress, they chair the Senate Judiciary Committee and block the nomination of pro-life Christian judges to the Supreme Court and Federal Courts.

What does Scripture say about the heart and mind of God on abortion? Scripture provides answers through the words of Abraham, Moses, King David, Job, Isaiah, Jeremiah, Luke, the Apostle Paul, and other authors of Scripture.

SCRIPTURE: Exodus 21:22-23 (KJV):

> If men strive, and hurt a woman with child, so
> that her fruit depart from her, and yet no
> mischief follow: he shall surely be punished,
> according as the woman's husband will lay
> upon him; and he shall pay as the judges
> determine. And if any mischief follow, then
> thou shall give him life for life.

COMMENTARY: In Exodus 21:22-23 God speaks to Moses, giving His law regarding death of an unborn child, revealing His heart and mind on abortion. If there is no "mischief" and the death of the unborn child is purely an accident, then the man who caused the unborn child's death is fined as determined by the husband and judge. However, if "mischief" is involved, then the penalty for killing the unborn child is the death penalty. The value of the life of the unborn child is the same as the value of the man guilty of the "mischief," hence the penalty of "life for life." In this passage God makes it perfectly clear that the penalty for deliberate killing an unborn child should be the death penalty. This does not mean that God would want us to impose the death penalty on anyone guilty of abortion. It does mean that we should change our laws to outlaw abortion. Cases involving the life of the mother pose a separate moral issue.

The Hebrew word for the unborn child in Ex. 21:22 is used throughout the Old Testament to refer to children before

and after birth ("hareh," word 2030, Strong's Exhaustive
Concordance of the Bible, James Strong, Ed.). See Gen.
16:11; 17:10,12,14; 19:36; 38:24,25; Ex. 21:22; 22:22; Lev.
12:2,5; 1 Sam. 4:19; 2 Sam. 11:5; 2Kin. 8:12; 15:16; Isa.
26:17,18; 49:15; 54:1; Jer. 31:8; Hos. 13:16; Am. 1:13. In
other words, a child is a child, a human life, before and after
birth.

SCRIPTURE: Psalm 127:3 (KJV): "Lo, children are a
heritage of the LORD: and the fruit of the womb is his
reward."

Deuteronomy 7:12-13 (KJV):

Wherefore it shall come to pass, if ye hearken to
these judgments, and keep, and do them, that
the LORD thy God shall keep unto thee the
covenant and the mercy which he swore unto
thy fathers: And he will love thee, and bless
thee, and multiply thee: he will also bless the
fruit of thy womb, and the fruit of thy land, thy
corn, and thy wine, and thine oil, the increase of
thy kind, and the flocks of thy sheep, in the land
which he swore unto thy fathers to give thee.

COMMENTARY: Psalm 127:3 states that children, the
"fruit of the womb," are a "reward" and "heritage of the
LORD." Deuteronomy 7:12-13 shows that one of God's
blessings upon His people if they are obedient to his
commandments is the "fruit of thy womb," the gift of having
children. All children are a blessing from God, and with the
blessing comes responsibility for proper care of the child,
before and after birth.

For <u>You formed my inward parts</u>; You covered
me in my mother's womb. I will praise You, for
<u>I am fearfully *and* wonderfully made;</u>
<u>marvelous are Your works</u>, and *that* my soul
knows very well. <u>My frame was not hidden</u>
<u>from You, when I was made in secret, *and*</u>
<u>skillfully wrought</u> in the lowest parts of the
earth. <u>Your eyes saw my substance, being yet</u>
<u>unformed, and in Your book they all were</u>
<u>written, the days fashioned for me, when *as yet*</u>
there were <u>none of them</u>.

<u>Job 31:15 (KJV)</u>: "Did not he that <u>made me in the</u>
<u>womb</u> make him? And did not one <u>fashion us in the womb?</u>"
<u>Isaiah 44:2 (KJV)</u>: "The <u>LORD that made thee, and</u>
<u>formed thee from the womb</u>, which will help thee…."
<u>Isaiah 44:24 (KJV)</u>: "The LORD…<u>that formed thee</u>
<u>from the womb</u>, I am the LORD that maketh all things; that
stretcheth forth the heavens alone; that spreadeth abroad the
earth by myself…."
<u>Isaiah 49:1,5 (KJV)</u>: "The LORD hath called me from
the womb…. And now, saith the <u>LORD that formed me from</u>
<u>the womb to be his servant</u>, to bring Jacob again to him …."
<u>Jeremiah 1:5 (KJV)</u>: "<u>Before I formed thee in the belly,</u>
<u>I knew thee</u>; and before thou camest forth out of the womb I
sanctified thee, and I ordained thee a prophet unto the nations."

<u>COMMENTARY</u>: These verses affirm that God forms
each person within the womb. Psalm 139:13-16, written by
King David, is one of the most beautiful passages in the Bible.
It states, "You formed my inward parts…I am fearfully *and*

---

¹⁴⁹ <u>Holy Bible</u>, New King James Version, 1982, <u>Thomas Nelson, Inc.</u>

wonderfully made…. I was made in secret, *and* skillfully wrought." These words imply that every person is formed by God within the womb, "fearfully and wonderfully made…skillfully wrought." Then David states that God "saw my substance, being yet unformed, and in Your book they all were written, the days fashioned for me, when *as yet there were* none of them." These words tell us that God sees every day of everyone's life before He forms them in the womb.

Job 31:15 uses the words "fashion us in the womb." Isaiah 49:5 states that God "formed" Isaiah" to be his servant, to bring Jacob" (Israel) back to him. Jeremiah 1:5 states that God "knew" Jeremiah before He formed him in the womb, and "sanctified" and "ordained" him to be "a prophet unto the nations." These passages inform us that God forms each person in the womb and that he creates people with a purpose, to serve Him.

The Declaration of Independence affirms that God creates "all men" and endows them with the right to life, describing these as "self-evident" truths. "We hold these truths to be self-evident, that all men are created equal, that they are endowed by their Creator with certain unalienable Rights, that among these are Life, Liberty and the pursuit of Happiness."

SCRIPTURE: Luke 1:13-15 (KJV):

But the angel said unto him, Fear not,
Zacharias: for thy prayer is heard; and thy wife
Elisabeth shall bear thee a son, and thou shalt
call his name John. And thou shalt have joy and
gladness; and many shall rejoice at his birth.
For he shall be great in the sight of the Lord,
and shall drink neither wine nor strong drink;

and he shall be filled with the Holy Ghost, even
from his mother's womb.

Luke 1:30-31 (KJV): "And the angel said unto her,
Fear not, Mary: for thou hast found favor with God. And,
behold, thou shalt conceive in thy womb, and bring forth a son,
and shalt call his name JESUS."

COMMENTARY: These passages contain prophecy of
angels about the conception and birth of Jesus and John the
Baptist. In Luke 1:13-15 the angel states that John will be
filled with the Spirit of God before birth, within his mother's
womb. In Luke 1:30-31 the angel tells Mary that she will
conceive and give birth to Jesus. These passages show that
God controls conception and birth, and that he forms a person
within the womb for a purpose. Luke 1:13-15 also raises the
question: How could anyone kill a child who could be filled
the Spirit of God in the womb?

SCRIPTURE: Luke 1:41-44 (KJV):

And it came to pass, that, when Elisabeth heard
the salutation of Mary, the babe leaped in her
womb; and Elisabeth was filled with the Holy
Ghost: And she spoke out with a loud voice,
and said, "Blessed art thou among women, and
blessed is the fruit of thy womb. And whence is
this to me, that the mother of my Lord should
come to me? For, lo, as soon as the voice of thy
salutation sounded in mine ears, the babe leaped
in my womb for joy."

Luke 18:15-16 (KJV): "And they brought unto him also
infants, that he would touch them: but when his disciples saw

it, they rebuked them. But Jesus called them unto him, and said, 'Suffer little children to come unto me, and forbid them not: for of such is the kingdom of God.'"

COMMENTARY: Luke 1:41-44 is the story of the meeting of Mary, when she was pregnant with Jesus, with Elisabeth, when she was pregnant with John the Baptist. John the Baptist "leaped…for joy" within his mother's womb when he heard the voice of the mother of Jesus. How can anyone abort a child that is able to recognize the voice of the mother of Jesus and jump for joy within his mother's womb?

The Greek word for the unborn child in Luke 1:41-44 is used in the New Testament to refer to children before and after birth ("brephos" word 1025, The Word Study Concordance, George Wigram and Ralph Winter, Ed. 1972 & 1978). It is used to refer to baby Jesus wrapped in swaddling clothes (Luke 2:12) and lying in a manger (Luke 2:16), the little children (infants) brought to Jesus (Luke 18:15), young children (Acts 7:19), a young child (2 Tim 3:15), and newborn babies (1 Pet. 2:2). In other words, a child is a child before and after birth.

SCRIPTURE: Genesis 18:10-15 (KJV):

And he said, I will certainly return unto thee
according to the time of life; and, lo, Sarah thy
wife shall have a son. And Sarah heard it in the
tent door, which was behind him. Now
Abraham and Sarah were old and well stricken
in age; and it ceased to be with Sarah after the
manner of women. Therefore, Sarah laughed
within herself, saying, "After I am waxed old
shall I have pleasure, my lord being old also?"
And the LORD said unto Abraham, "Wherefore

did Sarah laugh, saying, Shall I of a surety bear
a child, which am old? Is anything too hard for
the LORD? At the time appointed I will return
unto thee, according to the time of life, and
Sarah shall have a son." Then Sarah denied,
saying, "I laughed not;" for she was afraid. And
he said, "Nay; but thou didst laugh."

Romans 4:19 (KJV): "And being not weak in faith, he
considered not his own body now dead, when he was about a
hundred years old, neither yet the deadness of Sarah's womb."

COMMENTARY: Genesis 18:10-15 and Romans 4:19
are about Abraham and Sarah. The key words in Genesis
18:10-15 are: "Is anything too hard for the LORD?" God made
Sarah, who was very old and no longer able to have children,
conceive and bear a child, to fulfill His promise to give
Abraham many descendants. Note that Sarah "laughed within
herself", but the LORD who sees the heart and mind knew that
she had laughed. Romans 4:19 is about Abraham faith that he
would have a child with Sarah as promised by God, even
though he was about a hundred years old and his wife was
barren. This passage shows that God is able to miraculously
cause conception and birth regardless of the age or physical
condition of the father or mother.

DECLARATION OF INDEPENDENCE. The
Declaration of Independence is a pro-life document. First, it
affirms that all men have a God-given right to life. Second, it
affirms that all men are created equal. In other words, from
conception until birth God creates each person in his or her
mother's womb, and makes that person equal in value to all
other persons.

Voting with the Declaration of Independence requires voting Republican because it is a pro-life document.

CONCLUSION. God makes his position on abortion clear through scripture. In Exodus 21:22-23 God tells Moses that the penalty for the deliberate killing of an unborn child is the death penalty. This does not mean that God would want us to assume jurisdiction to impose the death penalty on everyone one guilty of abortion. However, it does mean that they are nevertheless deserving of death under God's laws and that we should therefore change our laws to outlaw abortion. Cases involving the life of the mother pose a separate moral issue, but that does not justify using "life of the mother" as an excuse for the murder of unborn children.

The Declaration of Independence affirms that God creates "all men" and endows them with certain God-given inalienable rights, which include the right to life. The right to life begins at conception, not birth. A mother's duty to care for her child begins at conception, not birth. A mother who abuses that right of her child by using drugs or alcohol during pregnancy endangers the health of her child.

The founding fathers of the United States understood that the "self-evident" truths and "inalienable rights" cited in the Declaration of Independence were common-sense teachings of Scripture. Job 31:15; Isaiah 44:2; 44:24; 49:5 and Jeremiah 1:5 affirm that God forms each person within the womb. In Psalm 139:13-16 King David teaches that everyone is "formed" and "fearfully and wonderfully made" and "skillfully wrought" by God within the womb, and that God sees every day of a person's life before He forms him or her in the womb. Genesis 18:10-15 and Romans 4:19 show that God is able to cause conception and birth regardless of the age of

the father and mother. Psalm 127:3 and Deuteronomy 7:12-13
teach that children are a blessing from the Lord. That blessing
brings responsibility for proper care of the child, before and
after birth.

Luke 1:13-15; 30-31 prophesizes the conception and
birth of Jesus and John the Baptist, showing that God controls
conception and birth and forms a person within the womb for a
purpose. Luke 1:13-15 and 1:41-44 raise the question: How
could anyone kill an unborn child who is filled the Spirit of
God and be able to recognize the voice of the mother of Jesus
and jump for joy within the womb?

The Hebrew word used in the Old Testament and the
Greek word used in the New Testament to refer to unborn
children are the same words used to refer to children after
birth. In other words, a child is a child before and after birth,
as precious as baby Jesus lying in a manger (Luke 2:12,16) and
the little children brought to Jesus (Luke 18:15-16).

Many ancient cultures practiced child sacrifice. Most
Americans cannot begin to understand how any people could
be so cruel and evil to sacrifice children on stone alters to
secure the blessings of their false gods. If any group of
Americans sacrificed a child on an altar today, most Americans
would be horrified and demand the death penalty. Abortion is
child sacrifice. In the world today, unwanted children are
sacrificed on the altar of convenience by an ungodly, godless
people who do whatever is right in their own eyes and seek
first not to love and serve God but to serve themselves.

Scripture reveals the heart and mind of God and His
laws, which are rooted in His unchanging character. A
candidate's stand on abortion speaks volumes about them; it

reveals their heart and mind and the condition of their moral compass. Comparing a candidate's position on abortion with Scripture reveals whether or not the candidate's heart and mind are in sync with God and His laws, or whether the candidate simply does whatever is right in his own eyes. Every American who votes for any Democrat has the blood of American children on his hands.

CHAPTER 8.4

SCRIPTURE ON HOMOSEXUALITY AND SAME-SEX MARRIAGE

INTRODUCTION. This chapter tackles homosexuality and same-sex marriage because a candidate's position on these issues should be a deciding factor for Christians. Homosexuals include Lesbians, Gays, Bisexuals, and Transvestites (LGBT). Scripture very clearly reveals the heart and mind of God and His laws on homosexuality, laws rooted in His unchanging character. A candidate's position on these topics clearly reveals the heart and mind of the candidate in relation to the heart and mind of God and His laws.

Democrats are far more supportive of homosexuality and same-sex marriage than Republicans. This can be quickly proven by reference to the voting records of members of Congress.[150] Most Christian leaders remain silent, detached from reality, irrelevant, failures not only at providing moral leadership, but also at making it clear what it means to be a Christian.

Scripture reveals the heart and mind of God on homosexuality and same-sex marriage through the story of creation in Genesis, laws of God given through Moses in Leviticus, and letters from the Apostle Paul to Timothy and to the Romans and Corinthians.

SCRIPTURE: Genesis 2:18-24 (KJV):

---

[150] "Vote Scorecard," Family Research Council Action, http://www.frcaction.org, accessed July 9, 2008.

177

And the LORD God said, "It is not good that
the man should be alone; I will make him a help
meet for him." And out of the ground the
LORD God formed every beast of the field, and
every fowl of the air; and brought them unto
Adam to see what he would call them: and
whatsoever Adam called every living creature,
that was the name thereof. And Adam gave
names to all cattle, and to the fowl of the air,
and to every beast of the field; but for Adam
there was not found a help meet for him. And
the LORD God caused a deep sleep to fall upon
Adam, and he slept: and he took one of his ribs,
and closed up the flesh instead thereof; And the
rib, which the LORD God had taken from man,
made he a woman, and brought her unto the
man. And Adam said, "This is now bone of my
bones, and flesh of my flesh: she shall be called
Woman, because she was taken out of Man.
Therefore, shall a man leave his father and his
mother, and shall cleave unto his wife: and they
shall be one flesh."

COMMENTARY: Genesis 2:18-24 is the story of
God's creation of man, then woman from man to be a suitable
companion for man, and finally marriage as a special union
between one man and one woman wherein "they shall be one
flesh." Note that God created woman very different from man,
to make her a suitable companion for man. Another man
would not be a suitable companion. Note that in God's design
for marriage, the man leaves his father and mother (his family),
to form a special "one flesh" union with his wife, which we
call marriage, and to start a new family. The new marriage

couple is then responsible to be obedient to the dominion mandate to "be fruitful and multiply," which is impossible in a same-sex marriage.

SCRIPTURE: Leviticus 18:22-26 (KJV):

Thou shalt not lie with mankind, as with womankind: it is abomination. Neither shalt thou lie with any beast to defile thyself therewith: neither shall any woman stand before a beast to lie down thereto: it is confusion. Defile not ye yourselves in any of these things: for in all these the nations are defiled which I cast out before you: And the land is defiled: therefore, I do visit the iniquity thereof upon it, and the land itself vomiteth out her inhabitants. Ye shall therefore keep my statutes and my judgments, and shall not commit any of these abominations; neither any of your own nation, nor any stranger that sojourneth among you.

COMMENTARY: In Leviticus 18:22-26 Moses recites commandments directly from God to the Israelites. God commands that men not have sexual relations with other men or beasts because is an "abomination." He states that it defiles the men who do it and their nations. God punishes a nation defiled by these sins. God warns the Israelites to keep His statutes and judgments, to not commit these abominations, and to not even allow a stranger who lives among them to "commit any of these abominations." The word "abomination" is used to describe something that is extremely offensive to God, an extreme perversion of His design and law.

SCRIPTURE: Leviticus 20:13-16 (KJV):

If a man also lies with mankind, as he lieth with a woman, both of them have committed an abomination: they shall surely be put to death; their blood shall be upon them. And if a man take a wife and her mother, it is wickedness: they shall be burnt with fire, both he and they; that there be no wickedness among you. And if a man lie with a beast, he shall surely be put to death: and ye shall slay the beast. And if a woman approach unto any beast, and lie down thereto, thou shalt kill the woman, and the beast: they shall surely be put to death; their blood shall be upon them.

COMMENTARY: In Leviticus 20:13-16 God states His law regarding two men having sex. God declares it is an "abomination" (extreme perversion) which must be punished by death. The same penalty applies to a man who has sex with his wife and her mother and to a man or woman who has sex with an animal. This does not mean that we should impose the death penalty for sodomy. It does mean we should not support candidates who are so strongly opposed to God and His laws.

SCRIPTURE: Romans 1:16-32 (KJV):

For I am not ashamed of the gospel of Christ: for it is the power of God unto salvation to everyone that believeth; to the Jew first, and also to the Greek. For therein is the righteousness of God revealed from faith to faith: as it is written, "The just shall live by faith." For the wrath of God is revealed from heaven against all ungodliness and unrighteousness of men, who hold the truth in unrighteousness; Because that which may be known of God is manifest in them; for God hath shewed it unto them. For the invisible things of him from the creation of the world are clearly seen, being understood by the things that are made, even his eternal power and Godhead; so that they are without excuse: Because that, when they knew God, they glorified him not as God, neither were thankful; but became vain in their imaginations, and their foolish heart was darkened. Professing themselves to be wise, they became fools, and changed the glory of the uncorruptible God into an image made like to corruptible man, and to birds, and fourfooted beasts, and creeping things. Wherefore God also gave them up to uncleanness through the lusts of their own hearts, to dishonor their own bodies between themselves: Who changed the truth of God into a lie, and worshipped and served the creature more than the Creator, who is blessed forever. Amen. For this cause God gave them up unto vile affections: for even their women did change the natural use into that which is against nature: And likewise also the men, leaving the natural use of the woman, burned in their lust one toward another; men with men working that which is unseemly, and receiving in themselves that recompence of their error which was meet. And even as they did not like to retain God in their knowledge, God gave them over to a reprobate mind, to do those things which are not convenient; Being filled with all unrighteousness, fornication, wickedness, covetousness, maliciousness; full of envy, murder, debate, deceit, malignity; whisperers, Backbiters, haters of God, despiteful, proud, boasters, inventors of evil things, disobedient to parents, Without understanding, covenant breakers, without natural affection, implacable, unmerciful: Who knowing the judgment of God, that they which commit such things are worthy of death, not only do the same, but have pleasure in them that do them.

COMMENTARY: In Romans 1:16-32 Paul reveals the heart and mind of God on homosexuality and another ungodliness and unrighteousness. First, he states that God reveals His wrath against "all ungodliness and unrighteousness of men, who hold the truth in unrighteousness." Then he explains why men choose ungodliness and unrighteousness and suffer the wrath of God. First, it is because they know what can be known about God because God has shown it to them. Second, it is because the "invisible things" of God are "clearly seen" because they are understood from observing the things that God created. These "invisible things" of God that are "clearly seen" include His "eternal power and Godhead" so they are "without excuse." Third, it is because although they knew God, they did not glorify Him as God and were not thankful, but became "vain in their imaginations" and their "foolish heart was darkened." Claiming to be wise, they became fools, and exchanged the glory of "uncorruptible God" for an image of "corruptible man," etc.

Then Paul explains what God did to these ungodly, unrighteous fools. First, He gave them up to their own lusts, to dishonor their bodies "between themselves" because they rejected the truth of God for a lie, and "worshiped and served" God's creation more than the Creator. Second, He gave them up to "vile affections." Women changed the "natural use" of their bodies for that "against nature." Men likewise rejected "natural use of the woman," "burned in their lust" for other men, and did "unseemly" things with other men. As a result, they received due punishment for their wrongdoing. Third, because they rejected God, He gave them up to a "reprobate mind," to do thing which are "not convenient."

Then Paul lists the wrongdoing of these reprobate men and women: "all unrighteousness, fornication, wickedness, covetousness, maliciousness; full of envy, murder, debate, deceit, malignity; whisperers, backbiters, haters of God, despiteful, proud, boasters, inventors of evil things, disobedient to parents, without understanding, covenant-breakers, without natural affection, implacable, unmerciful." Finally, Paul ends by saying that they not only did all these evil things, but actually took pleasure in doing them, although they knew the "judgment of God" meant they were deserving of death for their wrongdoing."

SCRIPTURE: 1 Corinthians 6:9-10 (New KJV):

Do you not know that the unrighteous will not inherit the kingdom of God? Do not be deceived. Neither fornicators, nor idolaters, nor adulterers, nor homosexuals, nor sodomites, nor thieves, nor covetous, nor drunkards, nor revilers, nor extortioners will inherit the kingdom of God" (1 Cor. 6:9-10, NKJV). [151]

---

[151] Holy Bible, New King James Version, Thomas Nelson, Inc., 1982.

COMMENTARY: 1 Corinthians 6:9-10 states that the "unrighteous will not inherit the kingdom of God" and that this includes "homosexuals" and "sodomites."

SCRIPTURE: 1 Timothy 1:9-10 (NKJV):

Knowing this: that the law is not made for a righteous person, but for *the* lawless and insubordinate, for *the* ungodly and for sinners, for *the* unholy and profane, for murderers of fathers and murderers of mothers, for manslayers, for fornicators, for sodomites, for kidnappers, for liars, for perjurers, and if there is any other thing that is contrary to sound doctrine….

COMMENTARY: 1 Timothy 1:9-10 shows that God considers homosexuals who commit sodomy to be "lawless…insubordinate…ungodly…sinners…unholy and profane."

CONCLUSION. Scripture is very clear about marriage and homosexuality. God created man male and female, and marriage to be a special union between one man and one woman (Genesis 2:18-24). He designed the family as the most fundamental unit in society, critical to its stability and proper function. Homosexuality and same-sex marriage are extreme perversions of God's design for man, woman, sex, marriage, and family. Homosexual acts are abominations to God deserving of the death penalty. There is absolutely no way that any individual or nation can ignore God's design for sex, marriage, and family without severe consequences.

Homosexuals call those who oppose them "homophobic," berating them with totally false accusations of fear of homosexuals. The opposite may be true. They may rightfully have greater fear and respect for God than man, and rightfully feel some of the same disgust for the extreme sexual perversion of homosexuality that God feels toward those who have so greatly perverted his design for man, woman, marriage, and family. Friends of the homosexual movement demonstrate greater fear of man than God, extreme ignorance, and extreme foolishness.

A candidate's positions on same-sex marriage and homosexuality should be deciding factors in voting because these sins are extremely offensive to God and because this subject area is so critically important to the future of our nation. Democrats are far more supportive of the homosexual lifestyle and same-sex marriage than Republicans. See Vote Scorecards of Family Research Council Action and Family Alliance. Any American who votes for any Democrat or in any way helps Democrats gain control of the Presidency, Congress or any other political office will answer to God for supporting a lifestyle which is an extreme perversion of God's design for man, woman, and marriage.

CHAPTER 9.0

VOTING FOR THE CONSTITUTION AND THE DECLARATION OF INDEPENDENCE

SECTION REVIEW. This section shows what voting in accordance with principles and laws embodied in the Declaration of Independence, Constitution, and Bill of Rights requires. The first chapter discusses the Declaration of Independence, the second the Constitution, and the third the Bill of Rights.

CHAPTERS:
9.1 Declaration of Independence
9.2 Constitution
9.3 Bill of Rights

CHAPTER 9.1

VOTING FOR THE
DECLARATION OF INDEPENDENCE

INTRODUCTION. This chapter addresses basic principles embodied in the Declaration of Independence. First, it discusses the "most important principle" that the United States was founded upon. Second, it reviews the very long list of "causes for separation" from Great Britain. Third, it briefly mentions efforts to resolve problems with Great Britain. Fourth, it reviews the final section, the actual declaration of independence from Great Britain. Finally, it discusses rights cited within the Declaration of Independence i.e. the rights to life, liberty, pursuit of happiness, and the right to bear arms. See Appendixes for full text of Declaration of Independence.

FOUNDING PRINCIPLE OF UNITED STATES. What is the most important principle that the United States was founded upon? Now let me rephrase the question to further clarify exactly what I am asking. What is the most important, most fundamental, most irreplaceable principle that the United States was founded upon? Answer: The United States was founded upon the principle that: (1) God created all things seen and unseen and all laws that govern all things seen and unseen; (2) God creates all men equal with "certain unalienable Rights," (3) "to secure these rights, governments are instituted," (4) "whenever any…government becomes destructive of these ends, it is the Right of the People to alter or to abolish it, and to institute new government;" (5) this new government must be established in accordance with God's laws to protect the God-given unalienable rights of all men.[152]

This most important, most fundamental, most irreplaceable principle that the United States was founded upon is partially stated and partially implied in the Declaration of Independence.

> We hold these truths to be self-evident, that all men are created equal, that they are endowed by their Creator with certain unalienable Rights, that among these are Life, Liberty and the pursuit of Happiness.--That to secure these rights, Governments are instituted among Men, deriving their just powers from the consent of the governed, --That whenever any Form of Government becomes destructive of these ends, it is the Right of the People to alter or to abolish it, and to institute new Government, laying its foundation on such principles and organizing its powers in such form, as to them shall seem most likely to effect their Safety and Happiness.[153]

<u>CAUSES FOR SEPARATION</u>. The first sentence of the Declaration of Independence announces its purpose: to "declare the causes which impel them to the separation" from Great Britain. It cites, as justification, the "<u>Laws of nature and Nature's God</u>."[154]

> When in the Course of human events, it becomes necessary for one people to dissolve the political bands which have connected them

---

[152] "Declaration of Independence," U.S. National Archives & Records Administration, http://www.archives.gov/exhibits/charters/declaration.html.
[153] Ibid.
[154] Ibid.

with another, and to assume among the powers of the earth, the separate and equal station to which the Laws of Nature and of Nature's God entitle them, a decent respect to the opinions of mankind requires that they should declare the causes which impel them to the separation.[i]

The founding fathers understood that: (1) God created all things seen and unseen and all laws that govern all things seen and unseen; (2) these laws justified the Declaration of Independence from Great Britain; and (3) these laws were the legal foundation for the establishment of a new, independent nation.

The first cause for separation cited refers to God as the Creator who continues to create all men equal. This belief is based upon Scripture. God told the prophet Jeremiah: "Before I formed thee in the belly, I knew thee; and before thou [came] forth out of the womb I sanctified thee, and I ordained thee a prophet unto the nations" (Jer. 1:5, KJV). Job said, "Did not he that made me in the womb make him? and did not one fashion us in the womb?" (Job 31:15, KJV). King David said, "I will praise thee; for I am fearfully and wonderfully made: marvelous are thy works; and that my soul know[s] right well. My substance was not hid from thee, when I was made in secret, and curiously wrought in the lowest parts of the earth. Thine eyes did see my substance, yet being unperfected; and in thy book all my members were written, which in continuance were fashioned, when as yet there was none of them" (Ps. 139: 14-16, KJV). See also Beck. 11:5; Isa. 44:2, 24; 49:1-5; Jer. 1:5; Luke 1:15,41-44.

The first cause for separation then states that God gives every man "certain unalienable Rights, that among these are

Life, Liberty and the pursuit of Happiness."[155] It states "that to secure these rights, Governments are instituted among Men, deriving their just powers from the consent of the governed" and "that whenever any Form of Government becomes destructive of these ends, it is the Right of the People to alter or to abolish it, and to institute new Government, laying its foundation on such principles and organizing its powers in such form, as to them shall seem most likely to effect their Safety and Happiness."[156] "Unalienable Rights" are God-given rights which no man or government has the right to take away from any man. It is the violation of these rights, which God gives to every man, that justify the Declaration of Independence from Great Britain and the formation of a new government.

The Declaration states that "Governments long established should not be changed for light and transient causes" but when there is a "long train of abuses and usurpations…it is their right, it is their duty, to throw off such Government, and to provide new Guards for their future security."[157] These "new Guards" are the protections embodied in the U.S. Constitution.

The next section of the Declaration of Independence gives an incredibly long list of the "repeated injuries and usurpations" of the "King of Great Britain…all having in direct object the establishment of an absolute Tyranny over these States."[158] These abuses justified the Declaration of Independence from Great Britain.

---

[155] Ibid.
[156] Ibid.
[157] Ibid.
[158] Ibid.

He has <u>refused his Assent to Laws</u>, the most wholesome and necessary for the public good.

He has <u>forbidden his Governors to pass Laws</u> of immediate and pressing importance, unless suspended in their operation till his Assent should be obtained; and when so suspended, he has utterly neglected to attend to them.

He has <u>refused to pass other Laws</u> for the accommodation of large districts of people, unless those people would relinquish the right of Representation in the Legislature, a right inestimable to them and formidable to tyrants only.

He has <u>called together legislative bodies at places</u> unusual, uncomfortable, and <u>distant</u> from the depository of their public Records, for the <u>sole purpose of fatiguing them into compliance</u> with his measures.

He has <u>dissolved Representative Houses repeatedly, for opposing</u> with manly firmness his <u>invasions on the rights of the people</u>.

He has <u>refused</u> for a long time, after such dissolutions, to cause <u>others to be elected</u>; whereby the Legislative powers, incapable of Annihilation, have returned to the People at large for their exercise; the State remaining in the mean time exposed to all the dangers of invasion from without, and convulsions within.

He has [endeavored] to prevent the population of these States; for that purpose <u>obstructing the Laws for Naturalization</u> of Foreigners; refusing to pass others to encourage their migrations hither, and raising the conditions of new Appropriations of Lands.

He has <u>obstructed the Administration of Justice</u>, by refusing his Assent to Laws for establishing Judiciary powers.

He has <u>made Judges dependent on his Will alone</u>,

for the tenure of their offices, and the amount and payment of their salaries.

He has <u>erected a multitude of New Offices</u>, and <u>sent hither swarms of Officers to harass</u> our people, and eat out their substance.

He has <u>kept among us</u>, in times of peace, <u>Standing Armies</u> without the Consent of our legislatures.

He has affected to render the <u>Military</u> independent of and <u>superior to the Civil power</u>.

He has combined with others to <u>subject us to a jurisdiction foreign to our constitution</u>, and unacknowledged by our laws; giving his Assent to their Acts of pretended Legislation:

For Quartering large <u>bodies of armed troops among us</u>:

For <u>protecting them</u>, by a mock Trial, <u>from punishment for any Murders</u> which they should commit on the Inhabitants of these States:

For <u>cutting off our Trade</u> with all parts of the world:

For **<u>imposing Taxes on us without our Consent</u>**:

For <u>depriving</u> us in many cases, of the benefits of <u>Trial by Jury</u>:

For <u>transporting</u> us beyond Seas to be <u>tried for pretended offences</u>

For <u>abolishing the free System of English Laws</u> in a [neighboring] Province, establishing therein an <u>Arbitrary government</u>, and enlarging its Boundaries so as to render it at once an example and fit instrument for introducing the same <u>absolute rule</u> into these Colonies:

For taking away our Charters, <u>abolishing our most valuable Laws</u>, and altering fundamentally the Forms of our Governments:

For <u>suspending our own Legislatures</u>, and declaring themselves invested with power to legislate for us in all cases whatsoever.

He has <u>abdicated Government</u> here, by declaring us

out of his Protection and <u>waging War against us.</u>
He has <u>plundered our seas, ravaged our Coasts,</u>
<u>burnt our towns, and destroyed the lives of our</u>
<u>people</u>. He is at this time transporting <u>large Armies</u>
<u>of foreign Mercenaries</u> to [complete] the works of
<u>death, desolation and tyranny</u>, already begun with
circumstances of Cruelty & perfidy scarcely
paralleled in the most barbarous ages, and totally
unworthy the Head of a civilized nation.
He has <u>constrained our fellow Citizens</u> taken
Captive on the high <u>Seas to bear Arms against their</u>
<u>Country,</u> <u>to become the executioners of their friends</u>
<u>and Brethren,</u> or to fall themselves by their Hands.
He has <u>excited domestic insurrections</u> amongst us,
and has [endeavored] to bring on the inhabitants of
our frontiers, the <u>merciless Indian Savages</u>, whose
known rule of warfare, is an undistinguished
<u>destruction of all ages, sexes</u> and conditions.[159]

<u>EFFORTS AT RECONCILLIATION</u>. After listing the
many abuses of the King of Great Britain, the Declaration of
Independence briefly states the efforts the Colonies made to
resolve their problems with Great Britain, and the total lack of
positive response to their efforts.

<u>In every stage</u> of these Oppressions We have <u>Petitioned</u>
<u>for Redress in the most humble terms</u>: Our repeated
Petitions have been <u>answered only by repeated injury</u>.
A Prince whose character is thus marked by every act
which may define a <u>Tyrant, is unfit</u> to be the <u>ruler of a</u>
<u>free people</u>.[160]

---

[159] Ibid.
[160] Ibid.

<u>FINAL SECTION</u>. The final section of the Declaration of Independence states,

> We, therefore, the Representatives of the united States of America, in General Congress, Assembled, <u>appealing to the Supreme Judge of the world</u>...solemnly publish and declare, That these United Colonies are, and of Right ought to be <u>Free and Independent States</u>; that they are <u>Absolved from all Allegiance to the British Crown</u>, and that <u>all political connection</u> between them and the State of Great Britain, is and ought to be <u>totally dissolved</u>; and that as Free and Independent States, they have full Power to levy War, conclude Peace, contract Alliances, establish Commerce, and to do all other Acts and Things which Independent States may of right do. [161]

The appeal to the "Supreme Judge of the world" is an appeal to God. The last sentence of the Declaration of Independence states, "And for the support of this Declaration, with a firm reliance on the protection of divine Providence, we mutually pledge to each other our Lives, our Fortunes and our sacred Honor."[162] "Firm reliance on the protection of divine Providence" means firm reliance on God.

<u>VOTING FOR LIFE</u>. Voting with the Declaration of Independence requires voting Republican because it is a pro-life document. First, it affirms that all men have a god-given right to life. Second, it affirms that all men are created equal. In other words, from conception until birth God creates each person in his or her mother's womb, and makes that person equal in value to all other persons. The right to life begins at

---

[161] Ibid.
[162] Ibid.

conception, not birth. A mother's duty to care for her child begins at conception, not birth. A mother who abuses that right with drugs or alcohol endangers the health of her child. All of these views are based upon Scripture which is discussed in later chapters.

<u>VOTING FOR LIBERTY AND PURSUIT OF HAPPINESS</u>. Voting with the Declaration of Independence requires voting Republican because Republicans support the rights to liberty and the pursuit of happiness infinitely better than Democrats. Republicans want lower taxes for all Americans. They want all Americans to have the right and freedom to keep more of their hard-earned money, which enables the pursuit of happiness. Democrats always want the government to do more to care for Americans, which requires higher taxes and less freedom for all Americans. All of this is discussed in greater detail in later chapters.

<u>VOTING FOR RIGHT TO BEAR ARMS</u>. Voting with the Declaration of Independence requires voting Republican because Republicans better support the right to bear arms. The entire Declaration of Independence is an argument for the right of the people to bear arms and to use those arms to overthrow any government which violates their God-given rights to life, liberty, and the pursuit of happiness. It is not argument for them to be able to bear lower-capacity arms, but an argument to be able to bear the exact same arms that would be used against them by the government.

<u>CONCLUSION</u>. What does the Declaration of Independence teach us about the Founding Fathers? First, that they had a biblical worldview. They understood that: (1) God created all things seen and unseen and all laws that govern all things seen and unseen; (2) God creates all men equal with

"certain unalienable Rights that [...include] Life, Liberty and the pursuit of Happiness;" (3) "to secure these rights, Governments are instituted among Men, deriving their just powers from the consent of the governed;" (4) "whenever any…Government becomes destructive of these ends, it is the Right of the People to alter or to abolish it, and to institute new Government;" (5) this new government must be established in accordance with God's laws to protect the God-given unalienable rights of all men.[163]

What does voting for and with the Declaration of Independence require? First and foremost, it requires voting Republican because Republicans better support all these principles that the United States was founded upon. Second, it requires voting Republican because Republicans better support the rights to life, liberty, the pursuit of happiness, and the right to bear arms.

---

[163] Ibid.

CHAPTER 9.2

VOTING FOR THE CONSTITUTION

INTRODUCTION. What does voting in accordance with principles embodied in the Constitution of the United States require? Before trying to answer this question, this chapter will lay a foundation of understanding regarding: (1) law and government, (2) jurisdiction; (3) the basic duty of government, and (4) the purpose, organization, and contents of the Constitution.

LAW AND GOVERNMENT. Consider the importance of law to government. The legislative branch makes laws. The executive branch enforces the laws. The judicial branch decides cases and controversies with respect to application of the laws. In other words, the federal government makes, enforces, and decides cases or controversies regarding federal laws.

DEFINITION OF JURISDICTION. Jurisdiction is one of the most important legal principles taught in law school. Black's Law Dictionary defines jurisdiction as, "A term of large and comprehensive import, and embraces every kind of judicial action...." It is the "power and authority of a court to hear and determine a judicial proceeding."[164]

Black's Law Dictionary actually takes a couple pages to fully define the broad subject of jurisdiction. Readers of this book only need to know that the jurisdiction of the federal government is the "power and authority" that it has under the

---

[164] Henry Campbell Black, Black's Law Dictionary, 5th Ed., 1979, p 766.

Constitution to make, enforce, and make judgments regarding application of federal law. In other words, the United States Constitution defines the responsibility and limits of power of the United States government.

<u>BASIC DUTY OF GOVERNMENT</u>. "YOU CANNOT DICTATE MORALITY" read a full-page newspaper advertisement in large, bold letters. It was many years ago, but I could never forget it. Many Americans, like Biden, believe that abortion should be legal because no one has the right to "legislate morality" or impose their morality on someone else. When asked when life began, Obama said the answer to that question was "above his pay grade." But it was not above his pay grade to decide that the unborn child must die if not wanted by the mother. He actually said that he would not want one of his daughters to be punished by being forced to give birth to an unwanted child. Were Senators Obama and Biden, and right or wrong? Does government have the jurisdiction (power and authority) to dictate morality?" Anyone who cannot properly answer these simple questions cannot begin to understand the role, jurisdiction, or limits of authority of government.

Understanding the most basic, fundamental duty of government is essential to understanding the jurisdiction of government. In his letter to the Romans, the Apostle Paul helps one understand the most basic, fundamental duty of government. Romans 13:1-7 states:

> Let every soul be in subjection to the higher
> powers: for there is no power but of God; and
> the powers that be are ordained of God.
> Therefore, he that resist[s] the power,
> withstand[s] the ordinance of God: and they that

withstand shall receive to themselves judgment.
For <u>rulers are not a terror to the good work, but
to the evil</u>. And would thou have no fear of the
power? do that which is good, and thou shalt
have praise from the same: for he is a minister
of God to thee for good. But if thou do that
which is evil, be afraid; for he <u>bear[s] not the
sword in vain: for he is a minister of God</u>, an
avenger for wrath to him that doeth evil.
Wherefore ye must needs be in subjection, not
only because of the wrath, but also for
conscience' sake. For this cause ye <u>pay tribute
also; for they are ministers of God's service</u>,
attending continually upon this very thing.
<u>Render to all their dues: tribute to whom tribute
is due; custom to whom custom; fear to whom
fear; honor to whom honor</u> (Rom 13:1-7, ASV).

In other words, government officials are "ministers of
God" with jurisdiction (power, authority, and responsibility) to
impose morality and punish evildoers. The primary reason
they have a duty to punish criminal acts is not because they
harm other citizens or because punishment best serves the
accused, the victim, others, or the government, but because the
criminal acts are morally wrong, they demand justice, and it is
their God-given duty to ensure justice in accordance with
God's laws as they are revealed through Scripture.

<u>PURPOSE OF CONSTITUTION</u>. To protect the God-
given unalienable rights of life, liberty, and the pursuit of
happiness, and to protect citizens from the abuses of power of
the King of Great Britain, the Founding Fathers drafted a
Constitution which made the federal government of the United
States a government of enumerated powers. Each branch of

government only had the powers granted to it by the Constitution. All other powers were reserved to the states. This book will concentrate on parts of the Constitution that state what powers are granted to the federal government, not on administrative sections.

ORGANIZATION OF CONSTITUTION. The Constitution is divided into a preamble and seven articles. The short preamble states:

> We the People of the United States, in Order to form
> a more perfect Union, establish Justice, insure
> domestic Tranquility, provide for the common
> [defense], promote the general Welfare, and secure
> the Blessings of Liberty to ourselves and our
> Posterity, do ordain and establish this Constitution
> for the United States of America.[165]

The preamble states the general purpose of the Constitution. It does not grant any powers to any branch of the federal government. If, for example, "promote the general Welfare" granted any authority, it would grant virtually unlimited authority to all branches of the federal government, which would destroy the intent of the signers to create a government of enumerated powers where each branch only had those powers granted to it by the Constitution.

ARTICLE I. The first three articles of the Constitution grant powers to the three branches of the federal government. The first, longest, most important article grants powers to a Congress. Article I is divided into ten sections. Section 1 states, "All legislative Powers herein granted shall be vested in

---

[165] "Constitution of the United States," U.S. National Archives & Records Administration, http://www.archives.gov/exhibits/charters /constitution.html.

a Congress of the United States, which shall consist of a Senate and House of Representatives." Sections 2-7 state how members of Congress are elected, serve, are paid, etc. See Appendix B for text.

Section 7 addresses raising taxes, "All Bills for raising Revenue shall originate in the House of Representatives; but the Senate may propose or concur with Amendments as on other Bills." The remainder of Section 7 reviews how bills are voted upon, passed, and become law. See Appendix B for text.

Section 8 states powers granted to Congress. Note that there is no mention of education, healthcare, or any other social programs.

> *The <u>Congress shall have Power</u> To lay and*
> *<u>collect Taxes, Duties, Imposts and Excises, to</u>*
> *<u>pay the Debts</u> and provide for the common*
> *<u>Defence and general Welfare</u> of the United*
> *States; but all Duties, Imposts and Excises shall*
> *be uniform throughout the United States;*
> *To <u>borrow Money</u> on the credit of the United*
> *States;*
> *To <u>regulate Commerce with foreign Nations,</u>*
> *<u>and among</u> the several <u>States</u>, and with the*
> *Indian Tribes;*
> To establish an uniform Rule of <u>Naturalization</u>,
> and uniform Laws on the subject of
> <u>Bankruptcies</u> throughout the United States;
> To <u>coin Money</u>, regulate the Value thereof, and
> of foreign Coin, and fix the Standard of
> Weights and Measures;

To provide for the <u>Punishment of counterfeiting</u> the Securities and current Coin of the United States;

To establish <u>Post Offices</u> and post Roads;

To <u>promote</u> the Progress of <u>Science and useful Arts,</u> by securing for limited Times to Authors and Inventors the <u>exclusive Right</u> to their respective <u>Writings and Discoveries</u>;

To constitute <u>Tribunals</u> inferior to the supreme Court;

To define and <u>punish Piracies</u> and Felonies committed on the high Seas, and Offences against the <u>Law of Nations</u>;

To <u>declare War</u>, grant Letters of Marque and Reprisal, and <u>make Rules</u> concerning <u>Captures</u> on Land and Water;

To raise and <u>support Armies</u>, but no Appropriation of Money to that Use shall be for a longer Term than two Years;

To provide and maintain a <u>Navy</u>;

To make <u>Rules</u> for the Government and Regulation of the <u>land and naval Forces</u>;

To provide for calling forth the <u>Militia to execute the Laws</u> of the Union, <u>suppress Insurrections and repel Invasions</u>;

To provide for <u>organizing, arming, and disciplining, the Militia</u>, and for governing such <u>Part of them</u> as may be employed in the <u>Service of the United States</u>, reserving to the States respectively, the Appointment of the Officers, and the Authority of training the Militia according to the discipline prescribed by Congress;

To exercise exclusive Legislation in all Cases
whatsoever, over such <u>District</u> (not exceeding
<u>ten Miles square</u>) as may, by Cession of
particular States, and the Acceptance of
Congress, become the <u>Seat of the Government
of the United States</u>, and to exercise like
Authority over all Places purchased by the
Consent of the Legislature of the State in which
the Same shall be, for the Erection <u>of Forts,
Magazines, Arsenals, dock-Yards, and other
needful Buildings</u>;--And
To <u>make all Laws</u> which shall be necessary and
proper for carrying into <u>Execution the foregoing
Powers</u>, and all other Powers vested by this
Constitution in the Government of the United
States, or in any Department or Officer thereof.

Section 9 states limitations on the powers of Congress.
Section 10 states rules regarding states (treaties, duties on
imports or exports, etc.). See Appendix B for text of these
sections.

<u>ARTICLE II.</u> The second article of the Constitution
grants powers to the President, the executive branch of the
government. It is divided into four sections. Section 1 states
how the President is elected, serves, is paid, etc. See Appendix
B for text. Section 2 states powers granted to the President.
Note that there is no mention of education, healthcare, or any
other social programs.

The <u>President shall be</u> <u>Commander in Chief</u> of
the Army and Navy of the United States, and of
the Militia of the several States, when called
into the actual Service of the United States; he

may require the Opinion, in writing, of the
principal Officer in each of the executive
Departments, upon any Subject relating to the
Duties of their respective Offices, and he shall
have Power to grant Reprieves and Pardons for
Offences against the United States, except in
Cases of Impeachment.
He shall have Power, by and with the Advice
and Consent of the Senate, to make Treaties,
provided two thirds of the Senators present
concur; and he shall nominate, and by and with
the Advice and Consent of the Senate, shall
appoint Ambassadors, other public Ministers
and Consuls, Judges of the supreme Court, and
all other Officers of the United States, whose
Appointments are not herein otherwise provided
for, and which shall be established by Law: but
the Congress may by Law vest the Appointment
of such inferior Officers, as they think proper,
in the President alone, in the Courts of Law, or
in the Heads of Departments.
The President shall have Power to fill up all
Vacancies that may happen during the Recess
of the Senate, by granting Commissions which
shall expire at the End of their next Session.

Section 3 states how President will work with Congress
(State of Union, etc.). Section 4 states grounds for
impeachment of the President, Vice President, and all "civil
Officers of the United States." See Appendix B for text.

ARTICLE III. The third article of the Constitution
grants powers to the Supreme Court and federal courts, the
judicial branch of the federal government. It is divided into

three sections. Section 1 states how the judges will serve, be paid, etc. Section 3 addresses treason against the United States. Only Section 2 states powers of the courts: Note that there is no mention of education, healthcare, or any other social programs.

The <u>judicial Power</u> shall extend to <u>all Cases</u>, in Law and Equity, arising under this Constitution, the Laws of the United States, and Treaties made, or which shall be made, under their Authority;--to all Cases affecting Ambassadors, other public Ministers and Consuls;--to all Cases of admiralty and maritime Jurisdiction;-- to <u>Controversies</u> to which the <u>United States</u> <u>shall be a Party</u>;--to <u>Controversies between two</u> <u>or more States</u>;-- <u>between a State and Citizens</u> <u>of another State</u>;--<u>between Citizens of different</u> <u>States</u>;--between Citizens of the same State claiming Lands under Grants of different States, and between a State, or the Citizens thereof, and foreign States, Citizens or Subjects.
In all <u>Cases affecting Ambassadors, other</u> <u>public Ministers</u> and Consuls, and those in which a State shall be Party, the supreme Court shall have original Jurisdiction. In all the other Cases before mentioned, the supreme Court shall have appellate Jurisdiction, both as to Law and Fact, with such Exceptions, and under such Regulations as the Congress shall make.
The <u>Trial of all Crimes</u>, except in Cases of Impeachment, <u>shall be by Jury</u>; and such Trial shall be held <u>in the State</u> where the said Crimes shall have been committed; but when not committed within any State, the Trial shall be at

such Place or Places as the Congress may by
Law have directed.

ARTICLE IV and ARTICLE V. The fourth article of
the Constitution only addresses issues related to the states. The
fifth article of the Constitution states the rules regarding
proposal and ratification of amendments to the Constitution.
These articles have no bearing on this book.

ARTICLE VI. The sixth article declares "this
Constitution, and the Laws of the United States which shall be
made in Pursuance thereof…the supreme Law of the Land; and
the Judges in every State shall be bound thereby…." It also
states that "Senators and Representatives…and the Members
of…State Legislatures, and all executive and judicial
Officers…of the United States and of the…States, shall be
bound by Oath or Affirmation, to support this Constitution; but
no religious Test shall ever be required as a Qualification to
any Office…"[166] Note that the requirement of "no religious
test" only applies to federal and state government officials. It
has absolutely nothing to do with qualification for immigration
or citizenship, as some Democrats have stated.

ARTICLE VII. The seventh and final article of the
Constitution only deals with details of ratification of the
Constitution by the states in 1787. It has no bearing on this
book.

CONCLUSION. So, what does the Constitution say
about jurisdiction of the federal government? First,
government of the United States is a government of
enumerated powers; each branch only has those powers
granted by the Constitution. Article I grants powers to

---

[166] Ibid.

Congress (Senate and House of Representatives). Article II grants powers to the executive branch (President). Article III grants powers to the judicial branch (Supreme Court and federal courts). No part of the Constitution grants any authority regarding education, healthcare, or any other social programs. Detailed discussion of all powers granted to the federal government is beyond the scope of this book. This book concentrates on the primary problem, the exercise of powers not granted by the Constitution.

During the 2008 election, Senator Obama often quoted the words "I am my brother's keeper" to explain what motivates him to government service. However, these are not words used by Christ, but words used by Cain after killing his brother Abel (Gen. 4:9). They have nothing to do with government. Most Republicans advocate a smaller federal government, lower taxes, and greater freedom. Most Democrats want a government that does more to help the people, which means more socialism, more redistribution of wealth, higher taxes and less freedom for citizens of the larger, more powerful government, all in violation of the powers granted to the federal government by the U.S. Constitution.

Most readers probably need clarification by what is meant by "less freedom." Greater taxes to pay for more government benefits means most Americans must work longer each year just to pay their taxes. More government benefits mean the government is taking more by force from most taxpayers to very ineffectively process and redistribute the funds to other taxpayers in the form of government benefits. In other words, taxpayers are forced to pay the school tuition, doctor bills and other bills of other taxpayers and much of the money they are forced to pay is spent paying for the larger government needed to ineffectively manage the government programs.

So, having a government that does more to take care of its people means Americans work longer each year just to pay their taxes and have less "liberty" and less of their own money to spend however they wish in their personal "pursuit of happiness." In other words, they have less of two of three God-given inalienable rights the United States government was established to protect. Also, more money flowing through government to schools and businesses means more improper government control of and less freedom for schools and businesses. It also means more fraud, more government waste, and more improper influence of government officials.

The objective of Democrats to increase the size and cost of government to provide more benefits to citizens violates the limited powers granted to the federal government by the U.S. Constitution. The spending on social programs is unconstitutional. The federal government is a government of enumerated powers; each branch only has those powers granted to it by the Constitution. No part of the Constitution grants any power to establish social programs. This is discussed in greater detail in the chapter on the Constitution.

If elected, Democrats will continue to increase the size and cost of government, a cost which must be passed on to the taxpayers one way or another, through individual or corporate taxes. Taxpayers are the only source of income for government. There is no such thing as a free lunch. More government benefits must be paid for by taxpayers.

VOTING FOR THE BILL OF RIGHTS

INTRODUCTION. What does voting according to principles embodied in the Bill of Rights require? To answer this question, this chapter will review: (1) history/definition of Bill of Rights; (2) rights granted by the ten amendments. The First and Second Amendments are discussed in much greater detail in separate chapters. Most other amendments are not discussed in detail because they are not critical to voting Christian values in the coming election. See Appendix C for full text of the Constitution.

HISTORY/DEFINITION OF BILL OF RIGHTS. In 1789 Congress ratified the first ten amendments to the Constitution, known as the "Bill of Rights."[167] Although all of the amendments are important for protection of freedoms enjoyed by Americans, this book will only concentrate on the few cited herein.

FIRST AMENDMENT. The First Amendment grants the rights to freedom of speech, religion, press, and assembly. It states:

> Congress shall make no law respecting an establishment of religion, or prohibiting the free exercise thereof; or abridging the freedom of speech, or of the press; or the right of the people peaceably to assemble, and to petition the Government for a redress of grievances.[168]

---

[167] "Bill of Rights," U.S. National Archives Records Administration, http://www.archives.gov/exhibits/charters/constitution.html.

See separate chapter on Freedom of Religion, which addresses both freedom of religion and freedom of speech of Christians.

SECOND AMENDMENT. The Second Amendment grants the right to bear arms. It states: "A well-regulated Militia, being necessary to the security of a free State, the right of the people to keep and bear Arms, shall not be infringed."[169] See separate chapter on Right to Bear Arms.

THIRD AMENDMENT. The Third Amendment only addresses soldiers staying in the homes of citizens with the permission of the owner. It states, "No Soldier shall, in time of peace be quartered in any house, without the consent of the Owner, nor in time of war, but in a manner to be prescribed by law."[170]

FOURTH AMENDMENT. The Fourth Amendment guards citizens from "unreasonable searches and seizures" and warrants without "probable cause." It states:

> The right of the people to be secure in their persons, houses, papers, and effects, against unreasonable searches and seizures, shall not be violated, and no Warrants shall issue, but upon probable cause, supported by Oath or affirmation, and particularly describing the place to be searched, and the persons or things to be seized.[171]

---

[168] "Bill of Rights," U.S. National Archives & Records Administration, http://www.archives.gov/exhibits/charters/constitution.html.
[169] Ibid.
[170] Ibid.

FIFTH AMENDMENT. The Fifth Amendment grants citizens the right to freedom from prosecution unless there is "indictment by Grand Jury," "due process of law," and no double jeopardy. It also guarantees just compensation for property taken for public use.

> No person shall be held to answer for a capital,
> or otherwise infamous crime, unless on a
> presentment or indictment of a Grand Jury,
> except in cases arising in the land or naval
> forces, or in the Militia, when in actual service
> in time of War or public danger; nor shall any
> person be subject for the same offence to be
> twice put in jeopardy of life or limb; nor shall
> be compelled in any criminal case to be a
> witness against himself, nor be deprived of life,
> liberty, or property, without due process of law;
> nor shall private property be taken for public
> use, without just compensation.[172]

SIXTH AMENDMENT--RIGHT TO ATTORNEY. The Sixth Amendment grants every American accused of a crime the right to a criminal defense attorney. It states:

> In all criminal prosecutions, the accused shall
> enjoy the right to a speedy and public trial, by
> an impartial jury of the State and district
> wherein the crime shall have been committed,
> which district shall have been previously
> ascertained by law, and to be informed of the
> nature and cause of the accusation; to be

---

[171] Ibid.
[172] Ibid.

confronted with the witnesses against him; to
have compulsory process for obtaining
witnesses in his favor, and to have the
Assistance of Counsel for his defence.[173]

Note that there is no right to an attorney for civil cases.
There is only a right to an attorney when it is a criminal case of
the government versus the accused citizen.

SEVENTH AMENDMENT. The Seventh Amendment
grants the right to trial by jury. It states:

In Suits at common law, where the value in
controversy shall exceed twenty dollars, the
right of trial by jury shall be preserved, and
no fact tried by a jury, shall be otherwise re-
examined in any Court of the United States,
than according to the rules of the common
law.[174]

EIGHTH AMENDMENT. The Eighth Amendment
protects citizens from excessive bail. It states: "Excessive bail
shall not be required, nor excessive fines imposed, nor cruel
and unusual punishments inflicted."[175]

NINTH AMENDMENT. The Ninth Amendment
makes it clear that Americans have other rights not listed in the
Constitution or Bill of Rights. It states, "The enumeration in
the Constitution, of certain rights, shall not be construed to
deny or disparage others retained by the people."[176] In other

---

[173] Ibid.
[174] Ibid.
[175] Ibid.
[176] Ibid.

words, the fact that the Constitution and Bill of Rights list and describe certain rights does not mean these are the only rights of citizens.

TENTH AMENDMENT. The tenth amendment states the vitally important principle that "the powers not delegated to the United States by the Constitution, nor prohibited by it to the States, are reserved to the States respectively, or to the people."[177] This vitally important amendment is additional confirmation that the federal government only has those powers that are specifically granted to it by the Constitution.

RIGHTS NOT GRANTED BY BILL OF RIGHTS. Many Americans mistakenly believe that they have many rights not granted by the Constitution or Bill of Rights. This greatly impacts politics and government.

RIGHT TO EDUCATION. The U.S. Constitution does not grant any American the right to an education. The United States government has no constitutional authority to make any laws regarding what person or organization provides or pays for education. The federal government has no authority to grant college student loans. Many state constitutions may grant citizens the right to a public education paid for by other citizens, but there is no right to any education under the Constitution of the United States.

RIGHT TO HEALTHCARE. The U.S. Constitution does not grant any American the right to any healthcare paid for by other Americans. The United States government has no constitutional authority to make any laws regarding what persons or organizations provide or pay for healthcare.

---

[177] Ibid.

    <u>CONCLUSION</u>. The Bill of Rights, the first ten amendments to the Constitution, grants all Americans the rights of freedom of religion, freedom of speech, right to bear arms, right to a criminal defense attorney, and other rights enumerated therein. The ninth amendment protects other rights of the people. The tenth amendment makes it clear that the federal government only has those powers granted to it by the Constitution, and that all other powers are reserved to the states. No part of the Constitution or Bill of Rights grants any American any right to education, healthcare, or any other social or economic benefits paid for by other Americans.

CHAPTER 10.0

VOTING FOR RIGHTS AND FREEDOMS

<u>SECTION REVIEW</u>. This section shows what voting for rights and freedoms requires. The first chapter shows what voting for liberty and the pursuit of happiness requires. The second chapter shows what voting for freedom of speech and freedom of religion requires.

<u>CHAPTERS</u>:
10.1 Voting for Liberty and the Pursuit of Happiness
10.2 Voting for Freedom of Speech and
Freedom of Religion

CHAPTER 10.1

VOTING FOR LIBERTY AND
THE PURSUIT OF HAPPINESS

<u>INTRODUCTION</u>. Liberty and the "pursuit of happiness" are the second and third God-given inalienable rights listed in the first paragraph of the Declaration of Independence. "Life," the first inalienable right listed, is addressed in a prior chapter entitled "Abortion." An inalienable right is a God-given right that no man has a right to take away from another man. Patrick Henry's famous words, "Give me liberty, or give me death!" express the sentiment of most Americans. Americans greatly treasure the freedoms they enjoy as citizens of the United States.

<u>DEFINITION OF LIBERTY</u>. Today most Americans have a totally different understanding of the meaning of liberty than that given by God in scripture. Most believe that freedom is the right to do whatever is right in your own eyes, so long as doing so does not harm another person. That is totally contrary to Scripture. The words, "Every man did that which was right in his own eyes" (Judges 17:5-7; 21:24-25) describe a period of lawlessness in Israel (See Deut. 12:7-9; Prov. 12:15; 21:2). God commanded the Israelites to not do whatever was right in their own eyes, but to obey His commandments. King David said, "I will walk at liberty: for I seek thy precepts" (Ps. 119:45). In other words, true liberty is found through submission to God and obedience to His laws, not through doing whatever is right in your own eyes.

<u>FOUNDING FATHERS AND LIBERTY</u>. Most Americans also have a totally different understanding of the

meaning of true liberty than our nation's Founding Fathers. The Founding Fathers were never willing to exchange their freedom for government benefits. They even protested taxes on tea. In total contrast, today many Americans are willing to give up their liberty and live under much greater government taxes in exchange for government benefits. That is one of the major factors that divide Americans between Republicans and Democrats. See further discussion below, under Pursuit of Happiness.

BILL OF RIGHTS. In 1789 Congress ratified the first ten amendments to the Constitution, known as the "Bill of Rights."[178] The Bill of Rights defines key rights and freedoms of Americans. The First Amendment grants the rights to freedom of speech, religion, press, and assembly. The Second Amendment grants the right to bear arms. See chapters on Freedom of Religion, Right to Bear Arms, and Bill of Rights for discussion of rights and freedoms.

PURSUIT OF HAPPINESS. Most Americans are probably uncertain about the meaning of "pursuit of happiness." Basically, "pursuit of happiness" means the freedom to work and earn, keep, and spend money to pursue one's own happiness. Few politicians ever mention the "pursuit of happiness", but it plays a key role in every national election. Most Republicans want smaller government and lower taxes. They want all Americans to have the right and freedom to keep more of their hard-earned money, which enables the pursuit of happiness.

Democrats always want a larger government which does more to take care of its people and they are willing to

---

[178] "Bill of Rights," U.S. National Archives & Records Administration, http://www.archives.gov/exhibits/charters/constitution.html.

have others pay higher taxes to fund it. If asked individually, most Democrats are probably not personally willing to pay higher taxes, and most Democratic politicians would never tell their supporters that they have to personally pay higher taxes to receive more government benefits. Democrats and the Democratic Platform always claim that they only want to raise taxes on the "wealthy few" who are not paying their "fair share", but that is a lie. Totally contrary to what Democrats and the Democratic Platform claim, the middle class does not pay its fair share of taxes and the wealthy pay far more than their fair share. All of this is discussed in greater detail in chapter on Truth on Taxes.

DECLARATION OF INDEPENDENCE. Voting with the Declaration of Independence requires voting Republican because Republicans support the right to liberty infinitely better than Democrats. First, more Republicans support God's definition of liberty, which requires obedience to God's commandments, not doing whatever is right in your own eyes. Second, Republicans want smaller government and lower taxes, which means greater liberty to exercise the pursuit of happiness. Third, more Republicans more strongly support the right to bear arms, so important to the Founding Fathers not just for hunting or personal protection, but for the establishment and defense of the United States.

CONSTITUTION. The Constitution of the United States of America was designed to strictly limit the power and authority of the federal government, and to reserve all other powers to the people and the states. In other words, the Constitution was designed to maximize the freedom of the people. However, countless years of voting to increase the size and power of the federal government have greatly increased federal taxes and greatly reduced the power of the people to engage in the pursuit of happiness. In other words, continually voting to increase the role of the federal government has greatly reduced the ability of Americans to keep and spend the money that they have earned.

VOTING FOR FREEDOM OF SPEECH AND FREEDOM OF RELIGION

INTRODUCTION. Freedom of speech and freedom of religion are two of the most important rights of every American. They are also the most infringed upon and threatened rights of Christians. The First Amendment to the Constitution grants the rights freedom of speech and freedom of religion. It states:

> Congress shall make no law respecting an establishment of religion, or prohibiting the free exercise thereof; or abridging the freedom of speech, or of the press; or the right of the people peaceably to assemble, and to petition the Government for a redress of grievances.[179]

DEMOCRATS AGAINST CHRISTIANS. Democrats have repeatedly tried to enact laws to silence Christians, to eliminate their competition during national elections. No group of Americans has more restrictions on its freedom of speech and freedom of religion than Christians. The U.S. Supreme Court actually approved the use of laws against anti-abortion protestors laws that were designed to be used against organized crime. During 2008, Democrats tried to enact legislation to silence Christian and conservative talk shows. The Obama Administration's attempt to force Catholic and other religious institutions to provide contraceptives, abortions, abortive drugs, and other medical products or procedures that violated

---

[179] "Bill of Rights," U.S. National Archives & Records Administration, http://www.archives.gov/exhibits/charters/constitution.html.

their religious or moral convictions was one of the most egregious violations of the First Amendment to the U.S. Constitution by a President.[180]

A law nicknamed the LBJ law because President Lyndon Baines Johnson signed it to silence his critics, threatens the tax-exempt status of any church or religious organization that endorses any candidate. It is a totally unconstitutional violation of the First Amendment. It is a tool effectively used by Democrats to silence Christians. Every religious leader has a duty to provide moral guidance to his congregation regarding all areas of life, to include politics. The Founding Fathers would be absolutely shocked to learn that pastors have been silenced in the name of "separation of church and state." Today most judges fail to realize that these laws are clear violations of freedom of speech and freedom of religion.

The author of this book had the honor of asking U.S. Supreme Court Justice Anthony Scalia one question during his visit to Regent University. He asked why the Supreme Court permitted the voice of moral leaders to be silenced. Justice Scalia asked if he would give the same rights to an ACLU attorney. When he said that he would be inclined to do so, Scalia said that he did not have a logical problem, but that the hands of the Supreme Court were tied by Congress, meaning by the LBJ law. Justice Scalia should be respected for his response. Many liberal judges show little respect for laws enacted by Congress or state legislatures. However, the author respectfully disagrees. The Supreme Court is one of the three branches of the federal government with responsibility to serve as part of the checks and balances established by the Founding

---

[180] "Where Do the Candidates Stand on Life: Mitt Romney, Barack Obama," National Right to Life Committee, http://www.nrlc.org.

Fathers. It has a duty to correct Congress when they enact a law that is so clearly a violation of the U.S. Constitution's protections of freedom of religion and freedom of speech. See Bill of Rights, Appendix C.

SEPARATION OF CHURCH AND STATE. Most Americans believe in separation of church and state, but differ sharply in what they believe it means. Many believe that the words "separation of church and state" are in the U.S. Constitution. They are not. They were first used by Thomas Jefferson to refer to the need to keep the church free from interference by government and to not have a state church improperly ruled by the government as in England. Over one hundred years later, they were used by the Supreme Court to define the limits of authority of church and state. Today many Americans believe in separation of church and state in a way that would be anathema to the Founding Fathers. Democrats have reversed the meaning of Jefferson's words, using them to justify action against the church and to silence Christian leaders, a violation of their rights to freedom of religion and freedom of speech. See Bill of Rights, Appendix C.

BELIEF IN GOD. Today many Americans believe that separation of church and state means that teachers and elected officials cannot rightfully be expected to believe in God or creation because these are matters of personal faith that do not belong in public schools, government, or the workplace. This is totally contrary to Scripture, common sense, and the beliefs of the Founding Fathers.

Belief in God and creation does not require faith. It only requires a modicum of common sense. "We hold these truths to be self-evident, that all men are created equal, that they are endowed by their Creator with certain unalienable

Rights…." (Declaration of Independence, Appendix A.) The United States was founded upon belief in God and creation. The Founding Fathers understood that belief in God, creation, and God's laws were common sense, self-evident truths. The most amazing common sense, self-evident truth embraced by the founding fathers was that God continues to create all men within their mothers, and to endow them with certain God-given unalienable rights which no man or government can rightfully take from another man. The Founding Fathers believed that it was the violation of these rights that justified the Declaration of Independence, Revolutionary War, and establishment of the United States of America.

Anyone who does not believe in God and creation is a fool. No fool should be trusted with any teaching or leadership position. King David said, "The fool has said in his heart, 'There is no God.'" (Psalm 14:1-3; 53:1-3). In other words, only a fool refuses to acknowledge the existence of God. Scripture teaches through King Solomon and other authors of Proverbs, that the fear of God is the beginning of wisdom.

Belief in God does not constitute endorsement of any religion. Many religions believe in God, and many individuals who are not part of any known religion believe in God. Belief in Christ is totally different. Neither Scripture nor the Founding Fathers stated that knowledge of Christ is a common sense, self-evident truth. God has not revealed Christ through creation. It takes acceptance of a gift of faith from God to believe in Christ because the cross is foolishness to man but the wisdom and power of God (1 Cor. 1:18-25). Belief in Christ as the Son of God is a tenant of one religion—Christianity.

ACKNOWLEDGMENT OF GOD. Do Christian and non-Christian teachers, professors, employers, judges, and government leaders have a right to impose their personal belief in God and creation upon their students, employees, courts, and citizens? Yes! All Americans have a duty to acknowledge God as the Creator of all things seen and unseen and of the laws that govern all things seen and unseen.

Why do all Americans, especially those in teaching or leadership positions, have a duty to acknowledge God? First, it is not because the Founding Fathers or Declaration of Independence acknowledged God. No one has any obligation to acknowledge anything just because the Founding Fathers acknowledged it. Second, it is not because Scripture acknowledges God. Scripture acknowledges Christ as Lord and Savior, but non-Christians cannot be required to acknowledge Christ as Savior. However, Scripture does explain why the Founding Fathers and the Declaration of Independence properly acknowledged God.

In his letter to the Romans, the Apostle Paul wrote,

For the wrath of God is revealed from heaven against all ungodliness and unrighteousness of men, who hold the truth in unrighteousness; Because that which may be known of God is manifest in them; for God hath shewed it unto them. For the invisible things of him from the creation of the world are clearly seen, being understood by the things that are made, even his eternal power and Godhead; so that they are without excuse: Because that, when they knew God, they glorified him not as God, neither were thankful; but became vain in their

imaginations, and their foolish heart was
darkened. Professing themselves to be wise,
they became fools..." (Romans 1:18-22, KJV).

First, many Americans believe that they have complete
freedom to choose whether or not to believe in God. They do
not. No man has any excuse for failure to believe in God
because God has revealed the "invisible things" about Himself,
including His "eternal power and Godhead," to all men so
"they are without excuse." These "invisible things" about God
are "clearly seen, being understood by the things that are
made." In other words, God reveals Himself to man through
creation. Also, "that which may be known of God is manifest
in them" (in all men). God personally reveals Himself to all
men.

Second, many Americans live as though they do not
presently answer to God for their actions. They are wrong. The
"wrath of God **is** revealed" (present tense) against "all
ungodliness and unrighteousness of men." In other words,
Americans are suffering the wrath of God today.

Third, Americans fail to understand why they suffer
God's wrath. They suffer because they "glorified him not as
God, neither were thankful." In other words, they suffer
because they failed to properly acknowledge God and be
thankful for His many blessings.

Fourth, Americans fail to understand how they suffer
the wrath of God. "Because... they glorified him not as God,
neither were thankful" they "became vain in their
imaginations, and their foolish heart was darkened. Professing
themselves to be wise, they became fools..." Those words
describe many Americans today. They think they are wise, but

they are fools. They cannot see the light of the truth because their hearts are darkened. They have become vain and foolish in their thinking.

Vain and foolish thinking are not the only ways Americans suffer God's judgment. The "wrath of God is revealed from heaven against all ungodliness and unrighteousness of men." In other words, Americans suffer the wrath of God for "all ungodliness and unrighteousness."

Consider the ignorance and foolishness of teachers and professors who believe that they can properly teach their students without teaching the self-evident, common sense truths embodied in the Declaration of Independence i.e. that God is the Creator of all things seen and unseen, to include all students, and the Creator of all laws that govern all things seen and unseen, to include all laws of mathematics and science, and laws that govern men and governments.

God has ordained that man must live by faith. Every man has a faith or religion that is his reason for living. The most important thing taught in schools is not reading, writing, arithmetic, or other academic subjects. It is faith. Today students are taught to not acknowledge or have faith in God and not to respect, fear, love or serve God or lead God-centered lives. They are taught that life is a meaningless product of evolutionary chance and that they should have faith in themselves, lead self-centered lives, and do whatever is right in their own eyes, without reference to God or His unchanging moral laws, laws rooted in His unchanging character.

Consider the ignorance of judges who have studied law for years, but refuse to acknowledge the Supreme Lawgiver, the God who created the laws that govern all things seen and unseen. They are fools who cannot be trusted to render wise judgments. Examples are liberal justices on the Supreme Court who rule totally contrary to God's laws.

Consider foolishness of government leaders who fail to properly acknowledge God. They cannot be trusted to enact, enforce, or properly adjudicate laws in accordance with God's laws. Examples include members of Congress who vote totally contrary to God's laws.

The greatest fools are those who have studied science or law but cannot see the Creator or Supreme Lawgiver; they cannot see the forest because there are so many trees. Many government leaders do great harm to our beloved nation by failing to acknowledge God, ask for His much-needed guidance and blessings, and making, enforcing, and judging laws in accordance with God's laws. Many teachers and professors do great injury to and handicap their students by teaching them that they can determine truth and right and wrong without God or His laws. All Americans, especially teachers and government leaders, have a duty to properly acknowledge God, pray for His guidance and blessings, and live and vote in accordance with His laws.[181]

CONCLUSION. The Founding Fathers of the United States had a godly, biblical understanding of the jurisdiction of church and state clearly reflected in the Declaration of Independence, which began with what they clearly understood to be the only proper justification for declaration of

---

[181] George Washington would not allow his troops to curse, for fear of losing God's blessings. All Americans should be familiar with the beautiful painting of General Washington during the Revolutionary War, kneeling in the snow, praying for God's guidance and blessing. Americans need godly Christian leaders like George Washington in government.

independence from Great Britain. That justification was based upon understanding that: (1) God created all things seen and unseen and all the laws that govern all things seen and unseen; (2) God continues to create all men equal, with certain God-given unalienable rights; and (3) only repeated extreme violation of these rights justified declaration of independence and the establishment of a new government.

Today most Americans, to include most lawyers and judges, have a totally wrong understanding of the jurisdiction of church and state and the simple self-evident, common-sense truths that this nation was founded upon. They exclude God, creation, and God's laws from politics, government, schools, and the workplace. They completely fail to recognize that all Americans have an absolute duty to properly acknowledge God in politics, government, schools, and the workplace in the same way that our nation's Founding Fathers acknowledged Him. They also completely fail to understand that failure to properly acknowledge, respect and fear God reduces one to vain thinking and foolishness because darkened hearts cannot see the light of truth. They fail to recognize this because they have already suffered the judgment of God due to their failure to properly acknowledge Him in all areas.

If Biden is elected and Democrats have a majority in the House and Senate, Congress will enact laws to further restrict the freedom of speech and freedom of religion of Christians. If Biden is elected, he will appoint liberal federal judges and/or Supreme Court Justices who do not understand or respect the limits of authority imposed on government by the Constitution and legislate from the bench to further restrict the freedom of speech and freedom of religion of Christians and other Americans.

CHAPTER 11.0

VOTING FOR THE TRUTH

<u>SECTION REVIEW</u>. This section addresses issues related to truth. The first chapter presents an alphabetical list of some of the many lies of politicians. The second chapter provides evidence that proves totally false the claims of Democrats that the "wealthy few" do not pay their fair share of taxes and that the middle class pays more than its fair share. The third chapter shows that the Democratic Platform rests on a foundation of lies, and that if you remove those lies, the Democratic Platform collapses.

<u>CHAPTERS</u>:
11.1 False Claims of Politicians
11.2 The Truth About Taxes
11.3 Democratic Platform: Foundation of Lies

FALSE CLAIMS OF POLITICIANS

INTRODUCTION. This critically important chapter exposes many false claims made by politicians to win votes. It presents a brief, alphabetical list of these claims, and references other chapters for additional facts and more detailed discussion.

ABORTION. Most Democrats and a few Republicans claim to be pro-choice but totally reject the right to choose of pro-life Americans. They actually want to force Americans who believe that abortion is murder to pay for abortions through taxpayer funding of abortions. That is the height of hypocrisy. President Obama is the perfect example. He actually overrode the votes of governors, state legislators, and pro-life Americans by funding Planned Parenthood, the nation's largest provider of abortions, in states where the governor and state legislators cut funding. Pro-choice Americans also claim that a child is not a child with a right to life until after birth. That is totally contrary to the position of God revealed through scripture. See chapter on Scripture on Abortion for verses and detailed discussion.

CONSTITUTION. Democrats falsely claim or imply that they support the Constitution better than Republicans. The entire purpose of the Constitution is to define the jurisdiction and limits of power of each branch of the federal government. Democrats totally reject the limits of power that the Constitution places on the federal government. Most Democrats and some Republicans believe that the Constitution grants rights to education and healthcare and other social or economic benefits. It does not. All Supreme Court rulings which grant these powers are unconstitutional. See chapters on Constitution, Supreme Court, Education, and Healthcare for detailed discussion.

<u>DECLARATION OF INDEPENDENCE</u>. Democrats believe that they better support the ideals embodied in the Declaration of Independence. The opposite is true. Republicans better support all the principles that the United States was founded upon, and the rights to life, liberty, and the pursuit of happiness, and the right to bear arms. See chapter on Declaration of Independence for detailed discussion.

<u>DEMOCRATIC PLATFORM</u>. The Democratic Platform is founded upon lies. If you remove those lies, the Democratic Platform collapses. See chapter on Democratic Platform for detailed explanation.

<u>EDUCATION</u>. Democrats tell some of their biggest lies regarding education. Hillary Clinton offered free college education to all families who earn less than $125,000/year (83% of all families) and debt free education to all others. She claimed that to pay for these benefits she would only raise taxes on the rich and corporations. The rich are already paying virtually all federal taxes. The top 1% is already paying about 27% of all federal income taxes. US corporations are already paying some of the highest corporate taxes in the world. College debt exceeds credit card debt in the United States. Obama doubled the national debt without giving free college. There is no way that Democrats can pay for all the educational benefits that they promise, but false promises win millions of votes.

231

GOVERNMENT—ROLE OF. Most Democrats and some Republicans state, imply, or simply believe that God and the Constitution support having a government that cares for its people through social and economic programs like education and healthcare. That is an absolute lie embraced by so many Americans. Neither scripture nor the Constitution support having a government that cares for its people through social or economic programs. See chapters on Constitution and Biblical Role of Government.

HEALTHCARE. Democrats tell some of their greatest lies regarding healthcare. They promise healthcare to all Americans by only raising taxes on the rich. The rich are already paying virtually all federal income taxes. The top 1% is already paying about 27% of all federal income taxes.

HOMOPHOBIC/HOMOSEXUALITY. Americans who oppose the homosexual lifestyle are called homophobic. That is not true. Phobic means fear. Americans who oppose the homosexual lifestyle are not afraid of homosexuals. They, like God, believe that homosexuality is a perversion of God's design for man and woman. See chapter on Homosexuality and Same-Sex Marriage.

RIGHT TO BEAR ARMS. Most Democrats and some Republicans falsely claim that Constitutional right to bear arms does not include assault weapons. Some even make the foolish and irrelevant comment that "You don't need an assault weapon to hunt deer." The Constitution does not say anything about hunting. It grants the right to bear arms suitable for a "Militia" for defense of government. The entire Declaration of Independence is justification for weapons needed to overthrow a government which fails to protect the rights to life, liberty, and the pursuit of happiness.

SAME-SEX MARRIAGE. Most Democrats and some Republicans support same-sex marriage. They say that it is a constitutional right. It is not. I was not for over 200 years and what is constitutional has not suddenly changed with the culture. Some actually believe that it is God's will. It is not. It is an extreme perversion of God's design for man, woman, and marriage. See chapter on Homosexuality and Same-Sex Marriage.

SEPARATION OF CHURCH AND STATE. Most Democrats and many Republicans believe that separation of church and state means that church leaders should not be able to endorse or recommend political candidates without their church losing its tax-exempt status. That is a lie; it is a violation of their constitutional First Amendment rights to freedom to speech and freedom of religion. Politics is faith in action and religious leaders have a duty to provide voting guidance to their people. See chapter on and Freedom of Speech and Freedom of Religion.

Most Democrats and some Republicans also believe that separation of church and state means that teaching belief in God and creation should be banned from public schools. The Declaration of Independence shows that the United States was founded upon belief in God and creation, and belief that God created the laws that govern men and nations. It is therefore illogical and unethical to claim that separation of church and state does not permit teaching God and creation in public schools. See chapter on Declaration of Independence.

SUPREME COURT. Democrats falsely claim that they are better able to select justices for the Supreme Court. Democrats never nominate, appoint, or confirm Supreme Court justices who will uphold the Constitution. To do so would be contrary to their core values. They only nominate, appoint, and confirm justices who will ignore the limits of power which the Constitution places on each branch of the federal government and grant totally unconstitutional education and healthcare benefits to Americans. Also, when Democrats have a majority in the Senate, they block pro-life Christians from the Supreme Court. See chapters on Supreme Court and Constitution.

TAXES. Democrats and the Democratic Platform claim that the "rich" or "wealthy few" do not pay their fair share of federal taxes, and that the poor and middle class pay more than their fair share. Those lies are proven false by facts cited in the chapters on Truth on Taxes and the Democratic Platform.

WOMEN'S WAGES. During the 2016 Democratic Convention, one of the speakers said that women earn only 79 cents for every dollar that men earn. That conveys a totally false impression of extreme sexual discrimination. Unmarried women earn 94 to 95 cents for every dollar that men earn. And some unmarried women also get pregnant, have children, and choose to leave the work force.

CONCLUSION. Politics is faith in action. It is a battle between truth and lies, right and wrong. A house divided against itself cannot stand. God is never on both sides of any war. Neither is he on both sides of the battle between Republicans and Democrats. Satan is the father of lies. Those who serve him use lies to advance their cause. This chapter presents an amazing list of lies used by Democrats to win votes. The Democratic Platform is founded upon lies. If you remove the lies, the platform collapses. See all chapters listed within this chapter for more detailed discussion.

THE TRUTH ABOUT TAXES

INTRODUCTION. First, President Trump reduced taxes for most Americans and American business. That is one reason markets hit record highs and unemployment hit record lows for black Americans, Hispanics, and all other Americans.

Second, Biden will raise taxes on Americans by 4.3 trillion dollars. That is a fact embodied in the 2020 Democratic National Platform. He needs money to fund all his social programs. Democrats always say that they will only raise taxes on the wealthy, but that is never true. They will raise income taxes, capital gains taxes, corporate taxes, etc.

Third, "fairness" in taxation is one of the primary themes of Democrats. It sounds so American, so right for a nation "with liberty and justice for all." All they ask in the name of fairness is that rich Americans pay their "fair" share of taxes. So why in the world would Republicans object?

Democrats and the Democratic Platform claim that "rich" or "the wealthy few" are not paying their fair share of taxes and should be taxed more to support the overtaxed "middle class." These statements are totally false. First, about half of Americans, mostly middle and lower class, do not pay any federal taxes. Second, the rich pay much higher taxes than the poor or middle class.

FEDERAL INCOME TAX RATES. Current official U.S. federal income tax rates range from 10% for the lowest income group to 37% for the highest income group. To verify this, go to www.irs.gov, find 2019 Instructions for Form 1040, and go to Tax Tables.

However, tax rates are only half of the story; deductions are the other half. The poor and middle class get many tax deductions that are phased out for the rich. The end result is that about half of Americans, mostly middle and lower class, do not pay any federal income taxes. In other words, they pay nothing to support the American soldiers who put their lives on the line for them. They pay nothing for the federal roads the travel on. They pay nothing for many benefits that they get from the federal government. Those who receive Social Security and Medicare benefits get far more that they paid for, the system is going bankrupt, and the national debt continues to rise dramatically. In other words, totally contrary to the lies being told by Democrats to win votes, the poor and middle class do not pay their fair share of taxes, and the rich pay far more than their fair share. The most vilified top 1% pays about 27% of all federal taxes.

How much federal taxes are actually paid by the rich, the middle class, and the poor? The lowest 20% (average income $15,900) earn 4% of the national income but pay only 1% of the taxes. The second 20% (average income $37,400) earn 8% of the income but pay only 4% of the taxes. The third 20% (average income $58,500) earn 13% of the income but pay only 9% of the taxes. The fourth 20% (average income $85,200) earn 20% of the income and pay 17% of the taxes. The next 10% (average income $120,700) earn 14% of the income and pay 14% of the taxes. The next 5% (average income $161,100) earn 10% of the income and pay 11% of the taxes. The next 4% (average income $277,200) earn 13% of the income but pay 17% of the taxes. The top 1% (average income 1,558,500) earn 18% of the income but pay 27% of the taxes. In other words, the bottom 60% of Americans pay much less than their share of federal taxes (14%), and the greatly and vilified top 1% pay far more than their share (27%).[182]

The foregoing only considers federal income tax. When you consider all taxes paid by Americans i.e. state and local income taxes, real estate taxes, sales taxes, fuel taxes, and all other taxes, then the poor and middle-class Americans pay more than above, and wealthy Americans pay far more.

WEALTHY AMERICANS. Democrats have continually stated or implied that wealthy Americans are somehow immoral or unethical because they did not really earn their wealth and do not pay their fair share of taxes. Americans should ask themselves whether Abraham, Job, and King Solomon, all extremely wealthy, were wealthy because they were dishonest or evil, or because they were obedient to God's laws and God's will, found favor with God, and were richly blessed by God.

Most wealthy men earn their money lawfully. They know how to make money, and they know how to use money to make more money. The DOW more than doubled in value during the past 8 years, and the real estate market has greatly improved. Many wealthy Americans know how to take advantage of these opportunities to multiply their money. There is absolutely nothing ethically or legally wrong with trying to multiply money through wise investments.

---

[182] Catherine Mulbrandon, "How Much Taxes Are Paid by the Poor, Middle Class and Rich," VisualizingEconomics, http://visualizingeconomics .com /2010/02/12/, February 2, 2012. Source of figures is Congressional Budget Office most recent figures (2005), http://www.cbo.gov/ftpdocs/88xx/ doc8885/EffectiveTaxRates.shtml.

CONCLUSION. During 2016 Hillary Clinton and during 2012 President Obama and other Democrats have said that they want to raise taxes on the "rich" to force them to pay their fair share to relieve the unfair tax burden on the "middle class." Why is this wrong? First, about 49% of Americans, mostly middle and lower class, do not pay any federal taxes. In other words, they are not paying their fair share of taxes.

Also, the U.S. Constitution makes the federal government a government of enumerated powers, where each branch only has those powers which are granted to it by the Constitution. There is absolutely no part of the Constitution that authorizes the social programs which now comprise most of the federal budget. Reduction or elimination of these programs would permit much lower tax rates and make it possible to eliminate the federal deficit and federal debt.

So how could federal tax laws be improved to ensure more "fairness" in taxation? One option would be a flat tax where all Americans pay the same rate. Most tax deductions and tax credits would be eliminated for all income levels. This would ensure that everyone paid their fair share and would greatly reduce tax fraud, tax preparation time, and the size, cost and workload of the Internal Revenue Service. A second but much more likely option would be to maintain current tax rates but eliminate most tax deductions and tax credits for all tax brackets. This would reduce tax fraud, tax preparation time, and the job of the Internal Revenue Service. A third but much less likely option would be to totally eliminate the federal income tax and fund the federal government with sales taxes. This would eliminate the need to complete a federal tax return and greatly reduce tax fraud and the size, cost and function of the Internal Revenue Service.

DEMOCRATIC PLATFORM:
FOUNDATION OF LIES

INTRODUCTION. A new Democratic Platform is published every four years. The 2012 Democratic Platform is a 63-page document that was published in 2012. The 2016 platform is a 55-page document that was published July 21, 2016. This chapter discusses the heart of the 2012 platform first, and then compares the 2016 platform, showing that the heart of the platform remains the same. Readers who do not want to read all the details in this lengthy chapter may jump to the chapter's conclusion for a quick summary.

When reading quotes from the platforms, ask the following questions: (1) Are the statements regarding Republicans, taxes, and other "facts" true? (2) Are the policies Constitutional? (3) Are the policies in agreement with laws and principles given by God through Scripture? As a Christian attorney, I was absolutely shocked by the degree to which the heart of Democratic Platform relies upon lies and deception. But do not take my word. Read it carefully. Verify every fact. Decide for yourself who is speaking the truth. Then read the Constitution; it is not long or complicated. Ask yourself, "Exactly what part of the Constitution grants authority for this policy or program?" Read chapter on Constitution and refer to full text of the Constitution, attached as an Appendix.

2012 DEMOCRATIC PLATFORM. The heart of the 2012 and 2016 Democratic Platforms is the same. The 2012 Democratic Platform states:

Reclaiming the economic security of the middle class is the challenge we must overcome today. That begins by restoring the basic values that made our country great, and restoring for everyone who works hard and plays by the rules the opportunity to find a job that pays the bills, turn an idea into a profitable business, care for your family, afford a home you call your own and health care you can count on, retire with dignity and respect, and, most of all, give your children the kind of education that allows them to dream even bigger and go even further than you ever imagined.

This has to be our North Star—an economy that's built not from the top down, but from a growing middle class, and that provides ladders of opportunity for those working hard to join the middle class.

This is not another trivial political argument. It's the defining issue of our time and at the core of the American Dream. And now we stand at a make-or-break moment, and are faced with a choice between moving forward and falling back.[183]

CORE ISSUE. These paragraphs make it clear that this issue, which is built on lies and deception as shown below and throughout this book, is the core issue of the Democrats. It is their "North Star." It is "not another trivial political argument."

---

[183] "2012 Democratic Platform," page 2, https://www.democrats.org/party-platform, downloaded 2/2/2016.

It is the "defining issue of our time and the core of the American Dream." In other words, the core issue of the Democratic Party is built on absolute lies about Republicans and the totally false claim that Democrats want equal opportunity for all Americans.

ECONOMIC SECURITY OF MIDDLE CLASS. What could possibly be wrong with the noble goal of "reclaiming the economic security of the middle class?" First, God forbids discrimination based on class or wealth. Exodus states, "Do not show favoritism to a poor person in a lawsuit" (Ex 23: 3). Leviticus states, "Do not pervert justice; do not show partiality to the poor or favoritism to the great, but judge your neighbor fairly" (Lev 19:15, NIV). Job declares that God "shows no partiality to princes and does not favor the rich over the poor, for they are all the work of his hands?" (Job 34: 19). That is why God's "tax rate" was exactly the same for the rich and the poor: 10%. See chapter on taxes.

Second, the Declaration of Independence states that: (1) God creates all men equal; (2) with "<u>certain unalienable Rights</u> that [...include] <u>Life, Liberty and the pursuit of Happiness</u>;" (3) "to secure these rights, Governments are instituted among Men." This clearly implies that all men are created equal and entitled to equal and fair treatment under the law, and that the responsibility of government is to ensure equal and fair treatment under the law. Protecting the right to "the pursuit of happiness" requires that the government protect every man's right to keep and spend money that he has lawfully earned, to enable his "pursuit of happiness."

Third, the Constitution does not grant any power, jurisdiction, or authority to any branch of the government to discriminate for or against any group of citizens based upon their class, wealth, or any other factor. The Founding Fathers never discriminated for or against any group based on class or wealth.

Fourth: "That the Commonwealth may be a nation of laws, and not of men." These words, inscribed in very large letters on the full length of the north side of the main courthouse in Cincinnati, Ohio, clearly state one of the most important principles that our nation was founded upon. The United States is governed by laws that apply to all men equally. It is not governed by men who have the right or freedom to show favoritism to the rich, poor, middle class, or any other class or group of citizens.

Fifth, it is not ethical or legal for a poor man to put a gun to the head of a rich man and take his money. It is also not ethical for the government to do the same thing, to forcefully take lawfully earned money from a rich man and give it to a poor man. The end does not justify the means.

Sixth, Democrats falsely claim that they want equal opportunity for all Americans. They want discrimination based upon class. They falsely claim that the "rich" or "the wealthy few" are not paying their "fair share" of taxes; the opposite is true. They falsely imply that the "middle class" are paying more than their fair share of taxes; the opposite is true. They falsely imply that if the "rich" or "the wealthy few" pay their "fair share" of taxes, that the additional money taken from them can be used to restore equal opportunity to the "middle class" through government programs that give educational, healthcare, and other benefits.

Democrats continually want to keep raising taxes on the rich to enable transfer of their money to federal programs that create opportunities for the poor and middle class. Even when most of the poor and middle class pay no taxes and even when the rich pay a far greater percentage, it is never enough. No matter how little the poor and middle class pay and no matter how much the rich pay, to win votes Democrats will always promise to take money from the rich and give it to the poor and middle class. So Democrats vote for whoever promises them the most financial benefit in the form of government benefits. Basically, they are voting to have the government forcefully take money from "rich" Americans and give it to them.

RESTORING BASIC VALUES. Republicans would completely agree with the second sentence in the quote from the Democratic Platform, "restoring the basic values that made our country great, and restoring for everyone who works hard and plays by the rules" all the opportunities that they deserve. However, Republicans would say that this can only be achieved by treating all Americans equally under the law, by having no discrimination based on class, wealth, or any other factor. Democrats do not want the equality of opportunity that they claim they want. They want discrimination based upon class and economic standing. That is why they are always talking about class. Again, the federal government has absolutely no authority, jurisdiction, or power under God's law or the Constitution to discriminate in any way based upon class or economic standing. It has a duty to apply the law equally to all citizens.

One must choose between equality of opportunity and equality of results; it is impossible to strive for both at the same time. Republicans and Democrats are in total agreement that all Americans should have equality of opportunity. However, Democrats are being totally dishonest when they claim that they want equality of opportunity for all Americans. They want discrimination based upon class or economic standing to achieve equality of results. President Obama, talking about the rich, said, "You didn't earn that!" Democrats have the attitude that the rich do not deserve the money they have, even if it was earned lawfully by work or investments.

"Restoring the basic values that made our country great" would require going back to the government policies of a time when the federal government did not offer any educational, healthcare, or other financial benefits to citizens. Politicians were not able to buy votes with promises of money in the form of government benefits. Americans had to earn their own money, not look to the government for handouts. The size and role of the federal government was limited to the powers granted to it by the Constitution. Taxes were much lower overall, so more Americans were able to keep and spend more of their own money.

<u>LIES ABOUT REPUB LICANS</u>. The Democratic Platform contains many lies about the Republicans. It states:

> The Republican Party has turned its back on the
> middle-class Americans who built this country.
> Our opponents believe we should go back to the
> top-down economic policies of the last decade.
> They think that if we simply eliminate
> protections for families and consumers, let Wall
> Street write its own rules again, and cut taxes
> for the wealthiest, the market will solve all our
> problems on its own. They argue that if we help
> corporations and wealthy investors maximize
> their profits by whatever means necessary,

whether through layoffs or outsourcing, it will
automatically translate into jobs and prosperity
that benefits us all. They would repeal health
reform, turn Medicare into a voucher program,
and follow the same path of fiscal
irresponsibility of the past administration—
giving trillions of dollars in tax cuts weighted
towards millionaires and billionaires while
sticking the middle class with the bill. But
we've tried their policies—and we've all
suffered when they failed.[184]

It is not enough to go back to where the country
was before the crisis. We must rebuild a strong
foundation that ensures it never happens again.

First and foremost, every single statement about
Republicans in this section of the Democratic Platform is
absolutely false. The amazing magnitude of the dishonesty of
Democrats is proven by the words in this section.

Commentary on "Republican Party has turned its back
on the middle class" and going "back to the top-down
economic policies of the last decade back to the top-down
economic policies of the last decade." The Republican Party
never turned its back on the middle class. They never wanted
to "eliminate protections for families and consumers, let Wall
Street write its own rules again, and cut taxes for the
wealthiest." The exact opposite is true. Between 2008 and
2012 a Republican Congress increased the tax rates for the
"wealthiest" Americans from 35% to 39.6%. For countless
years, Republicans have joined forces with Democrats to

---

[184] "2012 Democratic Platform," page 2, https://www.democrats.org/party-platform, downloaded 2/2/2016.

establish tax rates and credits and deductions which greatly favor the poor and middle class. See chapter on Taxation for details.

No Democrat ever heard any Republican "argue that if we help corporations and wealthy investors maximize their profits by whatever means necessary, whether through layoffs or outsourcing, it will automatically translate into jobs and prosperity that benefits us all." No Republican ever said this. So why is the Democratic Platform filled with so many statements that are such blatant lies? The answer is simply that the lies are believed by voters.

Commentary on "repeal health form" and "turn Medicare into a voucher program." No Republican running for president has advocated turning Medicare into a voucher program." The federal government has absolutely no jurisdiction, power, or authority to implement a national healthcare program. See chapter on healthcare for detailed discussion. However, Americans have paid taxes to support Medicare and therefore deserve to receive the Medicare benefits that they paid for; therefore, both Republicans and Democrats want to keep and support Medicare.

Commentary on "follow the same path of fiscal irresponsibility of the past administration—giving trillions of dollars in tax cuts weighted towards millionaires and billionaires while sticking the middle class with the bill." Again, these statements are totally and absolutely false. The exact opposite is true. For countless years, Republicans have joined forces with Democrats to establish tax rates and credits and deductions which greatly favor the poor and middle class. A Republican Congress just increased the tax rates for the "wealthiest" Americans. See chapter on Taxation for details. The Democratic Platform keeps repeating these false accusations because they are key parts of the foundation of the Democratic Platform.

<u>EQUAL OPPORTUNITY FOR ALL AMERICANS</u>. The Democratic Platform goes on to state some noble objectives.

> Democrats know that America prospers when we're all in it together. We see an America where everyone has a fair shot, does their fair share, and plays by the same rules. We see an America that out-educates, out-builds, and out-innovates the rest of the world.

Republicans would be in full agreement with all of these statements. They agree that "America prospers when we're all in it together." They want " an America where everyone has a fair shot, does their fair share, and plays by the same rules…an America that out-educates, out-builds, and out-innovates the rest of the world." However, Democrats do not want an America where everyone "plays by the same rules." They want discrimination based upon class and wealth. Democrats do not want an America where everyone "does their fair share." They want to give government benefits to those who have not earned them, a transfer of money from those who have earned it lawfully to those who have not earned it.

<u>END NOT JUSTIFY MEANS</u>. The Democratic Platform states great goals for America, but the end does not justify the means.

We see an America with greater economic

security and opportunity, driven by education,
energy, innovation and infrastructure, and a tax
code that helps to create American jobs and
bring down the debt in a balanced way. We
believe in deficit reduction not by placing the
burden on the middle class and the poor, but by
cutting out programs we can't afford and asking
the wealthiest to again contribute their fair
share.[185]

Republicans would agree with everything in this
paragraph except the discrimination based upon wealth or
class. Consider the absolute absurdity, impossibility, and
extreme dishonesty of Democrats who in this passage say
they do not want to ask the poor or middle class to do
anything to help reduce the national deficit. They only want
the "wealthiest to again contribute their fair share." They also
say that they want to cut "programs we can't afford." But they
are the ones who always want more programs and bigger
programs to do a better job of caring for the poor and the
middle class. And at the same time that their platform states
that they want to cut programs to reduce the deficit, under
President Obama they have introduced Obamacare, one of the
most expensive programs in the history of the United States,
a program that will cost as much as the United States
remaining at war for the remainder of its history.

<u>DIFFERENT VISIONS</u>. The Democratic Platform
gives a very false impression of the different visions of
Republican and Democrats.

We Democrats offer America the opportunity to

---

[185] "2012 Democratic Platform," page 2, https://www.democrats.org/party-platform, downloaded 2/2/2016.

move our country forward by creating an economy built to last and built from the middle out. Mitt Romney and the Republican Party have a drastically different vision. They still believe the best way to grow the economy is from the top down—the same approach that benefited the wealthy few but crashed the economy and crushed the middle class."[186]

Again, every statement about Republicans is an absolute lie. The Republican Party does not want to "grow the economy from the top down." Republicans want grow the economy by ensuring equal opportunity for all Americans, by not discriminating against anyone on the basis of race, class, or anything else. Democrats want discrimination based upon economic class. That is why they are always talking class.

Democrats falsely imply that Republicans implemented policies that "benefited the wealthy few but crashed the economy and crushed the middle class." Republicans did not advance policies that "benefited the wealth few" and they did not advance any policies that crashed the economy or crushed the middle class. The primary reason that the economy crashed is that mortgages were given to so many people who should not have qualified and who then defaulted. The federal regulations that enabled less financially qualified individuals to obtain mortgages were signed into law by a Democrat, President Clinton, not President Bush.

2016 DEMOCRATIC PLATFORM. Quotes from the 2016 platform show that the same false statements and promises are being made in 2016. The 2016 Democratic

---

[186] "2012 Democratic Platform," page 2, https://www.democrats.org/party-platform, downloaded 2/2/2016.

Platform begins by citing the accomplishments of the Obama Administration. It falsely states that Republican policies triggered the Great Recession. Again, it was President Clinton, who simply wanted to make home ownership more affordable to more Americans who signed into law regulations which enabled many Americans who never should have qualified for home loans to get mortgages, which led to the economic crash.

> Under President Obama's leadership, and thanks to the hard work and determination of the American people, we have come a long way from the Great Recession and the Republican policies that triggered it. American businesses have now added 14.8 million jobs since private-sector job growth turned positive in early 2010. Twenty million people have gained health insurance coverage. The American auto industry just had its best year ever. And we are getting more of our energy from the sun and wind, and importing less oil from overseas.

The jobs figure fails to note the millions of Americans who are not part of the statistics because they have given up on looking for a job. The health insurance figures fail to consider the insurance companies refusing to continue with Obamacare because they have lost so much money with it (Aetna, etc.) or the simple fact that Constitution does not give any branch of the federal government any authority to institute a national healthcare system. See chapter on Healthcare (Obamacare). The comments about "getting more of our energy from the sun and wind" win votes dishonestly because there is no significant increase in use of energy from the sun or wind.

The next paragraph lists the many problems that "too many Americans" still have after 8 years under the leadership of President Obama.

> But too many Americans have been left out and left behind. They are working longer hours with less security. Wages have barely budged and the racial wealth gap remains wide, while the cost of everything from childcare to a college education has continued to rise. And for too many families, the dream of homeownership is out of reach. As working people struggle, the top one percent accrues more wealth and more power. Republicans in Congress have chosen gridlock and dysfunction over trying to find solutions to the real challenges we face. It's no wonder that so many feel like the system is rigged against them.

So why do so many Americans have so many problems after 8 years under President Obama? Why should Americans vote for Hillary Clinton if she will continue the policies of the Obama Administration? The Democratic Platform does not answer these questions or take any responsibility for the fact that "too many Americans have been left out and left behind." Instead, as always, it dishonestly blames the rich ("top one percent") and Republicans.

Totally contrary to the false claims of Democrats, Americans are not victims of the wealthy or Republicans. This entire book reveals the moral depravity of Democratic principles and policies, and shows that Republican principles and policies are much more in line with God's principles and laws embodied in scripture, the Declaration of Independence, the Constitution, and the Bill of Rights. Also, as stated in the chapter on Truth on Taxes, the top one percent already pays about 27% of all federal taxes, much more than their fair share. And about half of Americans, mostly middle class, do not pay any federal taxes, so they are the ones who do not pay their fair share for national defense, the roads they travel on, etc.

The next paragraph contains more false statements and again presents the same totally wrong, unethical, solution that Democrats always present i.e. taking more money from the rich and giving it to the middle class.

> We will <u>ensure those at the top contribute to our country's future by establishing a multimillionaire surtax to ensure millionaires and billionaires pay their fair share</u>. In addition, we will shut down the "private tax system" for those at the top, immediately close egregious loopholes like those enjoyed by hedge fund managers, restore fair taxation on multi-million-dollar estates, and ensure millionaires can no longer pay a lower rate than their secretaries. At a time of near-record corporate profits, slow wage growth, and rising costs, we need to offer <u>tax relief to middle-class families—not those at the top.</u>

First, the next president cannot lawfully and will not establish "a multimillionaire surtax" to force the wealthy to pay higher taxes. That is a lie designed to win votes. Also, there is no "private tax system" for those at the top. That is another lie designed to win votes. Every statement in this paragraph is a lie designed to win votes. Also, note that after eight years of having President Obama in office, Democrats are still trying to win votes with the same false promise of "tax relief to the middle-class families—not those at the top" based upon the same false claim that the rich are not paying their fair share of taxes and the middle class are paying more than their fair share.

> We will offer tax relief to hard working,
> middle-class families for the cost squeeze they
> have faced for years from rising health care,
> childcare, education, and other expenses.
> Donald Trump and the Republican Party would
> do the opposite and provide trillions in tax cuts
> for millionaires, billionaires, and corporations at
> the expense of working families, seniors, and
> the health of our economy.

Again, Democrats make the same totally false statements about Republicans, claiming that they want to give millions in tax cuts to the rich at the expense of "working families and seniors. That is totally false. They repeat the same lies because they work, because they win votes.

CONCLUSION. Now consider how Democrats try to win votes. Consider the absolute impossibility of paying for the long list of government benefits that they promise. They promise to "everyone who works hard and plays by the rules the opportunity to find a job that pays the bills, turn an idea into a profitable business, care for your family, afford a home you call your own and health care you can count on, retire with dignity and respect, and, most of all, give your children the kind of education that allows them to dream even bigger and go even further than you ever imagined." They promise tuition-free college, healthcare for all Americans, Social

Security, Medicaid and/or Medicare, etc. They promise to provide all these benefits and to reduce the national deficit by only raising taxes on the "wealthy few."

In other words, Democrats promise to provide the majority of Americans with a very long list of extremely costly benefits and reduce the deficit without any cost to the vast majority of Americans, by only making the wealthiest pay their "fair share." Again, the claim that the wealthy few are not paying their fair share of taxes is an absolute lie. The opposite is true; they pay more than their fair share. Democrats falsely imply that the "middle class" are paying more than their fair share of taxes. Again, the opposite is true; many pay absolutely no federal taxes. See chapter on Taxes.

CHAPTER 12.0

CONCLUSION

<u>INTRODUCTION</u>. Trump or Biden--how would Christ vote? This chapter answers this question in sections. The first reviews voter guidance from Christian organizations (Chapter 2). The second discusses basic principles of living and voting Christian values (Chapter 3). The third addresses the current spiritual battle i.e. war on Trump, Democratic National Convention, Republican National Convention (Chapters 4-6).

The fourth addresses voting for the Supreme Court, because Supreme Court justices serve for life (Chapter 7). The fifth discusses the Covid-19 global epidemic. The sixth discusses jobs, the economy, and taxes because they are issues that dramatically affect every American and because the global epidemic so greatly impacted jobs and the economy (Chapters 7, 8, 11). Ideally all Americans would care more about whoever and whatever best served God and country, not their own finances, but that simply does not happen.

The seventh section addresses racism, because the death of George Floyd and others made it the hottest political issue of 2020 (Chapter 7). The eighth discusses other important issues of the 2020 election: national defense, law and order, healthcare, education, immigration, and the environment (Chapter 7).

The final sections discuss issues which should be of the greatest concern to Christians. The nineth discusses scripture on the Biblical role of government, abortion, homosexuality and same-sex marriage (Chapter 8). The tenth reviews principles embodied in the Declaration of Independence, Constitution, and Bill of Rights (Chapter 9). The eleventh addresses freedoms and rights (Chapters 7 and 10). The twelfth discusses issues related to truth (Chapter 11). The conclusion presents final findings and recommendations.

CONGRESSIONAL SCORECARDS OF CHRISTIAN ORGANIZATIONS. Voting with Congressional Scorecards produced by Christian organizations requires voting Republican. Democrats score amazingly low for voting Christian values on (1) Congressional Scorecard produced by National Right to Life and (2) Congressional Scorecard jointly produced by Family Research Council and Family Alliance. Most Republicans scored 100%. Most Democrats scored 0%. Trump did not serve in Congress, so he was not rated. Senators Obama, Biden, and Clinton all scored zero on both scorecards. They voted against Christian values every time they voted on family-related issues.

2020 PARTY PLATFORM COMPARISON. Voting with Christian voter guidance requires voting Republican. See Party Platform Comparison 2020 published by FRC Action (Family Research Council Action). Republicans support Christian values on all issues. Democrats oppose Christian values on all issues.

LIVING AND VOTING CHRISTIAN VALUES. First, Christians should realize that this election is first and foremost a spiritual battle, not a political battle. "We wrestle not against flesh and blood, but against principalities, against powers" (Eph. 6:12). Second, Christians should understand that politics is faith in action, and being a Christian requires living and voting Christian values, because "faith without works is dead" (James 2:20; 2:26, KJV). Third, Christians should realize that

God's ways are higher than man's ways, and voting Christian values requires voting biblical principles embodied in Scripture, the Declaration of Independence, the Constitution, and the Bill of Rights. As Christ said, "Ye do err, not knowing the Scriptures, nor the power of God" (Matt. 22:28-30, KJV).

THE AMERICAN CIVIL WAR OF THE 2020s. All Americans should realize that the current battle between Republicans and Democrats is, like the American Civil War of the 1860's, first and foremost a spiritual battle, not a political battle. Every Confederate soldier fought against the God who created all men equal. There has been an intense, unrelenting, full-time war against President Trump waged by Democrats and the media. Virtually every news program and political talk show attacks Trump. At this time, during September 2020, major television networks are conducting interviews with authors who have written books against Trump, but not with authors who have written books supporting Trump.

Democratic National Convention did not concentrate on their vision for America or Biden's accomplishments during 47 years in Washington, D.C. The Associated Press stated, "There has been one persistent theme in the Democratic National Convention...to portray President Donald Trump in highly personal ways as one unsuited for the White House both in skills and temperament. And no one, not even former President Barack Obama, has been holding back."[187]

Many speakers at the Republican Convention, in total contrast to those at the Democratic National Convention, talked about President Trump's incredibly long list of accomplishments. Five black Americans spoke and explained

[187] "Democratic Convention Takeaways: Make History, Pound Trump," Associated Press, August 19, 2020.

how Trump had done more for black Americans in 4 years
than Biden had in 47 years. Many speakers also spoke about
their vision for America and the policies needed to help
Americans realize the American dream. The remainder of this
chapter discusses issues related to this election.

SUPREME COURT. Voting for the Supreme Court
requires voting Republican. The president appoints Supreme
Court justices who serve for life. Trump and Republicans
support Supreme Court Justices who uphold the Constitution.
Biden and Democrats support Supreme Court justices who,
contrary to the Constitution, give the federal government
authority to grant healthcare, education, and other benefits not
mentioned or authorized by the Constitution. See chapters on
Supreme Court, Constitution, Healthcare, and Education.

GLOBAL PANDEMIC (COVID-19): No Christian
should vote based on anything related to the 2020 Covid-19
global pandemic. Christians should vote based on Christian
values they have before and after the global pandemic. No
American should believe the lies that Democrats always tell
about Republicans not caring about their fellow Americans.

Democrats claim that President Trump does not care
about Americans and that he failed to do everything possible to
save American lives. That is an absolute lie. Trump listed his
actions to combat Covid-19 as follows: (1) When Covid-19
virus hit, launched largest national mobilization since World
War II, invoking Defense Production Act, and produced
world's largest supply of ventilators. No American has been
denied a ventilator. (2) Shipped hundreds of millions of masks,
gloves and gowns to front line healthcare workers. (3) Rushed
supplies, testing kits, and personnel to nursing homes and
long-term care facilities. (4) Had Army Corps of Engineers

build field hospitals and Navy deploy hospital ships. (5) Developed largest, most advanced testing system in the world. America has tested more than all Europe and more than every nation in the Western Hemisphere combined. (6) Developed a wide array of effective treatments, including a powerful antibody treatment known as Convalescent Plasma that will save thousands of lives. (7) Reduced fatality rate by 80 percent since April. The European Union's fatality rate is nearly three times higher. See chapter on Global Pandemic (Covid-19).

<u>JOBS AND ECONOMY</u>. <u>Voting for jobs and the economy requires voting for Trump</u>. Trump is infinitely more qualified to deal with jobs and the economy than Joe Biden. Under President Trump, **markets hit record highs and unemployment hit record lows for black Americans, Hispanics, and all other Americans**. All that changed when the United States got hit by the global pandemic of Covid-19, which devasted the economies of many nations. Under President Trump, jobs and the economy can recover infinitely better than under Biden.

Trump's accomplishments related to jobs and the economy are as follows: (1) Produced best unemployment numbers ever recorded for African-Americans, Hispanic-Americans, and Asian-Americans. (2) Built strongest economy in the history of the world. (3) Passed record-setting tax and regulation cuts. (4) Achieved, for first time, American Energy Independence. (5) Approved Keystone XL and Dakota Access Pipelines. (6) Withdrew from job-killing Trans Pacific Partnership. (7) Ended the NAFTA nightmare and signed new U.S. Mexico Canada Agreement. (8) Took toughest, boldest, strongest, hardest hitting action against China in American history. (9) Ended unfair and costly Paris Climate Accord. See chapter on Jobs and the Economy.

One of Trump's sons said, "<u>My father only sees green</u>." In other words, <u>Trump is a businessman who thinks first and foremost about jobs and the economy for ALL Americans</u>. Many black Americans think first and foremost about race, and vote based on race. Christians should think first and foremost about God, and vote to love God more than man.

<u>TAXES</u>. <u>Voting for lower taxes requires voting Republican</u>. President Trump reduced taxes for most Americans. That is one reason markets hit record highs and unemployment hit record lows for black Americans, Hispanics, and all other Americans. <u>Biden will raise taxes by 4.3 trillion dollars, which may devastate the U.S. economy</u>. Democrats always say that they will only raise taxes on the wealthy, but that is never true. Biden will raise income taxes, capital gains taxes, corporate taxes, etc. See chapter Taxes for more facts.

Biden, Obama, Clinton, and Democrats tell many of their biggest lies about taxes, and the media never corrects them. They always claim that the "rich" or "wealthy few" are not paying their fair share of taxes and should be taxed more to support the overtaxed "middle class." That is totally false.

<u>All Americans can quickly verify the truth about taxes by taking a few minutes to go to www.cbo.gov (Congressional Budget Office)</u>, click on Taxes or Income Distribution and read the very short article entitled "The Distribution of Household Income and Federal Taxes, 2013" dated June 8, 2016. [188] <u>In 2013, the top 20% of Americans earned 53% of the income and paid 69% of federal taxes. The bottom 20% earned</u>

---

[188] Go to <u>www.cbo.gov</u> (Congressional Budget Office website), click on Taxes or Income Distribution and read article entitled "The Distribution of Household Income and Federal Taxes, 2013" dated June 8, 2016.

5% of income and paid only 1% of federal taxes. The middle 20% earned 14% of income and paid only 9% of federal taxes. Another article in the same area shows that figures for 2011 were almost exactly the same.

Americans can also go to www.irs.gov and search for 2019 Instructions for Form 1040. Go to Tax Tables. Federal income tax rates range from 10% for the lowest income group to 37% for the highest income group. However, actual tax rates are actually much lower for the poor and middle class due to countless tax deductions and credits that benefit the poor and middle class but are phased out for the wealthy. The end result is that about 49% of Americans, mostly lower and middle class, pay no federal income tax, the rich pay more than their fair share, and the most vilified top 1% pay about 27% of all federal taxes. Democrats will never quote these facts, because they want to win votes with lies and deception. See chapter Taxes for more facts.

SCRIPTURE ON TAXES. Voting for God's ideal on taxes requires voting Republican. What is God's ideal for taxes for the rich and the poor? God's "tax rate" for tithes is exactly the same rate for the rich and the poor: 10% (Lev. 27:30-32). See Deut. 12:5-11; 14:22-28; Num. 18:24-28; Mal. 3:8-10; Heb. 7:1-4. In 1 Sam. 8:8-20, God warned Israel that a king would charge exactly the same for the rich and the poor: 10%. No verse in the 66 books of the Bible even suggests charging higher tax rates for the rich.

Republicans and Democrats both agree on charging higher tax rates for the wealthy. Why then does God not advocate higher tax rates for the rich? No poor man has any legal or moral right to put a gun to the head of a rich man and demand his money. That is theft. The same principle applies to government. Governments do not have authority to take by force lawfully earned income from one person and give it to another. That is theft by government, and that is what the Democrats strongly advocate in every election. They win votes by promising government benefits not paid for by the poor or middle class, but only by "the rich."

RACISM, REPUBLICANS, AND TRUMP: Many Democrats and black Americans believe that most Republicans are racist. That is a lie. Republicans have ALWAYS strongly opposed all racism. It was Republicans, under President Abraham Lincoln, who fought the American Civil War, freed the slaves, and gave them the right to vote. Most of the 640,000 to 700,000 men who died in the Civil War were white Union soldiers fighting against slavery.[189] It was Democrats who formed the KKK, lynched countless black men, and killed white Republicans who opposed slavery.[190] Today over 90% of black Americans are Democrats. They vote with Confederate officers who formed the KKK and with Edmund Pettus, a Confederate general, Grand Dragon of the KKK, Democratic Senator, and the man after whom bridge at Selma is named.

Five black men spoke at the Republican National Convention. Herschel Walker, a top NFL football player and winner of the Heisman Trophy, said, "It hurt my soul to hear the terrible names that people called Donald. The worst one is racist... I take it as a personal insult that people would think I've had a 37-year friendship with a racist."[191] He ended by

---

[189] "Casualties Numbers and Battle Death Statistics For the American Civil War," www.historynet.com, downloaded June 3, 2020.

[190] "Ku Klux Klan," www.history.com, October 29, 2009; updated February 21, 2020; downloaded August 8, 2020. "Ku Klux Klan," www.wikipedia.com, downloaded June 4, 2020.

[191] "Herschel Walker Defends Trump in Passionate Speech... He's Not A

saying, "If you love America and want to make it better, Donald Trump is your president."[192]

Daniel Cameron, the first black Attorney General of Kentucky, said, "I also think about Joe Biden, who says, if you aren't voting for me, 'you ain't black.' Who argued that Republicans would put us 'back in chains.' Who says there is no 'diversity' of thought in the Black community? Mr. Vice President look at me, I am Black. We are not all the same, sir. I am not in chains. My mind is my own. And you can't tell me how to vote because of the color of my skin."[193] He said, "Joe Biden would destroy jobs, raise our taxes, and throw away the lives of countless unborn children. And he is captive to the radical left..."[194]

Clarence Henderson, civil rights activist and military veteran, said, "Joe Biden said if you don't vote for him you ain't black. If you vote for him, you don't know history.... It was the Republican Party that passed the 13th Amendment abolishing slavery; it was the Republican Party that passed the 14th Amendment giving black men citizenship; and it was the Republican Party that passed the 15th Amendment giving Black men the right to vote."[195] He said Trump gave "record funding to HBCUs (Historically Black Colleges)... created a record amount of jobs for the black community, and passed criminal justice reform... where 91 percent of the inmates released were black."[196] He ended by saying, "Donald Trump

Racist!!!," TMZ Sports, www.tmz.com, 8/25/2020.

[192] Ibid.

[193] "Daniel Cameron, Kentucky A.G., Speaks at the R.N.C.: Full Transcript," Maggie Astor, August 25, 2020.

[194] Ibid.

[195] "Civil Rights Leader Clarence Henderson: If You Vote for Biden 'You Don't Know History'," Katherine Rodriguez, www.Breitbart.com, 26 Aug 2020.

truly cares about black lives.... He has done more for black Americans in four years than Joe Biden has done in 50!"[197]

Senator Tim Scott, a black Republican senator from South Carolina, said, "Joe Biden said if a black man didn't vote for him, he wasn't truly black. Joe Biden said black people are a monolithic community. Joe Biden said poor kids can be just as smart as white kids. And while his words are one thing, his actions take it to a whole new level."[198] He then explained how Biden failed black Americans, but how Trump had done so much for them. See chapter on Republican National Convention for his long but eloquent speech.

Ja'Ron Smith, assistant to the president, said, "In the wake of the murder of Ahmaud Arbery, George Floyd, and LeGend Taliferro.... I have seen his true conscience. I just wish everyone could see the deep empathy he shows to families whose loved ones were killed in senseless violence."[199]

<u>RACISM AND POLICE</u>. The murder of George Floyd by police in Minneapolis in 2020 <u>RIGHTFULLY</u> provoked national and international outrage. Black lives matter. All lives matter equally because God creates all men equal. Statements by black Democrats give the false impression that countless unarmed black men are killed by police every year. See chapter on Racism for quotes by Senator Kamala Harris, Senator Cory Booker, Floyd family attorney, etc.

---

[196] Ibid.

[197] Ibid.

[198] "Republican Senator for South Carolina Tim Scott Speaks During the First Day of the Republican Convention at the Mellon Auditorium in Washington on Aug. 24, 2020." NBC News, updated Aug. 25, 2020.

[199] "Ja'Ron Smith, One of the Top Black Officials in the White House, Touts Trump's Empathy," Dartunorro Clark, NBC News, August 28, 2020.

Of the 1,004 people killed by police in 2019, only 19 were unarmed whites, and only 9 were unarmed blacks. About 18.5 policemen are killed for every unarmed black man killed by police. Black men are only 6% to 7% of the U.S. population, but black men kill about 40% of all policemen killed in the line of duty. In 2018 there were 7,407 black homicide victims.[200] Most were black men killed by black men, not by police. You will not hear these facts on the news, because it is a politically incorrect message not helpful to Democrats or the media, especially during a presidential election. See chapter on Racism for additional facts.

Democrats, like white supremacists, use racism to gain advantage over their political opponents. Senator Harris surged in the polls when she accused Biden of racism. Biden chose Senator Harris to be his Vice-President to win the votes of black Americans, women, and other Democrats. President Obama used the funeral of Congressman John Lewis to mobilize voters. Rev. Al Sharpton used the funeral of George Floyd and is now using the mothers of black men killed by police to mobilize voters.

NATIONAL SECURITY. Voting for national security requires voting Republican. Democrats, cannot be trusted to make national security or funding of the armed forces of the United States their top priority. Their top priority is taking care of Americans through costly, totally unconstitutional social programs outlined in the Democratic Platform (education, healthcare, etc.). Only Trump can be trusted to make national defense his top priority, to maintain military strength, and to

---

[200] C. Douglas Golden, "Tucker Carlson Does the Math on Police Shootings, Says This Is 'Not Even Close to Genocide'," The Western Journal, June 5, 2020.

properly defend Americans from all enemies, foreign and domestic. See chapter on National Security.

President Trump's national defense accomplishments include the following: (1) Spent $2.5 trillion on completely rebuilding military, which was badly depleted. (2) Gave 3 pay raises to our warriors. (3) Passed VA Accountability and VA Choice. (4) Obliterated ISIS Caliphate and killed its leader Abu Bakr al-Baghdadi. (5) Eliminated world's number one terrorist, Iranian General Qasem Soleimani (responsible for killing/wounding hundreds of American soldiers with Iranian-made Improvised Explosive Devices, etc.). (6) Kept America out of new wars, and troops are coming home. (7) Launched Space Force, first new branch of United States military since Air Force was created 75 years ago. (8) Got NATO partners to pay $130 billion more per year. (9) Achieved first Middle East peace deal in 25 years. (10) Recognized Israel's true capital, and moved our Embassy to Jerusalem for less than $500,000. (11) Recognized Israeli sovereignty over Golan Heights. (12) Withdrew from terrible, one-sided Iran Nuclear Deal. See chapter on National Defense.

LAW AND ORDER. All Americans should support peaceful protests but condemn the violence, rioting, looting, attacks on police, and destruction of buildings and police cars by lawless, violent protestors.

The entire chapter entitled The War on President Trump describes the intense, unrelenting, full-time, lawless war against President Trump waged by Democrats and the media. Scripture states that the law is a good thing, if used lawfully. Democrats have used the law unlawfully in many ways to try to get rid of President Trump and to block his nomination of Justice Kavanagh.

Scripture states that government officials are ministers of God. This entire book shows that President Trump is fighting to uphold laws and principles embodied in Scripture, the Declaration of Independence, the Constitution, and the Bill of Rights. Democrats and the media are waging war against God and the laws and principles that this nation was founded upon.

EDUCATION AND HEALTHCARE. Voting against totally unconstitutional federal education and healthcare benefits requires voting Republican. No part of Scripture or the Constitution gives the federal government authority to provide education or healthcare benefits to Americans. Congress cannot ethically or legally forcefully take money from one American to pay the education or healthcare bills of another American. See chapters on Education, Healthcare, Constitution, and Bill of Rights.

IMMIGRATION. Voting for legal immigration and against illegal immigration requires voting for Trump. Americans who want more protection from immigration of terrorists, illegal drug traffic, and illegal immigration should vote for Trump. Americans who want fewer restrictions on immigration and legalization of millions of illegal immigrants should vote for Biden.

President Trump's accomplishments related to borders and immigration are as follows: (1) Secured America's borders more than ever before. (2) Built 300 miles of border wall, are adding 10 miles/week, and will soon be complete. (3) Ended catch-and-release; stopped asylum fraud. (4) Took down human traffickers who prey on women and children. (5) Deported 20,000 gang members and 500,000 criminal aliens. See chapter on Immigration.

ENVIRONMENT. Any American who chooses to vote with Democrats because of concerns about the environment or climate change is choosing to serve "the creature more than the Creator" (see Rom. 1). Americans should not be deceived by dishonest election arguments about using renewable energy sources. After 8 years in office, President Obama did virtually nothing to change the energy usage of Americans. See chapter on Environment.

BIBLICAL ROLE OF GOVERNMENT. Voting for God's ideal for government requires voting Republican. Democrats believe that God's ideal is government that does more to care for its citizens. That is why President Obama said, "I believe that I am my brother's keeper!" and why he instituted national healthcare (Obamacare). That is why Biden and Clinton offered generous healthcare and education benefits which never could be afforded by taxpayers. But scripture shows that God's ideal is NOT government that does more to care for its people. 1 Samuel 8:8-20 shows that God wants his people to look to Him not government for their provision. He warned the Israelites how much a king would take from them (10%). Today Americans pay far more than 10% through many taxes (federal, state, and local income taxes, sales tax, fuel tax, real estate tax, etc.).

The founding fathers understood God's ideal, embodied in the Constitution, of smaller government, lower taxes, and greater personal freedom and responsibility for all citizens. They were fiercely independent men who greatly treasured their freedom and would not trade it for government benefits. The purpose of government is not to provide or care for citizens, but to protect life and liberty and thereby enable the pursuit of happiness. See chapters on Truth About Taxes and Biblical Role of Government.

HOMOSEXUALITY AND SAME-SEX MARRIAGE. Voting God's will on homosexuality and same-sex marriage means voting Republican. Scripture teaches that they are extreme perversions of God's design for man, woman, and marriage (Gen. 2:18-24; Lev. 18:22-26; 20:13-16; 1 Tim. 1:9-10; 1 Cor. 6:9-10; Rom. 1:16-32). Election of Democrats will continue to result in laws that promote homosexuality and same-sex marriage, which are so destructive to families, the most basic, fundamental unit of society and the backbone of our nation.

ABORTION. Voting God's will on abortion means voting Republican. Most Democrats are pro-choice. Most Republicans are pro-life. Scripture shows that in the eyes of God, abortion is murder. See Gen. 16:11; 17:10,12,14; 19:36; 38:24,25; Ex. 21:22-23; 22:22; Lev. 12:2,5; 1 Sam. 4:19; 2 Sam. 11:5; 2Kin. 8:12; 15:16; Isa. 26:17,18; 49:15; 54:1; Jer. 31:8; Hos. 13:16; Am. 1:13; Luke 2:12,16; 18:15-16, Ps. 139:13-16; Job 31:15; Is. 44:2; 44:24: 49:5; Jer. 1:5. See chapter on Abortion.

Most Americans fail to grasp the primary abortion-related issue, which is who pays for abortions. Pro-choice Democrats want to force Americans who consider abortion to be murder to pay for abortions. They only support the choices of those who agree with them. That is the ultimate in hypocrisy. The Constitution does not give the federal government authority to order any American to pay for abortions of other Americans. It is illegal and unethical to force any American to violate their deeply held moral or religious beliefs by paying for abortions.

Biden would continue the pro-abortion policies of President Obama, who used executive orders to divert funds to national and international pro-abortion groups. He refused to cut federal funds (taxpayer dollars) to Planned Parenthood, the nation's number one abortion provider. When several states cut state funds to Planned Parenthood, President Obama funded it with millions in U.S. taxpayer dollars.

DECLARATION OF INDEPENDENCE. The Declaration of Independence shows that the United States was founded upon belief that: (1) God created all things seen and unseen and all laws that govern all things seen and unseen; (2) God creates all men equal with "certain unalienable Rights…[that include] Life, Liberty and the pursuit of Happiness;" (3) "to secure these rights, Governments are instituted among Men, deriving their just powers from the consent of the governed;" (4) "whenever any…Government becomes destructive of these ends, it is the Right of the People to alter or to abolish it, and to institute new Government;" and (5) this new government must be established in accordance with God's laws to protect these God-given rights.[201]

Voting with and for the Declaration of Independence requires voting Republican. Most Americans who reject the most important principles that the United States was founded upon are Democrats, not Republicans. Most Americans who do not believe in God and creation are Democrats. Most Americans who reject the laws that God created to govern men and governments are Democrats. Any American who votes for any Democrat joins forces with these ungodly fools who reject God and His laws. Also, Republicans better support the rights

---

[201] Ibid.

to life, liberty, the pursuit of happiness, and the right to bear arms. See chapter on Declaration of Independence.

CONSTITUTION. <u>Voting for the Constitution requires voting Republican</u>. The primary purpose of the Constitution is to define and limit the powers of each branch of the federal government. The government of the United States is a government of enumerated powers. Each branch only has those powers granted to it by the Constitution. All other powers are reserved to the states and to the people. Article I grants powers to Congress (Senate and House of Representatives). Article II grants powers to the executive branch (President). Article III grants powers to the judicial branch (Supreme Court and federal courts). No part of the Constitution grants any branch responsibility or authority for healthcare or education or to care for the poor or the middle class. Democrats reject the limits of power imposed on the federal government by the Constitution. See chapters on Constitution, Truth on Taxes, Democratic Platform, etc.

BILL OF RIGHTS. <u>Voting with and for the Bill of Rights requires voting Republican</u>. The Bill of Rights, the first ten amendments to the Constitution, grants all Americans the rights of freedom of religion, freedom of speech, right to bear arms, right to a criminal defense attorney, etc. The ninth amendment protects other rights of the people. The tenth amendment states that the federal government only has those powers granted to it by the Constitution, and that all other powers are reserved to the people and the states. No part of the Bill of Rights grants any American any right to education, healthcare, or any other social or economic benefits paid for by other Americans.

JURISDICTION OF CHURCH AND STATE. Voting for proper jurisdiction of church and state requires voting Republican. Today most Americans, to include most lawyers and judges, have a totally wrong understanding of the jurisdiction of church and state and the self-evident common-sense truths our nation was founded upon. They exclude God, creation, and God's laws from politics, government, schools, and the workplace. They fail to recognize that the United States government was founded upon belief in God and creation, and that all Americans have a duty to properly acknowledge God in politics, government, schools, and the workplace in the same way that our nation's Founding Fathers acknowledged Him and asked for his guidance and blessing.

FREEDOM OF SPEECH AND FREEDOM OF RELIGION. Voting for freedom of speech and freedom of religion requires voting Republican. No group of Americans has more restrictions on its freedom of speech and freedom of religion than Christians. Democrats have tried to silence Christians, to eliminate their competition during elections. A law called the LBJ law, because President Lyndon Baines Johnson pushed it through to silence his critics, threatens a church with loss of tax-exempt status if it endorses a candidate. During 2008, Democrats tried to enact legislation to silence conservative talk shows.

No President did more to rob Christians of freedom of religion than President Obama. See chapter on Freedom of Speech and Freedom of Religion for details. If Biden is elected and Democrats have a majority in the House and Senate, Congress will enact laws to further restrict the freedom of speech and freedom of religion of Christians.

RIGHT TO BEAR ARMS AND GUN CONTROL.
Voting for the right to bear arms requires voting Republican.
The Declaration of Independence and Second Amendment
provide justification for the right to bear arms not for hunting
or self-defense, but for defense of good government or
overthrow of an abusive government that denies the God-given
rights of life, liberty, and the pursuit of happiness. Thus, both
provide justification for the ownership of military style
weapons needed for defense or overthrow of a government.

As an Army officer, I fired and qualified many times on
the .45 caliber pistol, 9mm pistol, and M-16 rifle, and fired
many other weapons. The only weapons used in the deadliest
school shooting in the United States were semi-automatic
pistols. They may be more deadly than rifles because they are
smaller, easier to conceal, quicker to aim and reload, and hold
many rounds. Millions of Americans own assault rifles.
Instituting a ban on assault rifles could result in greater use of
semi-automatic pistols, which may be even more deadly in
school shootings. However, Republicans and Democrats
should agree to reasonable background checks and reasonable
restrictions on who should be denied the right to bear arms.
See chapter on Gun Control.

LIES AND DECEPTION. Voting against lies and
deception means voting Republican. It is absolutely amazing
how much politicians use lies and deception to win votes.
However, a Republican who uses lies to win votes is a fool
who does not realize that the truth is on his side. On the other
hand, lies are an essential part of the political philosophy and
political arguments of Democrats. The entire chapter on False
Claims of Politicians presents an amazing alphabetical list of
false claims made by Democrats. These include lies about the
Declaration of Independence, Constitution, the role of

government, separation of church and state, supreme court, education, healthcare, abortion, homosexuality, same-sex marriage, right to bear arms, taxes, etc.

The Democratic Platform is founded upon lies. If you remove the lies, the Democratic Platform collapses. One of biggest lies is that so many Americans can enjoy so many government benefits without paying for them (healthcare, welfare, education, Social Security, Medicare, abortions, etc.). Democrats buy votes by promising "free" benefits to Americans paid for by other Americans. This gives them great political advantage. It is impossible to pay for all the totally unconstitutional education and healthcare benefits promised by Biden and other Democrats by just raising taxes on the rich, who already pay more than their share of taxes. See chapters on Democratic Platform and Taxes.

Why do so many Americans reward dishonest politicians with their support? How is it possible that so many Americans believe all the lies and deception and vote for whoever promises the greatest financial benefit? Why do they not care about what best serves God or the nation? The challenge for Christians is to see through all the lies and false promises and to discern how to vote Christian values.

CONCLUSION. The American Civil War of the 1860's was first and foremost a spiritual battle, not a political battle. Every Confederate soldier fought against the God who created all men equal. The American Civil War of the 2020's is a spiritual battle. Every vote is for or against the God who created the laws that govern men and governments.

Fear of God is the beginning of wisdom (Pr. 9:10; Ps. 111:10. See Job 28:28; Pr. 1:7; 15:33). Why did Confederate soldiers not fear the God who created all men equal? Why do Americans who support abortion and same-sex marriage not fear the wrath of the holy God who created man, woman, and marriage? And why do Americans put more faith in man and government than God, and want to trade their freedom as Americans for greater dependence on government? The answer is spiritual blindness. Romans 1 states that God gives those who fail to acknowledge Him over to vain thinking.

After committing adultery and murder, King David, the only man called a man after God's heart, said, "I have sinned against the Lord" (2 Sam. 12:13, KJV). He understood that every thought, word, and action is first and foremost for or against the God who created and sustains all life. He understood that His first and foremost duty was not to love his fellow man, but to love God with all his heart, mind, soul, and strength (Deut. 6:5; Matt. 22:37-40; Luke 10:27).

Americans should respect and fear God, not man, place their trust in God not man, and vote for men who will govern in obedience to His commandments. Christians should seek better understanding of God's laws, and follow Christ, living and voting in obedience to "the will of [the] Father." They should reach out to others, to lead them from darkness to light, from death to life, and challenge them to live and vote Christian values.

All this is done in vain if it is reluctant, sacrificial obedience to God's will. God is God in all areas of our lives, and we answer to Him for all of our thoughts, words, and actions. However, what God really wants is not reluctant obedience to His commandments but a heart to heart loving relationship with each man, woman, and child. The God who created every atom in every universe has chosen to need our love and devotion. Life apart from God is devoid of meaning. In Him we live and move and have our being.

Trump or Biden—how would Christ vote? This book shows that <u>voting with Christ requires voting Republican and voting for President Trump</u>. It is absolutely amazing how much Democrats are united in voting against Christian values. Democrats strongly align themselves against God and His laws in virtually all areas: freedom of speech, freedom of religion, biblical role of government, taxes, federal spending, appointment of judges, abortion, marriage, etc.

<u>Any vote for any Democrat is a vote against scripture, the Declaration of Independence, the Constitution, and the Bill of Rights</u>. No Christian should vote for any Democrat, not even pro-life Democrats. When Democrats control the House or the Senate, they block legislation based on God's laws. When Democrats have a majority in the Senate, they chair the Senate Judiciary Committee and block any pro-life Christian judges from becoming federal judges or Supreme Court Justices. Empowering Democrats enables them to defeat attempts by Christians to return our nation to the Christian principles upon which it was founded.

All Americans answer to God, not man, for everything done to ensure the election of men and women who will govern in accordance with God's laws. Every Christian has a duty to vote for the candidates who will best serve God. Failure to vote for the lesser of evils ensures election of the most evil. Contrary to popular opinion, the most loving thing to do is not to remain silent, be tolerant, avoid divisive issues or avoid being critical or judgmental, but to forcefully and emphatically challenge Christians to love and serve God in greater obedience to the laws and principles that God has revealed through Scripture.

President John F. Kennedy challenged Americans to a higher calling: "Think not what your country can do for you, but what you can do for your country." A much higher calling is: "Think not what God can do for you, but what you can do for God." The highest calling is the Greatest Commandment: "Thou shalt love the Lord thy God with all thy heart, and with all thy soul, and with all thy mind" (Deut. 6:5; Matt. 22:37-40; Luke 10:27). Every man, woman, and child is called by God to daily put on the full armor of God and to do battle for the Lord and to be salt and light in all areas of life, to include politics, law, and government. Jesus said, "I am come that they might have life, and that they might have it more abundantly" (John 10:11, KJV). This abundant life is only possible if one dies to self and lives for Christ.

BIBLIOGRAPHY

"2012 Democratic Platform." https://www.democrats.org/party-platform, accessed 2/2/2016.

"2015 Tax Rate Schedules." 2015 Internal Revenue Service Form 1040 Instructions, www.IRS.gov.

"2016 Democratic Platform." https://www.demconvention.com/ platform, accessed 8/19/2016.

"2016 Values Voter Presidential Voter Guide." Family Research Council Action, http://www.FRCAction.org, accessed June, 2016.

"2019 Tax Tables." 2019 Internal Revenue Service Form 1040 Instructions, www.IRS.gov.

"Abraham Lincoln Quotes." Thinkexist, http://thinkexist.com /quotes /abraham.lincoln. April 13, 2012.

"Apostles' Creed." Catechism of the Catholic Church. Wikipedia.org., http://en.wikipedia.org/ wiki/Apostles%27_Creed.

Astor, Maggie. "Daniel Cameron, Kentucky A.G., Speaks at the R.N.C.: Full Transcript." August 25, 2020.

Balkin, Karen, Ed. The War on Terrorism: Opposing Viewpoints. New York: Thomson Gale, 2005.

Barrasso, John. "President Trump is Right to Get Us Out of the Bad Paris Climate Accord: Senator Barrasso." USA Today. November 5, 2019.

Barton, David. The Bible, Voters & the 2008 Election. Aledo, Texas: Wallbuilder Press, 2008.

Bethany Monk. "Same-Sex Marriage to Become Plank in DNC Platform." Citizenlink, http://www.citizenlink.com, July 31, 2012.

"Bill of Rights." U.S. National Archives & Records Administration, http://www.archives.gov/ exhibits/charters/constitution.html.

Black, Henry Campbell. Black's Law Dictionary, 5th Ed., 1979, p 766.

Blakely, Jonathan. "One Top GOP Line of Attack: Kagan's Opposition to Military Recruitment at Harvard Law School's Office of Career Services." ABC News, http://abcnews.go.com/blogs/politics/2010/05/one-top-gop-line-of-attack-kagans-opposition-to-military-recruitment-at-harvard-law-schools-office-of-career-services/.

"BLM's #WhatMatters2020," www.blacklivesmatter.com, downloaded August 2, 2020.

Bondarchuk's, Sergei. Soviet film adaptation of Leo Tolstoy's book War and Peace.

Bracchi, Paul. "It May Have Been a Victory for Free Speech, But Why Did Breakfast Insult of Muslim's Faith Case Ever Come to Court?" Daily Mail, http://www.dailymail.co.uk/ news/article-1234680/ It-victory-free-speech-did-breakfast-insult=Muslims-faith-case-come-court.html.

Bradner, Eric, Gregory Krieg and Dan Merica "Democratic Convention Highlights: 6 Takeaways from Night 1." CNN, August 18, 2020.

Bruce, Mary. "Obama: Voters Face Starkest Contrast Since Johnson-Goldwater." ABC OTUS News, April 10, 2012.

Burke, Edmund. "Edmund Burke," Wikiquote, http://en.wikiquote.org/wiki/Edmund_Burke.

Byrne, Gary J. Crisis in Character. New York: Center Street Publishers, 2016.

"Can Congress Make Me Buy Health Insurance?" Citizenlink, http://www.citizenlink.com/2009/08/24/can-congress-make-me-buy-health-insurance/.

Carpenter, F.B. (1866). "Six Months at the White House," p. 282. Retrieved 2010-02-20. Quoted in "Abraham Lincoln and Religion." TheFreeDictionary, http://encyclopedia.thefreedictionary.com/Abraham+Lincoln+ and+religion #endnote_rf-17.

"Casualties Numbers and Battle Death Statistics For the American Civil War." Historynet, downloaded June 3, 2020.

Citron, Jamie. "We're Going to be the Edge," October 02, 2008, and "Friends of Barack Visit Ohio," October 06, 2008. LBGT link under "People" at http://pride.barackobama.com.

Clark, Dartunorro. "Ja'Ron Smith, One of the Top Black Officials in the White House, Touts Trump's Empathy." NBC News, August 28, 2020.

"Constitution of the United States." U.S. National Archives & Records Administration, http://www.archives.gov/ exhibits/charters/ constitution.html.

"Declaration of Independence." U.S. National Archives & Records Administration, http://www.archives.gov/exhibits/charters /declaration.html.

"The Developing Threat of Freedom of Conscience." Citizenlink, http://www.citizenlink.com/2011/04/15/the-developing-threat-of-freedom-of-conscience/.

D'Souza, Dinesh. America: Imagine a World Without Her. Regnery Publishing, 2014.

D'Souza, Dinesh, John Sullivan, Bruce Schooley. America: Imagine the World Without Her. America Film, LLC, 2014.

D'Souza, Dinesh. Hillary's America: The Secret History of the Democratic Party. Regnery Publishing, 2016.

"Democratic Convention Takeaways: Make History, Pound Trump." Associated Press, August 19, 2020.

Edelman, Adam. "Bill Clinton Got $17.6M from Big For-Profit University while Hillary Clinton Vowed 'Crackdown' on their 'Abusive Practices.'" New York Daily News, August 24, 2016.

"Effective Tax Rates." Congressional Budget Office, http://www.cbo.gov/ftpdocs/88xx/doc8885/EffectiveTaxRates.shtml.

Foust, Michael. "Obama: If Elected I Will Use the Bully Pulpit for Gay Causes." Baptist Press, Feb 28, 2008, http://www.bpnews.netbpnews.asp?id=27510 as quoted in October 2008 letter by James Dobson at http://www.citizenlink.com.

"FRC Action: Elena Kagan's Pro-Abortion Record is Far Outside the Mainstream." Family Research Council Action, http://www.frcaction.org. May 19, 2010.

"Full Text: Ivanka Trump's 2020 Republican National Convention Speech." ABC News, August 27, 2020.

"Full Text: Joe Biden's 2020 Democratic National Convention Speech." ABC News, August 21, 2020.

Gass, Nick. "Clinton mounts full-court press against media." http://www.politico.com/story/2016/08/Clinton-campaign-blasts-massive," downloaded August 24, 2016.

Golden, C. Douglas. "Tucker Carlson Does Math on Police Shootings, Says This Is 'Not Even Close to Genocide'." The Western Journal. June 5, 2020.

Haines, Tim. "Pompeo at 2020 RNC: Trump Has Held China Accountable for Covering Up the China Virus." www.realclearpolitics.com, August 25, 2020.

Hausknecht, Bruce. "Obamacare Decision Next Week: What's at Stake?" June 22, 2012, http://www.citizenlink.com.

"Herschel Walker Defends Trump in Passionate Speech... He's Not A Racist!!!" TMZ Sports, www.tmz.com. August 25, 2020.

Holy Bible, King James Version. Nashville: Thomas Nelson, Inc., 1982.

Holy Bible, New King James Version. Nashville: Thomas Nelson, Inc., 1982.

Holy Bible, New International Version. Grand Rapids: Zondervan Bible Publishing, 1973, 1978, 1984.

Holy Bible, Today's New International Version. Grand Rapids: Zondervan
     Bible Publishing, 2001, 2005.

"How Trump's Taxes Compare to Those of Other Presidents." The
     Washington Post. September 28, 2020.

"I Have a Dream Speech," www.History.com, Nov. 30, 2017, Updated
     January 15, 2020. Downloaded July 29, 2020.

"Ku Klux Klan," www.history.com, October 29, 2009; updated February
     21, 2020; downloaded August 8, 2020.

"Ku Klux Klan." Wikipedia, downloaded June 4, 2020.

Kornblut, Anne E. and Robert Barnes. "Kagan Would Emphasize Supreme
     Court Moving in New Direction." The Washington Post. May 11, 2010,
     http://www.washingtonpost.com/wp-dyn/content/article/2010/05/10/
     AR20100510001116.html.

Krieg, Gregory, Melissa Macaya, Kyle Blaine, Jessica Estepa. "Democratic
     National Convention 2020: Day 2," CNN August 19, 2020.

Lewis, David L. "Martin Luther King, Jr., American Religious Leader and
     Civil-Rights Activist," www.britannica.com. Accessed July 29, 2020.

Lorinov, Rob. "Obamacare: Dissenting Justices Opinion." Lorinov's Blog,
     http://roblorinov.wordpress.com/ 2012/06/28/ obamacare-dissenting-
     justices-opinion. June 28, 2012.

Mansfield, Stephen. The Faith of Barack Obama. Nashville, Dallas:
     Thomas Nelson Publisher, 2008.

"March 2008 Action Update." National Journal, http://nj.Nationaljournal
     .com /voteratings. As cited in Focus Action, http://www.citizenlink.org.
     March 7, 2008.

Mendell, David. Obama: A Promise of Change. New York: HarperCollins
     Publishers, 2008.

Monk, Bethany. "HHS Contraception Mandate Deadline Falls
     Wednesday." Citizenlink, http://www.citizenlink.com. July 31, 2012.

Mulbrandon, Catherine. "How Much Taxes Are Paid by the Poor, Middle Class and Rich." Visualizing Economics, http://visualizingeconomics.com/ 2010/02/12/. February 2, 2012.

Obama, Barack. The Audacity of Hope: Thoughts on Reclaiming the American Dream. New York: Crown Publishers, 2006.

Obama, Barack. "Call to Renewal Keynote Address." June 28, 2006. http://www.Barackobama.com.

Obama, Barack. Change We Can Believe In: Barack Obama's Plan to Renew America's Promise. New York: Three Rivers Press, 2008.

Obama, Barack. Dreams from My Father. New York: Three Rivers Press, 1995.

"Obama Distorts His Abortion Record in Third Debate." National Right to Life Committee, http://www.nrlc.org. October 16, 2008, accessed October 22, 2008.

"ObamaCare and the Power to Tax." Wall Street Journal. June 28, 2012.

"President Obama to Freedom of Religion: Nertz to You!" Family Research Council Action, http://www.frcaction.org. August 6, 2012

"The Presidential Record on Life: President Barack Obama 2009-present." National Right to Life, http://www.nrlc.org.

"President Trump's Accomplishments." Ohio Battleground Alliance, Ohio Women for Liberty. Accessed September 30, 2020.

"Pro-Life Group Proves That Obama Subsidizes Abortion," Citizenlink, http://www.citizenlink.com/2012/10/29/pro-life-group-proves-that-obamacare-subsidizes-abortion/.

Quinn, Melissa, Kathryn Watson, "Full Text: Pence Says 'The Choice in this Election is Whether America Remains America' in RNC Speech." CBS News, August 26, 2020.

"Report: Rev. Jeremiah Wright Has Affair with Another Man's Wife." Fox News, http://FOXNews.com. September 9, 2008.

"Republican Senator for South Carolina Tim Scott Speaks During the First Day of the Republican Convention at the Mellon Auditorium in Washington on Aug. 24, 2020." NBC News. Updated Aug. 25, 2020.

Roberts, Chief Justice. "Roberts: Our Decision Isn't About Whether Obamacare Is Sound Policy." Talking Points Memo Livewire, June 28, 2012, http://livewire.talkingpointsmemo.com/entries/roberts-our-decision-isnt-about-whether-obamacare-is.

Rodriguez, Katherine. "Civil Rights Leader Clarence Henderson: If You Vote for Biden 'You Don't Know History'." http://www.Breitbart.com, Aug 26, 2020.

Roy, Avik. "CBO: Obamacare Will Spend More, Tax More, and Reduce the Deficit Less Than We Previously Thought." Forbes, http://www.forbes.com. August 27, 2012,

Sanger, David E. "Tuesday's Debate Made Clear the Gravest Threat to the Election: The President Himself." The New York Times. September 30, 2020.

Sapet, Karrily. Political Profiles: Barack Obama. Greensboro, North Carolina: Morgan Reynolds Publishing, 2008.

Schweizer, Peter. Clinton Cash: The Untold Story of How and Why Foreign Governments and Businesses Helped Make Bill and Hillary Rich. New York: Harper Publishers, 2015.

"SCOTUS Obamacare Ruling: The Dissenting Opinion in It's Entirety." Patriots for America, http://patriotsforamerica. ning.com/ forum/topics/ scotus-obamacare-ruling-the-dissenting-opinion-in-it-s-entirety. June 28, 2012.

"Senator Barack Obama Record on Abortion, United States Senate, Illinois State Senate." National Right to Life Committee, http://www.nrlc.org, accessed August 28, 2008.

Smith, Allan. "Giuliani Tells NBC News He Will Attack Biden on Police Brutality Protests." NBC News. August 28, 2020.

"So-Called Hate Speech," Citizenlink, www.citizenlink.com/ 2010/03/citizenlink-so-called-hate-speech/.

"Sotomayor: A Policy Maker or a Jurist?" Family Research Council Action, http://www.frcaction.org. May 26, 2009.

Stanek, Jill. "Obama Blocked Born Alive Infant Protection Act." April 2, 2008. National Right to Life Committee, http://www.nrlc.org, accessed July 7, 2008.

Steele, Shelby. A Bound Man: Why We Are Excited about Barack Obama and Why He Can't Win. New York: Free Press, 2008.

Street, Paul. Barack Obama and the Future of American Politics. Boulder, Colorado: Paradigm Publishers, 2008.

Stone, Tyler. "Civil Rights Activist Clarence Henderson: If You Vote for Biden, You Don't Know History." August 26, 2020.

"Supreme Court Upholds Obama Health-care Reform." Catholic World News, http://www.catholicculture.org/ news/headlines/index.cfm? storyid=14767. June 28, 2012.

"Supreme Court's Obamacare Decision: Full Text." The Atlantic, http://www.theatlantic.com/politics/archive/2012/06/the-supreme-courts-obamacare-decision-full-text/259102/. June 28, 2012.

Thompson, Derek. "The Health Care Decision Explained in 1 Paragraph on SCOTUSblog." The Atlantic, http://www.theatlantic.com/business/ archive/2012/06/the-health-care-decision-explained-in-1-paragraph-on-scotusblog/259097/. June 28, 2012.

Titus, Herbert W. God, Man, and Law: The Biblical Principles. Oak Brook, Illinois: Institute in Basic Life Principles, 1994.

Tobias, Carol. "Statement by Carol Tobias, National Right to Life President." http://www.nrlc.org. April 12, 2012.

"Trump Accepts Republican Nomination for President at the 2020 RNC." NBC News. Aug. 28, 2020.

"UK Pastor Arrested Over Comments on Homosexuality." Citizenlink, http://www.citizenlink.com/2010/05/ citizenlink-uk-pastor-arrested-over-comments-on-homosexuality/.

"Values Voter Guide for 2008 Presidential Candidates." Family Research Council Action, http://www.frcaction.org, accessed July 9, 2008.

Van Der Vat, Dan. Pearl Harbor: The Day of Infamy—An Illustrated History. Introduction by Senator John McCain. New York: Basic Books, 2001.

"Vote Scorecard." Family Research Council Action, http://www.frcaction.org, accessed July 9, 2008.

"Vote Scorecard." Family Research Council Action, http://www.frcaction.org, accessed February 17, 2012.

"Vote Scorecard." Focus on the Family Action, http://www.citizenlink.org, accessed July 9, 2008.

"Vote Scorecard." National Right to Life Committee, http://www.nrlc.org, accessed July 7, 2008.

"Vote Scorecard." National Right to Life Committee, http://www.nrlc.org, accessed February 17, 2012.

Wagner, Heather. Barack Obama. New York: Chelsea House Publishers, 2008.

Walsh, Susan, Associated Press. "Donald Trump Jr., Speaks as He Tapes His Speech for the First Day of the Republican National Convention from the Andrew W. Mellon Auditorium in Washington, on Aug. 24, 2020." Aug. 24, 2020, Updated Aug. 25, 2020 by NBC News.

"What Defunding the Police Really Means." www.blacklivesmatter.com. July 6, 2020, downloaded August 2, 2020.

Whelan, Ed. "Obamacare Dissenting Opinion the Original Majority Opinion?" <u>Kansas Citian,</u> http://thekansascitian.blogspot.com/2012/06/obamacare-dissenting-opinion-original.html. June 28, 2012.

"Where Do the Candidates Stand on Life: John McCain, Barack Obama." <u>National Right to Life Committee,</u> http://www.nrlc.org, accessed August 28, 2008.

"Where Do the Candidates Stand on Life: Mitt Romney, Barack Obama." <u>National Right to Life Committee,</u> http://www.nrlc.org.

"Why Did Hillary Clinton Need a Private Server? The Answer Makes Bernie Sanders President." www.TheHuffingtonPost.com, downloaded March 7, 2016.

"Widdecombe and Gay Tory Defend Cornish BB Owners." <u>The Christian Institute,</u> http://www.christian.org.uk/news/ widdecombe-and-gay-tory-defend-cornish-bb-owners/.

APPENDIX A

DEFINING CHRISTIAN

<u>REASON FOR CHAPTER</u>. Many Americans think that simply believing in Christ makes one a Christian. That is totally contrary to the teachings of Christ.

<u>FIRST ELEMENT</u>. There are several vitally important elements of being a Christian. First, a Christian is someone who, like all Jews and Muslims, believes in God. He understands that:
1.   There is one true God, who always was, is, and ever shall be.
2.   He never changes. He is the same yesterday, today, and tomorrow.
3.   He created all things seen and unseen, and all laws that govern all things seen and unseen.
4.   He creates each man in His own image, knitting him together in his mother's womb.

A Christian understands that God's moral laws are rooted in His unchanging character. They do not change or evolve. They are the same today as they were when our universe was created. These include laws that govern men and governments. The United States was founded upon these self-evident, common sense truths, revealed by God through creation and Scripture and embodied in the Declaration of Independence and U.S. Constitution.

<u>SECOND ELEMENT</u>. Second, a Christian is someone who, unlike Jews or Muslims, believes in a triune God, one God in three persons: Father, Son, and Holy Spirit. This is not common sense. It is not revealed through creation. It is revealed through Scripture, and it takes a special gift of faith from God to believe.

Many Christians publicly profess their faith in God the Father, Son, and Holy Spirit through the Apostles' Creed, which briefly summarizes key tenants of the Christian faith.

1. **<u>I believe in God, the Father</u>** almighty, creator of heaven and earth.

2. **I believe in Jesus Christ**, His <u>only</u> Son, our <u>Lord</u>.

3. He was conceived by the power of the Holy Spirit and born of the Virgin Mary.

4. He suffered under Pontius Pilate, <u>was crucified</u>, died, and was buried.

5. He descended to the dead. On the third day <u>he rose again</u>.

6. He <u>ascended into heaven</u> and is <u>seated</u> at the <u>right hand of the Father</u>.

7. He will <u>come again</u> to <u>judge the living and the dead</u>.

8. **I believe in the Holy Spirit**,

9. the holy Catholic Church, the <u>communion of saints</u>,

10. the <u>forgiveness of sins</u>,

11. the <u>resurrection of the body</u>,

12. and <u>life everlasting</u>. Amen.[202]

A Christian believes that Christ is the Son of God and the Messiah and Savior whose coming was prophesied to the people of Israel. He believes that Christ is fully God and fully man and that if He was not both He could not be the perfect, blameless "Lamb of God" who made payment in full for the sins of man through His death on the cross. However, belief in all the foregoing does not make one a Christian. Satan and his demons believe in God; it does not make them Christians.

THIRD ELEMENT. Third, a Christian is a repentant sinner. "I love being Catholic, because I can do whatever I want and just go to confession," said a young lady. She is the perfect example of someone who is not a Christian because she is not repentant. No priest has the power to forgive the sins of anyone who is not repentant. Repentance means more than true regret for sin; it means turning from sin to obedience to God. King David provides the best example of true repentance:

> <u>Have mercy upon me, O God</u>, according to thy
> lovingkindness: according unto the multitude of
> thy tender mercies <u>blot out my transgressions.</u>
> Wash me thoroughly from mine iniquity, and cleanse me
> from my sin.

---

[202] The *Catechism of the Catholic Church* gives this English translation of the Apostles' Creed. The Catechism maintains the traditional division into twelve articles. See http://en.wikipedia.org/wiki/Apostles%27_Creed.

For I acknowledge my transgressions: and my sin is ever
         before me.
Against thee, thee only, have I sinned, and done this evil
         in thy sight: that thou mightest be justified when
         thou speakest, and be clear when thou judgest.
Behold, I was shapen in iniquity; and in sin did my
         mother conceive me.
Behold, thou desirest truth in the inward parts: and in the
         hidden part thou shalt make me to know
         wisdom.
Purge me with hyssop, and I shall be clean: wash me, and
         I shall be whiter than snow.
Make me to hear joy and gladness; that the bones which
         thou hast broken may rejoice.
Hide thy face from my sins, and blot out all mine
         iniquities.
Create in me a clean heart, O God; and renew a right
         spirit within me.
Cast me not away from thy presence; and take not thy
         Holy Spirit from me.
Restore unto me the joy of thy salvation; and uphold me
         with thy free spirit.
Then will I teach transgressors thy ways; and sinners
         shall be converted unto thee.
Deliver me from bloodguiltiness, O God, thou God of my
         salvation: and my tongue shall sing aloud of thy
         righteousness.
O Lord, open thou my lips; and my mouth shall shew
         forth thy praise.
For thou desirest not sacrifice; else would I give it: thou
         delightest not in burnt offering.
The sacrifices of God are a broken spirit: a broken and a
         contrite heart, O God, thou wilt not despise.
Do good in thy good pleasure unto Zion: build thou the
         walls of Jerusalem.
Then shalt thou be pleased with the sacrifices of
         righteousness, with burnt offering and whole
         burnt offering: then shall they offer bullocks
         upon thine altar. Psalm 51:1-19 (KJV).

Note that true repentance requires: (1) full acknowledgment of sin against God; (2) true regret for sin against God; (3) humble request for God's forgiveness; (4) cleansing and full restoration of relationship with God; (5) empowerment by God to do His will; (6) humble obedience to God's will.

<u>FOURTH ELEMENT</u>. Fourth, a Christian is someone who accepts Christ as Savior. He understands that God is holy, and that no man can meet God's standard of perfection. He understands that "all have sinned, and come short of the glory of God" (Rom 3:22-24). He understands that only Christ, the perfect Lamb of God, fully God and fully man, could make payment for man's sins. He understands that Christ died on the cross as payment in full for his sins, and that he can only be cleansed by faith in what Christ has done for him. "For God so loved the world, that he gave his only begotten Son, that whosoever believeth in him should not perish, but have everlasting life" (John 3:16, KJV). He knows that "a man is not justified by the works of the law, but by the faith of Jesus Christ" (Gal 2:16, KJV). Therefore he accepts Christ as his Savior, as the Lamb of God who made payment in full for his sins through death on the cross.

<u>FIFTH ELEMENT</u>. Fifth, a Christian is someone who accepts Christ as the Lord of his life. Christ said, "If any man will come after me, let him deny himself, and take up his cross, and follow me" (Mat. 16:23-25, KJV). He said, "And he that taketh not his cross, and followeth after me, is not worthy of me" (Matt. 10:38, KJV. See also Mark 8:34-35, Luke 9:22-24, KJV). Christ said, "My food is to do the will of Him who sent Me, and to finish His work" (John 4:34, NKJV). If a man believes in Christ and accepts Him as the Lord of his life, then he will take up his cross, dying to self, and follow Him.

Christ made it clear that one cannot be a Christian and live contrary to God's commandments. On Judgment Day Christ will reject many who claim to be Christians because they failed to live Christian values. Christ said,

> <u>Not everyone that saith unto me, "Lord, Lord," shall enter into the kingdom of heaven; but he that doeth the will of my Father</u> which is in heaven. Many will say to me in that day, "Lord, Lord, have we not prophesied in thy name? and in thy name have cast out devils? and in thy name done many wonderful works?" And then will I

291

profess unto them, I never knew you: depart from me, ye
that work iniquity (Matt. 7:21-23, KJV).

In other words, believing in Christ as Lord and Savior and doing
great miracles in His name does not make one a Christian. A Christian is a
follower of Christ who does "the will of my Father." Doing God's will
means living in obedience to His commandments. This does not mean that
anyone is saved by works. Man is saved by faith not works, but "faith
without works is dead" (James 2:20, KJV; see also James 2:17, 25-26). A
man who chooses to live contrary to God's commandments is not a
Christian because he is not repentant and he has not accepted Christ as Lord
and Savior.

SIXTH ELEMENT. Sixth, a Christian is empowered and guided
by the Spirit of God (the Holy Spirit). Jesus made it clear that being saved
required being "born again" and that this spiritual rebirth required not just
baptism with water, but being "born of…the Spirit." He said, "Except a
man be born of water and of the Spirit, he cannot enter into the kingdom of
God. That which is born of the flesh is flesh; and that which is born of the
Spirit is spirit. Marvel not that I said unto thee, 'Ye must be born again'"
(John 3:5-7, KJV).

When Christ gave the Great Commission to his disciples, he said,
"All power is given unto me in heaven and in earth. Go ye therefore, and
teach all nations, baptizing them in the name of the Father, and of the Son,
and of the Holy Ghost: Teaching them to observe all things whatsoever I
have commanded you…" (Matt. 28:18-20, KJV). Baptism in the name of
the Spirit (Holy Ghost) had special meaning. Jesus said, "For John truly
baptized with water; but ye shall be baptized with the Holy Ghost.… But ye
shall receive power, after that the Holy Ghost is come upon you: and ye
shall be witnesses unto me…unto the uttermost part of the earth" (Act 1:5-
8, KJV). In other words, part of being saved involved being "baptized with
the Holy Ghost", which resulted in being empowered by the Holy Spirit.

John states that believers in Christ would receive the "Spirit"
("Holy Ghost"). First he quotes Christ; then he explains the meaning of
Christ's words (in parentheses): " He that believeth on me, as the Scripture
hath said, out of his belly shall flow rivers of living water. (But this spake
he of the Spirit, which they that believe on him should receive: for the Holy
Ghost was not yet given; because that Jesus was not yet glorified)" (John
7:38-39, KJV). Acts 5:32 refers to the Holy Spirit as "the Holy Ghost,

whom God hath given to them that obey him" (Acts 5:32, KJV). In other words, being saved requires obedience to God's commandments, and God gives His Holy Spirit to those who are saved and therefore obedient to His will.

The Apostle Paul explains in great detail the role of the Spirit of God in empowering and guiding the believer to do the will of God.

> For they that are after the flesh do mind the things of the flesh; but they that are after the Spirit the things of the Spirit. For <u>to be carnally minded is death; but to be spiritually minded is life and peace</u>. Because the carnal mind is enmity against God: for it is not subject to the law of God, neither indeed can be. So then they that are in the flesh cannot please God. But ye are not in the flesh, but in the Spirit, if so be that the Spirit of God dwell in you. Now <u>if any man have not the Spirit of Christ, he is none of his</u>. And <u>if Christ be in you, the body is dead</u> because of sin; <u>but the Spirit is life</u> because of righteousness. But <u>if the Spirit</u> of him that raised up Jesus from the dead <u>dwell in you</u>, he that raised up Christ from the dead shall also quicken your mortal bodies by his Spirit that dwelleth in you. Therefore, brethren, we are debtors, not to the flesh, to live after the flesh. For <u>if ye live after the flesh, ye shall die</u>: but if ye through the Spirit do mortify the deeds of the body, ye shall live. For as many as are <u>led by the Spirit of God, they are the sons of God </u>(Rom 1:5-14, KJV).

<u>SEVENTH ELEMENT</u>. Seventh, a Christian is a person whose reason for living is Christ. Paul said, "For to me to live is Christ, and to die is gain"(Phil. 1:20-22). Christ said, "My meat is to do the will of him that sent me, and to finish his work" (John 4:34, KJV). Christ and Paul provide perfect examples of the total devotion and commitment required by someone whose reason for living is loving and serving God.

Christ also said, "He that loveth father or mother more than me is not worthy of me: and he that loveth son or daughter more than me is not worthy of me" (Matt. 10:36-38, KJV). If loving and serving God is not a man's top priority and primary objective, his reason for living, then he is in violation of the greatest commandment: "Thou shalt love the Lord thy God with all thy heart, and with all thy soul, and with all thy might" (Deut. 6:5, KJV. See also Matt. 22:37-38; Luke 10:27). He is also in violation of the first of the ten commandments: "Thou shalt have none other gods before me" (Deut. 5:7, KJV).

The author defines a man's faith or religion as his reason for living. Everyone has a faith or religion, a reason for living. A man's true faith or religion is the true reason he lives and votes that way that he does. A man who claims to be a Christian and attends church weekly but lives and votes contrary to Christian values is not a Christian.

CONCLUSION. A Christian is not simply someone who believes in God and accepts Christ as Savior. A Christian is someone who: (1) believes in the one true God, the Creator of all things seen and unseen (2) believes in a triune God, one God in three persons: Father, Son, and Holy Spirit; (3) is a repentant sinner; (4) is saved by faith in Christ as his Savior; (5) accepts Christ as Lord of his life; (6) is empowered and guided by the Holy Spirit; and (7) is a person whose purpose and reason for living is Christ.

DECLARATION OF INDEPENDENCE[203]

IN CONGRESS, July 4, 1776.

The unanimous Declaration of the thirteen united States of America,
When in the Course of human events, it becomes necessary for one people
to dissolve the political bands which have connected them with another,
and to assume among the powers of the earth, the separate and equal station
to which the Laws of Nature and of Nature's God entitle them, a decent
respect to the opinions of mankind requires that they should declare the
causes which impel them to the separation.
We hold these truths to be self-evident, that all men are created equal, that
they are endowed by their Creator with certain unalienable Rights, that
among these are Life, Liberty and the pursuit of Happiness.--That to secure
these rights, Governments are instituted among Men, deriving their just
powers from the consent of the governed, --That whenever any Form of
Government becomes destructive of these ends, it is the Right of the People
to alter or to abolish it, and to institute new Government, laying its
foundation on such principles and organizing its powers in such form, as to
them shall seem most likely to effect their Safety and Happiness. Prudence,
indeed, will dictate that Governments long established should not be
changed for light and transient causes; and accordingly all experience hath
shewn, that mankind are more disposed to suffer, while evils are sufferable,
than to right themselves by abolishing the forms to which they are
accustomed. But when a long train of abuses and usurpations, pursuing
invariably the same Object evinces a design to reduce them under absolute
Despotism, it is their right, it is their duty, to throw off such Government,
and to provide new Guards for their future security.--Such has been the
patient sufferance of these Colonies; and such is now the necessity which
constrains them to alter their former Systems of Government. The history
of the present King of Great Britain is a history of repeated injuries and
usurpations, all having in direct object the establishment of an absolute
Tyranny over these States. To prove this, let Facts be submitted to a candid
world.

---

[203] U.S. National Archives & Records Administration, "The Charters of
Freedom: The Declaration of Independence,"
http://www.archives.gov/exhibits/charters.

He has refused his Assent to Laws, the most wholesome and
necessary for the public good.
He has forbidden his Governors to pass Laws of immediate and
pressing importance, unless suspended in their operation till his
Assent should be obtained; and when so suspended, he has utterly
neglected to attend to them.
He has refused to pass other Laws for the accommodation of large
districts of people, unless those people would relinquish the right
of Representation in the Legislature, a right inestimable to them
and formidable to tyrants only.
He has called together legislative bodies at places unusual,
uncomfortable, and distant from the depository of their public
Records, for the sole purpose of fatiguing them into compliance
with his measures.
He has dissolved Representative Houses repeatedly, for opposing
with manly firmness his invasions on the rights of the people.
He has refused for a long time, after such dissolutions, to cause
others to be elected; whereby the Legislative powers, incapable of
Annihilation, have returned to the People at large for their
exercise; the State remaining in the mean time exposed to all the
dangers of invasion from without, and convulsions within.
He has endeavoured to prevent the population of these States; for
that purpose obstructing the Laws for Naturalization of Foreigners;
refusing to pass others to encourage their migrations hither, and
raising the conditions of new Appropriations of Lands.
He has obstructed the Administration of Justice, by refusing his
Assent to Laws for establishing Judiciary powers.
He has made Judges dependent on his Will alone, for the tenure of
their offices, and the amount and payment of their salaries.
He has erected a multitude of New Offices, and sent hither swarms
of Officers to harrass our people, and eat out their substance.
He has kept among us, in times of peace, Standing Armies without
the Consent of our legislatures.
He has affected to render the Military independent of and superior
to the Civil power.
He has combined with others to subject us to a jurisdiction foreign
to our constitution, and unacknowledged by our laws; giving his
Assent to their Acts of pretended Legislation:
For Quartering large bodies of armed troops among us:
For protecting them, by a mock Trial, from punishment for any

Murders which they should commit on the Inhabitants of these States:

For cutting off our Trade with all parts of the world:

For imposing Taxes on us without our Consent:

For depriving us in many cases, of the benefits of Trial by Jury:

For transporting us beyond Seas to be tried for pretended offences

For abolishing the free System of English Laws in a neighbouring Province, establishing therein an Arbitrary government, and enlarging its Boundaries so as to render it at once an example and fit instrument for introducing the same absolute rule into these Colonies:

For taking away our Charters, abolishing our most valuable Laws, and altering fundamentally the Forms of our Governments:

For suspending our own Legislatures, and declaring themselves invested with power to legislate for us in all cases whatsoever.

He has abdicated Government here, by declaring us out of his Protection and waging War against us.

He has plundered our seas, ravaged our Coasts, burnt our towns, and destroyed the lives of our people.

He is at this time transporting large Armies of foreign Mercenaries to compleat the works of death, desolation and tyranny, already begun with circumstances of Cruelty & perfidy scarcely paralleled in the most barbarous ages, and totally unworthy the Head of a civilized nation.

He has constrained our fellow Citizens taken Captive on the high Seas to bear Arms against their Country, to become the executioners of their friends and Brethren, or to fall themselves by their Hands.

He has excited domestic insurrections amongst us, and has endeavoured to bring on the inhabitants of our frontiers, the merciless Indian Savages, whose known rule of warfare, is an undistinguished destruction of all ages, sexes and conditions.

In every stage of these Oppressions We have Petitioned for Redress in the most humble terms: Our repeated Petitions have been answered only by repeated injury. A Prince whose character is thus marked by every act which may define a Tyrant, is unfit to be the ruler of a free people.

Nor have We been wanting in attentions to our Brittish brethren. We have warned them from time to time of attempts by their legislature to extend an unwarrantable jurisdiction over us. We have reminded them of the circumstances of our emigration and settlement here. We have appealed to their native justice and magnanimity, and we have conjured them by the ties of our common kindred to disavow these usurpations, which, would inevitably interrupt our connections and correspondence. They too have been deaf to the voice of justice and of consanguinity. We must, therefore, acquiesce in the necessity, which denounces our Separation, and hold them, as we hold the rest of mankind, Enemies in War, in Peace Friends.

We, therefore, the Representatives of the united States of America, in General Congress, Assembled, appealing to the Supreme Judge of the world for the rectitude of our intentions, do, in the Name, and by Authority of the good People of these Colonies, solemnly publish and declare, That these United Colonies are, and of Right ought to be Free and Independent States; that they are Absolved from all Allegiance to the British Crown, and that all political connection between them and the State of Great Britain, is and ought to be totally dissolved; and that as Free and Independent States, they have full Power to levy War, conclude Peace, contract Alliances, establish Commerce, and to do all other Acts and Things which Independent States may of right do. And for the support of this Declaration, with a firm reliance on the protection of divine Providence, we mutually pledge to each other our Lives, our Fortunes and our sacred Honor.

<u>***The 56 signatures on the Declaration appear in the positions indicated:***</u>

Column 1
Georgia:
Button Gwinnett
Lyman Hall
George Walton
Column 2
North Carolina:
William Hooper
Joseph Hewes
John Penn
South Carolina:
Edward Rutledge
Thomas Heyward, Jr.
Thomas Lynch, Jr.
Arthur Middleton
Column 3
Massachusetts:
John Hancock
Maryland:
Samuel Chase
William Paca
Thomas Stone
Charles Carroll of Carrollton
Virginia:
George Wythe
Richard Henry Lee
Thomas Jefferson
Benjamin Harrison

Thomas Nelson, Jr.
Francis Lightfoot Lee
Carter Braxton
Column 4
Pennsylvania:
Robert Morris
Benjamin Rush
Benjamin Franklin
John Morton
George Clymer
James Smith
George Taylor
James Wilson
George Ross
Delaware:
Caesar Rodney
George Read
Thomas McKean
<u>Column 5</u>
<u>New York:</u>
<u>William Floyd</u>
<u>Philip Livingston</u>
<u>Francis Lewis</u>
<u>Lewis Morris</u>
<u>New Jersey:</u>
<u>Richard Stockton</u>

CONSTITUTION OF THE UNITED STATES[204]

Note: The following text is a transcription of the Constitution in its original form. Items that are [underlined] hyperlinked have since been amended or superseded.

We the People of the United States, in Order to form a more perfect Union, establish Justice, insure domestic Tranquility, provide for the common defence, promote the general Welfare, and secure the Blessings of Liberty to ourselves and our Posterity, do ordain and establish this Constitution for the United States of America.

Article. I.
Section. 1.
All legislative Powers herein granted shall be vested in a Congress of the United States, which shall consist of a Senate and House of Representatives.

Section. 2.
The House of Representatives shall be composed of Members chosen every second Year by the People of the several States, and the Electors in each State shall have the Qualifications requisite for Electors of the most numerous Branch of the State Legislature.

No Person shall be a Representative who shall not have attained to the Age of twenty five Years, and been seven Years a Citizen of the United States, and who shall not, when elected, be an Inhabitant of that State in which he shall be chosen.

Representatives and direct Taxes shall be apportioned among the several States which may be included within this Union, according to their respective Numbers, which shall be determined by adding to the whole Number of free Persons, including those bound to Service for a Term of Years, and excluding Indians not taxed, three fifths of all other Persons. The actual Enumeration

---

[204] U.S. National Archives and Records Administration. "The Charters of Freedom: The Constitution of the United States," http://www.archives.gov/exhibits/charters.

shall be made within three Years after the first Meeting of the Congress of the United States, and within every subsequent Term of ten Years, in such Manner as they shall by Law direct. The Number of Representatives shall not exceed one for every thirty Thousand, but each State shall have at Least one Representative; and until such enumeration shall be made, the State of New Hampshire shall be entitled to chuse three, Massachusetts eight, Rhode-Island and Providence Plantations one, Connecticut five, New-York six, New Jersey four, Pennsylvania eight, Delaware one, Maryland six, Virginia ten, North Carolina five, South Carolina five, and Georgia three.

When vacancies happen in the Representation from any State, the Executive Authority thereof shall issue Writs of Election to fill such Vacancies.

The House of Representatives shall chuse their Speaker and other Officers; and shall have the sole Power of Impeachment.

Section. 3.

The Senate of the United States shall be composed of two Senators from each State, chosen by the Legislature thereof for six Years; and each Senator shall have one Vote.

Immediately after they shall be assembled in Consequence of the first Election, they shall be divided as equally as may be into three Classes. The Seats of the Senators of the first Class shall be vacated at the Expiration of the second Year, of the second Class at the Expiration of the fourth Year, and of the third Class at the Expiration of the sixth Year, so that one third may be chosen every second Year; and if Vacancies happen by Resignation, or otherwise, during the Recess of the Legislature of any State, the Executive thereof may make temporary Appointments until the next Meeting of the Legislature, which shall then fill such Vacancies.

No Person shall be a Senator who shall not have attained to the Age of thirty Years, and been nine Years a Citizen of the United States, and who shall not, when elected, be an Inhabitant of that State for which he shall be chosen.

The Vice President of the United States shall be President of the Senate, but shall have no Vote, unless they be equally divided.

The Senate shall chuse their other Officers, and also a President pro tempore, in the Absence of the Vice President, or when he shall exercise the Office of President of the United States.

The Senate shall have the sole Power to try all Impeachments. When sitting for that Purpose, they shall be on Oath or Affirmation. When the President of the United States is tried, the Chief Justice shall preside: And no Person shall be convicted without the Concurrence of two thirds of the Members present.

Judgment in Cases of Impeachment shall not extend further than to removal from Office, and disqualification to hold and enjoy any Office of honor, Trust or Profit under the United States: but the Party convicted shall nevertheless be liable and subject to Indictment, Trial, Judgment and Punishment, according to Law.

Section. 4.

The Times, Places and Manner of holding Elections for Senators and Representatives, shall be prescribed in each State by the Legislature thereof; but the Congress may at any time by Law make or alter such Regulations, except as to the Places of chusing Senators.

The Congress shall assemble at least once in every Year, and such Meeting shall <u>be on the first Monday in December</u>, unless they shall by Law appoint a different Day.

Section. 5.

Each House shall be the Judge of the Elections, Returns and Qualifications of its own Members, and a Majority of each shall constitute a Quorum to do Business; but a smaller Number may adjourn from day to day, and may be authorized to compel the Attendance of absent Members, in such Manner, and under such Penalties as each House may provide.

Each House may determine the Rules of its Proceedings, punish its Members for disorderly Behaviour, and, with the Concurrence of two thirds, expel a Member.

Each House shall keep a Journal of its Proceedings, and from time to time publish the same, excepting such Parts as may in their Judgment require Secrecy; and the Yeas and Nays of the Members of either House on any question shall, at the Desire of one fifth of those Present, be entered on the Journal.

Neither House, during the Session of Congress, shall, without the Consent of the other, adjourn for more than three days, nor to any other Place than that in which the two Houses shall be sitting.

Section. 6.

The Senators and Representatives shall receive a Compensation for their Services, to be ascertained by Law, and paid out of the Treasury of the United States. They shall in all Cases, except Treason, Felony and Breach of the Peace, be privileged from Arrest during their Attendance at the Session of their respective Houses, and in going to and returning from the same; and for any Speech or Debate in either House, they shall not be questioned in any other Place.

No Senator or Representative shall, during the Time for which he was elected, be appointed to any civil Office under the Authority of the United States, which shall have been created, or the Emoluments whereof shall have been encreased during such time; and no Person holding any Office under the

United States, shall be a Member of either House during his Continuance in Office.

Section. 7.

All Bills for raising Revenue shall originate in the House of Representatives; but the Senate may propose or concur with Amendments as on other Bills. Every Bill which shall have passed the House of Representatives and the Senate, shall, before it become a Law, be presented to the President of the United States: If he approve he shall sign it, but if not he shall return it, with his Objections to that House in which it shall have originated, who shall enter the Objections at large on their Journal, and proceed to reconsider it. If after such Reconsideration two thirds of that House shall agree to pass the Bill, it shall be sent, together with the Objections, to the other House, by which it shall likewise be reconsidered, and if approved by two thirds of that House, it shall become a Law. But in all such Cases the Votes of both Houses shall be determined by yeas and Nays, and the Names of the Persons voting for and against the Bill shall be entered on the Journal of each House respectively. If any Bill shall not be returned by the President within ten Days (Sundays excepted) after it shall have been presented to him, the Same shall be a Law, in like Manner as if he had signed it, unless the Congress by their Adjournment prevent its Return, in which Case it shall not be a Law. Every Order, Resolution, or Vote to which the Concurrence of the Senate and House of Representatives may be necessary (except on a question of Adjournment) shall be presented to the President of the United States; and before the Same shall take Effect, shall be approved by him, or being **disapproved by him, shall be repassed by two thirds of the Senate and House of Representatives, according to the Rules and Limitations prescribed in the Case of a Bill.**

Section. 8.

The Congress shall have Power To lay and collect Taxes, Duties, Imposts and Excises, to pay the Debts and provide for the common Defence and general Welfare of the United States; but all Duties, Imposts and Excises shall be uniform throughout the United States;
To borrow Money on the credit of the United States;
To regulate Commerce with foreign Nations, and among the several States, and with the Indian Tribes;
To establish an uniform Rule of Naturalization, and uniform Laws on the subject of Bankruptcies throughout the United States;
To coin Money, regulate the Value thereof, and of foreign Coin, and fix the Standard of Weights and Measures;
To provide for the Punishment of counterfeiting the Securities and current Coin of the United States;

To establish Post Offices and post Roads;
To promote the Progress of Science and useful Arts, by securing for limited Times to Authors and Inventors the exclusive Right to their respective Writings and Discoveries;
To constitute Tribunals inferior to the supreme Court;
To define and punish Piracies and Felonies committed on the high Seas, and Offences against the Law of Nations;
To declare War, grant Letters of Marque and Reprisal, and make Rules concerning Captures on Land and Water;
To raise and support Armies, but no Appropriation of Money to that Use shall be for a longer Term than two Years;
To provide and maintain a Navy;
To make Rules for the Government and Regulation of the land and naval Forces;
To provide for calling forth the Militia to execute the Laws of the Union, suppress Insurrections and repel Invasions;
To provide for organizing, arming, and disciplining, the Militia, and for governing such Part of them as may be employed in the Service of the United States, reserving to the States respectively, the Appointment of the Officers, and the Authority of training the Militia according to the discipline prescribed by Congress;
To exercise exclusive Legislation in all Cases whatsoever, over such District (not exceeding ten Miles square) as may, by Cession of particular States, and the Acceptance of Congress, become the Seat of the Government of the United States, and to exercise like Authority over all Places purchased by the Consent of the Legislature of the State in which the Same shall be, for the Erection of Forts, Magazines, Arsenals, dock-Yards, and other needful Buildings;--And
To make all Laws which shall be necessary and proper for carrying into Execution the foregoing Powers, and all other Powers vested by this Constitution in the Government of the United States, or in any Department or Officer thereof.

Section. 9.

The Migration or Importation of such Persons as any of the States now existing shall think proper to admit, shall not be prohibited by the Congress prior to the Year one thousand eight hundred and eight, but a Tax or duty may be imposed on such Importation, not exceeding ten dollars for each Person.
The Privilege of the Writ of Habeas Corpus shall not be suspended, unless when in Cases of Rebellion or Invasion the public Safety may require it.
No Bill of Attainder or ex post facto Law shall be passed.

No Capitation, or other direct, Tax shall be laid, <u>unless in Proportion to the Census or enumeration herein before directed to be taken.</u>
No Tax or Duty shall be laid on Articles exported from any State.
No Preference shall be given by any Regulation of Commerce or Revenue to the Ports of one State over those of another; nor shall Vessels bound to, or from, one State, be obliged to enter, clear, or pay Duties in another.
No Money shall be drawn from the Treasury, but in Consequence of Appropriations made by Law; and a regular Statement and Account of the Receipts and Expenditures of all public Money shall be published from time to time.

No Title of Nobility shall be granted by the United States: And no Person holding any Office of Profit or Trust under them, shall, without the Consent of the Congress, accept of any present, Emolument, Office, or Title, of any kind whatever, from any King, Prince, or foreign State.

Section. 10.

No State shall enter into any Treaty, Alliance, or Confederation; grant Letters of Marque and Reprisal; coin Money; emit Bills of Credit; make any Thing but gold and silver Coin a Tender in Payment of Debts; pass any Bill of Attainder, ex post facto Law, or Law impairing the Obligation of Contracts, or grant any Title of Nobility.

No State shall, without the Consent of the Congress, lay any Imposts or Duties on Imports or Exports, except what may be absolutely necessary for executing it's inspection Laws: and the net Produce of all Duties and Imposts, laid by any State on Imports or Exports, shall be for the Use of the Treasury of the United States; and all such Laws shall be subject to the Revision and Controul of the Congress.

No State shall, without the Consent of Congress, lay any Duty of Tonnage, keep Troops, or Ships of War in time of Peace, enter into any Agreement or Compact with another State, or with a foreign Power, or engage in War, unless actually invaded, or in such imminent Danger as will not admit of delay.

Article. II.
Section. 1.
The executive Power shall be vested in a President of the United States of America. He shall hold his Office during the Term of four Years, and, together with the Vice President, chosen for the same Term, be elected, as follows:

Each State shall appoint, in such Manner as the Legislature thereof may direct, a Number of Electors, equal to the whole Number of Senators and Representatives to which the State may be entitled in the Congress: but no

Senator or Representative, or Person holding an Office of Trust or Profit under the United States, shall be appointed an Elector.

The Electors shall meet in their respective States, and vote by Ballot for two Persons, of whom one at least shall not be an Inhabitant of the same State with themselves. And they shall make a List of all the Persons voted for, and of the Number of Votes for each; which List they shall sign and certify, and transmit sealed to the Seat of the Government of the United States, directed to the President of the Senate. The President of the Senate shall, in the Presence of the Senate and House of Representatives, open all the Certificates, and the Votes shall then be counted. The Person having the greatest Number of Votes shall be the President, if such Number be a Majority of the whole Number of Electors appointed; and if there be more than one who have such Majority, and have an equal Number of Votes, then the House of Representatives shall immediately chuse by Ballot one of them for President; and if no Person have a Majority, then from the five highest on the List the said House shall in like Manner chuse the President. But in chusing the President, the Votes shall be taken by States, the Representation from each State having one Vote; A quorum for this purpose shall consist of a Member or Members from two thirds of the States, and a Majority of all the States shall be necessary to a Choice. In every Case, after the Choice of the President, the Person having the greatest Number of Votes of the Electors shall be the Vice President. But if there should remain two or more who have equal Votes, the Senate shall chuse from them by Ballot the Vice President.

The Congress may determine the Time of chusing the Electors, and the Day on which they shall give their Votes; which Day shall be the same throughout the United States.

No Person except a natural born Citizen, or a Citizen of the United States, at the time of the Adoption of this Constitution, shall be eligible to the Office of President; neither shall any Person be eligible to that Office who shall not have attained to the Age of thirty five Years, and been fourteen Years a Resident within the United States.

In Case of the Removal of the President from Office, or of his Death, Resignation, or Inability to discharge the Powers and Duties of the said Office, the Same shall devolve on the Vice President, and the Congress may by Law provide for the Case of Removal, Death, Resignation or Inability, both of the President and Vice President, declaring what Officer shall then act as President, and such Officer shall act accordingly, until the Disability be removed, or a President shall be elected.

The President shall, at stated Times, receive for his Services, a Compensation, which shall neither be increased nor diminished during the Period for which he shall have been elected, and he shall not receive within that Period any other Emolument from the United States, or any of them.

Before he enter on the Execution of his Office, he shall take the following Oath or Affirmation:--"I do solemnly swear (or affirm) that I will faithfully execute the Office of President of the United States, and will to the best of my Ability, preserve, protect and defend the Constitution of the United States."

Section. 2.
The President shall be Commander in Chief of the Army and Navy of the United States, and of the Militia of the several States, when called into the actual Service of the United States; he may require the Opinion, in writing, of the principal Officer in each of the executive Departments, upon any Subject relating to the Duties of their respective Offices, and he shall have Power to grant Reprieves and Pardons for Offences against the United States, except in Cases of Impeachment.
He shall have Power, by and with the Advice and Consent of the Senate, to make Treaties, provided two thirds of the Senators present concur; and he shall nominate, and by and with the Advice and Consent of the Senate, shall appoint Ambassadors, other public Ministers and Consuls, Judges of the supreme Court, and all other Officers of the United States, whose Appointments are not herein otherwise provided for, and which shall be established by Law: but the Congress may by Law vest the Appointment of such inferior Officers, as they think proper, in the President alone, in the Courts of Law, or in the Heads of Departments.
The President shall have Power to fill up all Vacancies that may happen during the Recess of the Senate, by granting Commissions which shall expire at the End of their next Session.

Section. 3.
He shall from time to time give to the Congress Information of the State of the Union, and recommend to their Consideration such Measures as he shall judge necessary and expedient; he may, on extraordinary Occasions, convene both Houses, or either of them, and in Case of Disagreement between them, with Respect to the Time of Adjournment, he may adjourn them to such Time as he shall think proper; **he shall receive Ambassadors and other public Ministers; he shall take Care that the Laws be faithfully executed**, and shall Commission all the Officers of the United States.

Section. 4.
The President, Vice President and all civil Officers of the United States, shall be removed from Office on Impeachment for, and Conviction of, Treason, Bribery, or other high Crimes and Misdemeanors.

Article III.

Section. 1.
The judicial Power of the United States shall be vested in one supreme Court, and in such inferior Courts as the Congress may from time to time ordain and establish. The Judges, both of the supreme and inferior Courts, shall hold their Offices during good Behaviour, and shall, at stated Times, receive for their Services a Compensation, which shall not be diminished during their Continuance in Office.

Section. 2.
The judicial Power shall extend to all Cases, in Law and Equity, arising under this Constitution, the Laws of the United States, and Treaties made, or which shall be made, under their Authority;--to all Cases affecting Ambassadors, other public Ministers and Consuls;--to all Cases of admiralty and maritime Jurisdiction;--to Controversies to which the United States shall be a Party;--to Controversies between two or more States;-- between a State and Citizens of another State;--between Citizens of different States;--between Citizens of the same State claiming Lands under Grants of different States, and between a State, or the Citizens thereof, and foreign States, Citizens or Subjects.
In all Cases affecting Ambassadors, other public Ministers and Consuls, and those in which a State shall be Party, the supreme Court shall have original Jurisdiction. In all the other Cases before mentioned, the supreme Court shall have appellate Jurisdiction, both as to Law and Fact, with such Exceptions, and under such Regulations as the Congress shall make.
The Trial of all Crimes, except in Cases of Impeachment, shall be by Jury; and such Trial shall be held in the State where the said Crimes shall have been committed; but when not committed within any State, the Trial shall be at such Place or Places as the Congress may by Law have directed.

Section. 3.
Treason against the United States, shall consist only in levying War against them, or in adhering to their Enemies, giving them Aid and Comfort. No Person shall be convicted of Treason unless on the Testimony of two Witnesses to the same overt Act, or on Confession in open Court.
The Congress shall have Power to declare the Punishment of Treason, but no Attainder of Treason shall work Corruption of Blood, or Forfeiture except during the Life of the Person attainted.

Article. IV.
Section. 1.
Full Faith and Credit shall be given in each State to the public Acts, Records, and judicial Proceedings of every other State. And the Congress may by general Laws prescribe the Manner in which such Acts, Records and Proceedings shall be proved, and the Effect thereof.

Section. 2.

The Citizens of each State shall be entitled to all Privileges and Immunities of Citizens in the several States.

A Person charged in any State with Treason, Felony, or other Crime, who shall flee from Justice, and be found in another State, shall on Demand of the executive Authority of the State from which he fled, be delivered up, to be removed to the State having Jurisdiction of the Crime.

<u>No Person held to Service or Labour in one State, under the Laws thereof, escaping into another, shall, in Consequence of any Law or Regulation therein, be discharged from such Service or Labour, but shall be delivered up on Claim of the Party to whom such Service or Labour may be due.</u>

Section. 3.

New States may be admitted by the Congress into this Union; but no new State shall be formed or erected within the Jurisdiction of any other State; nor any State be formed by the Junction of two or more States, or Parts of States, without the Consent of the Legislatures of the States concerned as well as of the Congress.

The Congress shall have Power to dispose of and make all needful Rules and Regulations respecting the Territory or other Property belonging to the United States; and nothing in this Constitution shall be so construed as to Prejudice any Claims of the United States, or of any particular State.

Section. 4.

The United States shall guarantee to every State in this Union a Republican Form of Government, and shall protect each of them against Invasion; and on Application of the Legislature, or of the Executive (when the Legislature cannot be convened), against domestic Violence.

Article. V.

The Congress, whenever two thirds of both Houses shall deem it necessary, shall propose Amendments to this Constitution, or, on the Application of the Legislatures of two thirds of the several States, shall call a Convention for proposing Amendments, which, in either Case, shall be valid to all Intents and Purposes, as Part of this Constitution, when ratified by the Legislatures of three fourths of the several States, or by Conventions in three fourths thereof, as the one or the other Mode of Ratification may be proposed by the Congress; Provided that no Amendment which may be made prior to the Year One thousand eight hundred and eight shall in any Manner affect the first and fourth Clauses in the Ninth Section of the first Article; and that no State, without its Consent, shall be deprived of its equal Suffrage in the Senate.

Article. VI.

All Debts contracted and Engagements entered into, before the Adoption of this Constitution, shall be as valid against the United States under this Constitution, as under the Confederation.

This Constitution, and the Laws of the United States which shall be made in Pursuance thereof; and all Treaties made, or which shall be made, under the Authority of the United States, shall be the supreme Law of the Land; and the Judges in every State shall be bound thereby, any Thing in the Constitution or Laws of any State to the Contrary notwithstanding.

The Senators and Representatives before mentioned, and the Members of the several State Legislatures, and all executive and judicial Officers, both of the United States and of the several States, shall be bound by Oath or Affirmation, to support this Constitution; but no religious Test shall ever be required as a Qualification to any Office or public Trust under the United States.

Article. VII.

The Ratification of the Conventions of nine States, shall be sufficient for the Establishment of this Constitution between the States so ratifying the Same. The Word, "the," being interlined between the seventh and eighth Lines of the first Page, the Word "Thirty" being partly written on an Erazure in the fifteenth Line of the first Page, The Words "is tried" being interlined between the thirty second and thirty third Lines of the first Page and the Word "the" being interlined between the forty third and forty fourth Lines of the second Page.

Attest William Jackson Secretary

Done in Convention by the Unanimous Consent of the States present the Seventeenth Day of September in the Year of our Lord one thousand seven hundred and Eighty seven and of the Independence of the United States of America the Twelfth In witness whereof We have hereunto subscribed our Names,

G°. Washington
President and deputy from
Virginia
Delaware
Geo: Read
Gunning Bedford jun
John Dickinson
Richard Bassett
Jaco: Broom
Maryland
James McHenry
Dan of St Thos. Jenifer
Danl. Carroll
Virginia
John Blair
James Madison Jr.
North Carolina
Wm. Blount
Richd. Dobbs Spaight
Hu Williamson
South Carolina
J. Rutledge
Charles Cotesworth Pinckney
Charles Pinckney
Pierce Butler
Georgia
William Few
Abr Baldwin
New Hampshire
John Langdon
Nicholas Gilman
Massachusetts
Nathaniel Gorham
Rufus King
Connecticut
Wm. Saml. Johnson
Roger Sherman
New York
Alexander Hamilton

New Jersey
Wil: Livingston
David Brearley
Wm. Paterson
Jona: Dayton
Pennsylvania
B Franklin
Thomas Mifflin
Robt. Morris
Geo. Clymer
Thos. FitzSimons
Jared Ingersoll
James Wilson
Gouv Morris

APPENDIX D

BILL OF RIGHTS[205]

The Preamble to The Bill of Rights **Congress of the United States** begun and held at the City of New-York, on Wednesday the fourth of March, one thousand seven hundred and eighty nine.

THE Conventions of a number of the States, having at the time of their adopting the Constitution, expressed a desire, in order to prevent misconstruction or abuse of its powers, that further declaratory and restrictive clauses should be added: And as extending the ground of public confidence in the Government, will best ensure the beneficent ends of its institution.

RESOLVED by the Senate and House of Representatives of the United States of America, in Congress assembled, two thirds of both Houses concurring, that the following Articles be proposed to the Legislatures of the several States, as amendments to the Constitution of the United States, all, or any of which Articles, when ratified by three fourths of the said Legislatures, to be valid to all intents and purposes, as part of the said Constitution; viz.

ARTICLES in addition to, and Amendment of the Constitution of the United States of America, proposed by Congress, and ratified by the Legislatures of the several States, pursuant to the fifth Article of the original Constitution.

Note: The following text is a transcription of the first ten amendments to the Constitution in their original form. These amendments were ratified December 15, 1791, and form what is known as the "Bill of Rights."

---

[205] U.S. National Archives and Records Administration, "The Charters of Freedom: The Bill of Rights,"
http://www.archives.gov/exhibits/charters.

Amendment I

Congress shall make no law respecting an establishment of religion, or prohibiting the free exercise thereof; or abridging the freedom of speech, or of the press; or the right of the people peaceably to assemble, and to petition the Government for a redress of grievances.

Amendment II

A well regulated Militia, being necessary to the security of a free State, the right of the people to keep and bear Arms, shall not be infringed.

Amendment III

No Soldier shall, in time of peace be quartered in any house, without the consent of the Owner, nor in time of war, but in a manner to be prescribed by law.

Amendment IV

The right of the people to be secure in their persons, houses, papers, and effects, against unreasonable searches and seizures, shall not be violated, and no Warrants shall issue, but upon probable cause, supported by Oath or affirmation, and particularly describing the place to be searched, and the persons or things to be seized.

Amendment V

No person shall be held to answer for a capital, or otherwise infamous crime, unless on a presentment or indictment of a Grand Jury, except in cases arising in the land or naval forces, or in the Militia, when in actual service in time of War or public danger; nor shall any person be subject for the same offence to be twice put in jeopardy of life or limb; nor shall be compelled in any criminal case to be a witness against himself, nor be deprived of life, liberty, or property, without due process of law; nor shall private property be taken for public use, without just compensation.

Amendment VI

In all criminal prosecutions, the accused shall enjoy the right to a speedy and public trial, by an impartial jury of the State and district wherein the crime shall have been committed, which district shall have been previously ascertained by law, and to be informed of the nature and cause of the accusation; to be confronted with the witnesses against him; to have compulsory process for obtaining witnesses in his favor, and to have the Assistance of Counsel for his defence.

Amendment VII
In Suits at common law, where the value in controversy shall exceed twenty dollars, the right of trial by jury shall be preserved, and no fact tried by a jury, shall be otherwise re-examined in any Court of the United States, than according to the rules of the common law.

Amendment VIII
Excessive bail shall not be required, nor excessive fines imposed, nor cruel and unusual punishments inflicted.

Note: The capitalization and punctuation in this version is from the Amendment IX
The enumeration in the Constitution, of certain rights, shall not be construed to deny or disparage others retained by the people.

Amendment X
The powers not delegated to the United States by the Constitution, nor prohibited by it to the States, are reserved to the States respectively, or to the people.
enrolled original of the Joint Resolution of Congress proposing the Bill of Rights, which is on permanent display in the Rotunda of the National Archives Building, Washington, D.C.

APPENDIX E

CONGRESSIONAL SCORECARD: FRC ACTION AND FAMILY POLICY ALLIANCE

INTRODUCTION. This Appendix contains details of the issues which Republicans and Democrats voted on the Congressional Scorecards of FRC Action and Family Policy Alliance (Citizenlink), as outlined in Chapter 2.3.

2008 SENATE SCORECARD. Senators were evaluated on 7 critical "pro-family" issues. The legislation included:

Issue 1: An amendment to the Lobby Reform Act to protect grassroots organizations from unfair regulation of lobbying activities;

Issue 2: The Embryonic Stem Cell Research Act, a bill funding embryonic stem cell research that required destruction of human embryos;

Issue 3: An amendment to the State Children's Health Insurance Program to allow states to provide health insurance for unborn children;

Issue 4: An amendment to the State, Foreign Operations and Related Programs Appropriations Act to prevent funding of international groups "that support or participate in coercive abortion or involuntary sterilization programs;"

Issue 5: An amendment to the same Act that would have funded international organizations "that perform and promote abortions as a method of family planning;

Issue 6: A "thought crimes amendment" to the Department of Defense Authorization that "would establish federal 'hate crimes' for certain violent acts based on the actual or perceived race, religion, disability, gender identity or sexual orientation of any person;" and

Issue 7: Confirmation of Judge Southwick, nominated by President Bush, to the U.S. Court of Appeals.

Senate Republicans sponsored all 4 bills, amendments or motions supporting Christian values. No Democrat sponsored any pro-Christian, pro-family values legislation, but they did sponsor 3 bills or amendments contrary to Christian values. Most Senate Democrats supported all anti-Christian legislation opposed by Republicans (Issues 1,2,4,5,6). They opposed all pro-Christian values legislation supported by Republicans (Issue 3) and opposed confirmation of conservative federal judge who supports Christian values (Issue 7).

Most Senate Republicans opposed: (1) laws regulating lobbying that inhibit Christian organizations from providing information to the public on matters before Congress (Issue 1); (2) federal funds for embryonic stem cell research that require destruction of human embryos (Issue 2); (3) federal funds for international groups that support abortion or involuntary sterilization (Issues 4,5); (4) hate crimes laws that wrongfully criminalize thoughts not just actions regarding "race, religion, disability, gender identity or sexual orientation" (Issue 6). Most Republicans supported: (1) confirmation of a federal judge who supports Christian values (Issue 7) and (2) laws that permit states to have health insurance for unborn children (Issue 3).

<u>2008 HOUSE OF REPRESENTATIVES SCORECARD</u>. Representatives were evaluated on 16 "pro-family" issues. The legislation included:
<u>Issue 1</u>: A motion to recommit the Embryonic Stem Cell Research Act that would ensure that taxpayer funds were not used for human cloning."
<u>Issue 2</u>: The Embryonic Stem Cell Research Act, which would fund stem cell research that required destruction of human embryos.
<u>Issue 3</u>: A motion to recommit the Head Start Reauthorization bill that would remove a provision that "prevents faith-based organizations from hiring according to their faith.
<u>Issue 4</u>: Federal Hate Crimes Act, a "thought crimes bill" that "would establish federal 'hate crimes' for certain violent acts based on the actual or perceived race, religion, disability, gender identity or sexual orientation of any person."
<u>Issue 5</u>: Human Cloning Protection Act, a bill that would allow "the creation of cloned human embryos for destructive research."
<u>Issue 6</u>: Embryonic Stem Cell Research Act, a bill funding embryonic stem cell research that required destruction of human embryos.
<u>Issue 7</u>: An amendment to the State, Foreign Operations and Related Programs Appropriations Act that would require "a third of HIV/AIDs prevention funding to be spent for 'abstinence-until-marriage' and 'be-faithful' programs.
<u>Issue 8</u>: A amendment to the State, Foreign Operations and Related Programs Appropriations Act that would allow "taxpayer funded

contraceptives to be given to international organizations that perform and promote abortions as a method of family planning."

Issue 9: An amendment to same Act that would have "upheld the prohibition against federal funding of international organizations that perform and promote abortions as a method of family planning."

Issue 10: State, Foreign Operations and Related Programs Appropriations Act, a bill that undermines the funding of "abstinence-until-marriage" and "be-faithful" programs and the prohibition of federal funding of "international organizations that perform or promote abortions as a method of family planning."

Issue 11: An amendment to the Financial Services and General Government Appropriations Act that restricts funding of needle exchange programs in the District of Columbia.

Issue 12: An amendment to the same Act that "strips the Federal Communications Commission of the authority to reinstitute" the…"Fairness Doctrine"…that would "order broadcasters to give equal air time to both sides of controversial issues."

Issue 13: Another amendment to the same Act that would prevent federal funds from being used by the District of Columbia for domestic partner benefits.

Issue 14: An amendment to the Labor, Health and Human Services and Education Appropriations Act that would restrict use of federal funds for abortions by withholding $331 million appropriated to Planned Parenthood, the nation's leading abortion provider, for "family planning services."

Issue 15: The Children's Health and Medicine Protection Act, a bill that reauthorizes and expands the State Children's Health Insurance Program. It undermines health coverage for unborn children, allows states to provide family planning services for individuals not eligible for Medicaid, and undermine abstinence education.

Issue 16: The Employment Non-Discrimination Act, it provides special protection for homosexuals not given to other employees and radically transforms workplace discrimination law.

In the House of Representatives, Republicans sponsored 7 pro-family, pro-Christian bills, amendments, or motions, and Democrats sponsored 8 contrary to Christian values. A Republican and a Democrat jointly sponsored only 1 of the 16 issues. Most Democrats in the House supported all anti-Christian values legislation supported by Republicans and opposed all pro-Christian values legislation supported by Republicans.

Most Republicans in the House, like Republicans in the Senate, opposed: (1) federal funds for embryonic stem cell research that requires the destruction of human embryos (Issues 2,6); (2) federal funds for groups that support abortion (Issues 8,9,10); (3) hate crimes laws which wrongfully criminalize thoughts not just actions regarding "race, religion, disability, gender identity or sexual orientation" (Issue 4). House Republicans also opposed: (1) use of taxpayer funds for cloning human embryos for destructive research (Issues 1,5); (2) legislation that prevents faith-based organizations from hiring according to their faith for the Head Start Program (Issue 3); (3) a law which would require part of HIV/AIDs prevention funding to be spent for "abstinence-until-marriage" and "be-faithful" programs (Issues 7,10); (4) restrictions on funds for needle exchange programs in the District of Columbia (Issue 11); (5) the 'Fairness Doctrine,' which would inhibit Christian broadcasters by forcing them to give equal time to both sides of issues (Issue 12); (6) use of federal funds by the District of Columbia for domestic partner benefits (Issue 13); (7) use of federal funds for abortions by Planned Parenthood (Issue 14); (8) allowing states to fund family planning for those not eligible for Medicaid and requiring states to fund family planning as part of Medicaid (Issue 15); (9) granting special consideration on the basis of "sexual orientation" not extended to other employees in the workplace (Issue 16). House Republicans supported state health coverage for unborn children and state abstinence education programs (Issue 15).

2012 SENATE SCORECARD. Senators were evaluated on 7 "pro-family" issues. The legislation included:

Issue 1: An amendment to the FAA Authorization Bill that would repeal Obamacare, the national health care law called the Patient Protection and Affordable Care Act, a law that funded abortion, denied conscience protections, and instituted health care rationing.

Issue 2: A Continuing Resolution to fund abortion in the District of Columbia that did not exclude funding for Planned Parenthood.

Issue 3: An amendment to the Department of Defense and Full Year Continuing Appropriations Act of 2011 that would prevent funding of the health care act (Patient Protection and Affordable Care Act), a law that funded abortion, denied conscience protections, and instituted health care rationing.

Issue 4: An amendment to the Department of Defense and Full Year Continuing Appropriations Act of 2011 that would prevent funding of Planned Parenthood, the nation's largest abortion provider.

Issue 5: A vote on John McConnell for U.S. District Judge. Nominated by President Obama, there was evidence that he would not be an impartial judge and that he would legislate from the bench.

Issue 6: A vote on Goodwin Liu for U.S. Court of Appeals Circuit Judge. Nominated by President Obama, there was evidence that he would be an activist judge and replace the Constitution with personal views.

Issue 7: A bill that would authorize the President to make appointments to thousands of government positions without Senate confirmation.

2012 HOUSE OF REPRESENTATIVES SCORECARD. Representatives were evaluated on 10 "pro-family" issues. The legislation included:

Issue 1: The Repealing the Job-Killing Health Care Law would repeal Obamacare, the national health care law called the Patient Protection and Affordable Care Act, a law that funded abortion, denied conscience protections, and instituted health care rationing.

Issue 2: An amendment to the Full-Year Continuing Appropriations Act that would prevent funding of Planned Parenthood, the nation's largest abortion provider.

Issue 3: A Continuing Resolution with funding for abortion in the District of Columbia and funding for Planned Parenthood.

Issue 4: The Scholarships for Opportunity and Results Act would reauthorize the D.C. Opportunity Scholarship Program to allow students in the District of Columbia to attend the school of their choice.

Issue 5: An amendment to the Department of Defense and Full Year Continuing Appropriations Act of 2011 that would prevent funding of Obamacare, the national health care law called the Patient Protection and Affordable Care Act, a law that funded abortion, denied conscience protections, and instituted health care rationing.

Issue 6: An amendment to the Department of Defense and Full Year Continuing Appropriations Act of 2011 that would prevent funding of Planned Parenthood, the nation's largest abortion provider.

Issue 7: The No Taxpayer Funding of Abortion Act was an amendment that would permanently prevent federal funds from paying for abortions and health care plans.

CONGRESSIONAL SCORECARD: NATIONAL RIGHT TO LIFE

INTRODUCTION. This Appendix contains details of the issues which Republicans and Democrats voted on the Congressional Scorecard of National Right to Life as outlined in Chapter 2.4.

2008 SENATE SCORECARD. Senators were evaluated on 7 critical "pro-family" issues. The legislation included:

Issue 1: Regulation of "grassroots lobbying" groups. Amendment (No. 20) to 2007 Lobby Reform Act (S.1) This "infringed on rights protected by the First Amendment, and would inhibit groups from providing…information to members of the public about matters under consideration in Congress." It would "require registration and reporting by certain activists and groups who spend money to encourage members of the general public to communicate with members of Congress or other federal officials about legislative and policy matters." Violations were punishable by fines up to $200,000 and prison up to 10 years.

Issue 2: Stem Cell Research Enhancement Act (S. 5). This bill "would mandate federal funding of the type of stem cell research that requires the killing of human embryos."

Issue 3: Medicare prescription drug price controls (Senate Bill 3). This bill would prevent "older people from being allowed to spend their own money…to save their own lives through access to unrationed prescription drugs under Medicare. Under the guise of allowing "government negotiation" the bill would authorize the imposition of price controls that would limit access to and discourage the development of innovative life-saving medicines."

Issue 4: Health Insurance for Unborn Child. Amendment (No. 2535) to H.R. 976, a bill to reauthorize the State Children's Health Insurance Program (SCHIP). "The State Children's Health Insurance (SCHIP) program is a federal program that provides funds to states primarily to provide health services to children of low-income families. The Amendment states that a covered child "includes, at the option of a State, an unborn child."

Issue 5: Banning Funding of Organizations that Support Coercive

Abortion Programs. Amendment (No. 2707) to the Senate State, Foreign Operations and Related Programs Appropriations Act 2008 (H.R. 2764). The Kemp-Kasten Anti-Coercion law has been in effect since 1985. It prohibits U.S. "population assistance" funds from going to any organization that "supports or participates in the management of a program of coercive abortion or involuntary sterilization." "However, in crafting the Fiscal Year 2008 State-Foreign Operations Appropriations Bill (H.R. 2764), the Senate Appropriations Committee removed the traditional Kemp-Kasten language…. Senator Sam Brownback (R-Ks.) offered an NRLC-backed amendment…to restore the…Kemp-Kasten anti-coercion language."

Issue 6: Funding International Abortion Groups. Amendment (No. 2719) to the Senate State, Foreign Operations and Related Programs Appropriations Act 2008 (H.R. 2764). "Known as the "Boxer Amendment to overturn pro-life "Mexico City Policy"... Under the pro-life "Mexico City Policy," private overseas organizations that "perform or actively promote abortion as a method of family planning" are not eligible to receive funds for "population assistance." Pro-abortion Senator Boxer (D-Ca.) offered an amendment to prohibit enforcement of any pro-life policy.

Issue 7: Prohibition on Abortion Services in Indian Health Programs. Vitter amendment to Senate Bill 1200. The federal government funds health programs for American Indians. During the 1970s, it paid for abortions. Funding of abortions was stopped in the 1980s, but this policy depended on annual renewal of the Hyde Amendment. On February 26, 2008, , Senator Vitter (R-La.) offered an NRLC-backed amendment to permanently prohibit coverage of abortion (except to save the life of the mother, or in cases of rape or incest)."

Note the types of legislation supported by Republicans and Democrats in the Senate. Most Republicans opposed: (1) laws regulating lobbying that would inhibit Christian organizations from providing information to the public on matters before Congress (Senate issue 1); (2) federal funds for embryonic stem cell research that require the destruction of human embryos (Senate issue 2); (3) laws that would impose "price controls that would limit access to and discourage the development of innovative life-saving medicines" for elderly Americans using Medicare (Senate Issue 3); (4) federal funds for international groups that support abortion or involuntary sterilization (Senate issue 5,6);and (5) federal funds for abortions by American Indians (Senate issue7). Most Republicans supported: (1) laws that permit states to have health insurance for unborn children (Senate issue 4). Most Senate Democrats supported all anti-Christian legislation opposed by Republicans and opposed all pro-Christian values legislation supported by Republicans.

<u>2008 HOUSE OF REPRESENTATIVES SCORECARD</u>.

Representatives were evaluated on 7 critical "pro-family" issues. The legislation included:

Issue 1: Prohibition on Funding of Human Cloning. Stem Cell Research Enhancement Act" (H.R. 3) Anti-Cloning Amendment. "On January 11, 2007, the House of Representatives debated H.R. 3, authored by Rep. Diana DeGette (D-Co.) and Mike Castle (R-De.), a bill that would mandate federal funding of the type of stem cell research that requires the killing of human embryos in order to harvest their stem cells. The embryos would be those "donated from in vitro fertilization clinics, [and that] were created for the purposes of fertility treatment," after authorization by the parents. The bill, which NRLC strongly opposed, is intended to overturn the pro-life policy that President Bush announced on August 9, 2001, under which federal funds do not support research that requires the killing of human embryos. The House Democratic leadership brought the bill to the floor under a "closed rule," which allowed the pro-life side to offer only a single proposed modification to the bill. This amendment (technically called a "motion to recommit with instructions") would have added language to the bill to <u>prohibit any of the funds</u> authorized by the bill from being given to labs or other entities that <u>do research on stem cells obtained from human embryos created by cloning</u>. NRLC is opposed to human cloning, so NRLC supported this anti-human-cloning motion/amendment."

Issue 2: Stem Cell Research. Embryonic Stem Cell Research Enhancement Act (H.R. 3). H.R. 3 was "a bill that <u>would mandate federal funding of the type of stem cell research that requires the killing of human embryos</u> in order to harvest their stem cells."

Issue 3: Medicare Prescription Drug Price Negotiation Act (H.R. 4). This bill "would effectively <u>prevent older people from being allowed to spend their own money, if they choose, to save their own lives through access to unrationed prescription drugs under Medicare</u>. Under the guise of "government negotiation" the bill would result in the imposition of price controls that would limit access to and discourage the development of innovative life-saving medicines."

Issue 4: Phony Ban on Human Cloning. Human Cloning Protection Act (H.R. 2560). This bill (H.R. 2560) is "deceptively titled "The Human Cloning Prohibition Act." But in reality H.R. 2560 does not ban any human cloning at all. H.R. 2560 would <u>allow the creation of any number of cloned human embryos, for the specific purpose of harvesting their stem cells or using them in other research that will kill them</u>. H.R.

2560 actually bans only allowing a human clone to live, by implanting her or him "into a uterus or the functional equivalent of a uterus," or "to ship, mail, transport, or receive" such an embryo. NRLC strongly opposes this "clone-and-kill bill."

Issue 5: Embryonic Stem Cell Research Enhancement Act of 2007 (S. 5). This bill "would mandate federal funding of the type of stem cell research that requires the killing of human embryos. This bill would overturn President Bush's policy that prohibits such funding."

Issue 6: International Abortion Funding. Amendment (H.AMDT. 368) to the State, Foreign Operations and Related Programs Appropriations Act, 2008 (H.R. 2764). This amendment was known as the "Smith-Stupak Amendment" to protect the pro-life "Mexico City Policy." "Under President Bush's pro-life "Mexico City Policy," private overseas organizations that "perform or actively promote abortion as a method of family planning" are not eligible to receive funds under the U.S. foreign aid program for "population assistance." The Fiscal Year 2008 State-Foreign Operations Appropriations Bill (H.R. 2764) contained language, authored by pro-abortion Rep. Nita Lowey (D-NY), designed to undermine the "Mexico City Policy" by requiring the U.S. Agency for International Development (USAID) to provide pro-abortion organizations with certain U.S.-funded contraceptive supplies. Pro-life Representatives Chris Smith (R-NJ) and Bart Stupak (D-Mi.) offered an amendment, which was strongly supported by NRLC, to remove the pro-abortion language from the bill."

Issue 7: Restrict Funding to Planned Parenthood. Amendment (H.AMDT. 594) to the Labor, Health and Human Services, and Education Appropriations Act, 2008 (H.R. 3043). This amendment would deny federal "family-planning" funds to Planned Parenthood. "Title X ("Title 10") of the Public Health Service Act provides more than $300 million annually for grants to state and private entities for "family planning" programs. Although federal law does not permit such funds to be used to pay for abortions, large amounts of Title X funds go to organizations that operate abortion clinics, including affiliates of the Planned Parenthood Federation of America (PPFA), the nation's largest abortion provider. On July 19, 2007, during consideration of the Fiscal Year 2008 appropriations bill for the federal Department of Health and Human Services, pro-life Congressman Mike Pence (R-In.) offered an amendment to prohibit any Title X funds from going to any arm of Planned Parenthood."

Note that most Republicans in the House, like Republicans in the Senate, opposed: (1) federal funds for embryonic stem cell research that requires the destruction of human embryos (House issues 2,4,5); (2) laws that would impose "price controls that would limit access to and discourage the development of innovative life-saving medicines" for elderly Americans using Medicare (House Issue 3); (3) federal funds for international groups that support abortion or involuntary sterilization (House issue 6). House Republicans also opposed: (1) taxpayer funds for cloning human embryos for destructive research (House issue 1) and (2) federal funds for Planned Parenthood, the nation's largest abortion provider (House issue 7). Most Democrats in the House supported all anti-Christian values legislation supported by Republicans and opposed all pro-Christian values legislation supported by Republicans. No Democrat sponsored any pro-Christian, pro-life legislation, but they did sponsor all bills and amendments contrary to Christian values. Republicans sponsored all bills and amendments that support Christian values.

<u>2012 SENATE SCORECARD</u>. Senators were evaluated on 5 critical "pro-family" issues. The legislation included:

<u>Issue 1</u>: Repeal Obamacare health care law. This was an amendment to completely repeal Obamacare, the Patient Protection and Affordable Care Act, the "massive health care restructuring law enacted March 2010. The PPACA contained many provisions that would implement government –imposed rationing of life-saving health care and included federal funding of abortion.

<u>Issue 2</u>: Block funding of Obamacare health care law. This bill was an attempt to block funding of Obamacare, the Patient Protection and Affordable Care Act discussed above.

<u>Issue 3</u>: Cut federal funding of Planned Parenthood. This was a bill to cut all federal funding to Planned Parenthood Federation of American (PPFA), the nation's number one provider of abortions.

<u>Issue 4</u>: Prevent Obama abortion mandates. This bill, the Respect for Rights of Conscience Act, would amend the Obamacare law to permit employers and health insurers to refuse to cover services to which they had a moral or religious objection, services such as abortion.

<u>Issue 5</u>: "Disclose Act" to restrict political free speech. This bill, opposed by NRLC, was designed to restrict freedom of "political speech about members of Congress, candidates for Congress, and ongoing developments in Congress."

<u>2012 HOUSE OF REPRESENTATIVES SCORECARD</u>. Representatives were evaluated on 9 critical "pro-family" issues. The legislation included:

<u>Issue 1</u>: H.R.2 to repeal Obamacare health care law. This was an

amendment to completely repeal Obamacare, the Patient Protection and Affordable Care Act, the "massive health care restructuring law enacted March 2010. The PPACA contained many provisions that would implement government –imposed rationing of life-saving health care and included federal funding of abortion.

Issue 2: Cut federal funding of Planned Parenthood. This was a bill to cut all federal funding to Planned Parenthood Federation of American (PPFA), the nation's number one provider of abortions.

Issue 3: Block funding of Obamacare health care law. This amendment blocked funding of the Patient Protection and Affordable Care Act, the "massive health care restructuring law enacted March 2010. The PPACA…would implement government –imposed rationing of life-saving health care and included federal funding of abortion. "

Issue 4: Cut federal funding of Planned Parenthood. This was a bill to cut all federal funding to Planned Parenthood Federation of American (PPFA), the nation's number one provider of abortions.

Issue 5: The No Taxpayer Funding of Abortion Act (H.R.3) would permanently block the use of federal funds for abortion and health insurance coverage of abortions by federal programs.

Issue 6: This amendment would block the use of federal funds to train abortionists. It would also establish conscience protections that would prohibit any medical facility to discriminate against any doctor, nurse, or medial provider who refused to "provide, pay for, provide coverage of, or refer for abortions"

Issue 7: The Protect Life Act would "repeal and/or correct all of the pro-abortion components" of Obamacare, the Patient Protection and Affordable Care Act, the "massive health care restructuring law.

Issue 8: The Prenatal Nondiscrimination Act is a ban on sex-selection abortions. This law would make it illegal to knowingly: (1) perform an abortion based upon sex of child, (2) to use force or threats to coerce sex-based abortion, (3) to "solicit or accept funds" for sex-based abortions, and (4) to transport a woman across state lines or into the nation for sex-based abortion.

Issue 9: Repeal of Obamacare health care law. This was an amendment to completely repeal Obamacare, the Patient Protection and Affordable Care Act, the "massive health care restructuring law enacted March 2010. The PPACA contained many provisions that would implement government –imposed rationing of life-saving health care and included federal funding of abortion.